SPITFIRE

SPITFIRE

A Test Pilot's Story

Jeffrey Quill

OBE AFC FRAeS

Foreword by Sir George Edwards OM CBE FRS FEng

ARROW BOOKS

Arrow Books Limited
62-65 Chandos Place, London WC2N 4NW

An imprint of Century Hutchinson Ltd

London Melbourne Sydney Auckland
Johannesburg and agencies throughout
the world

First published by John Murray (Publishers) Ltd 1983

Arrow edition 1985
Reprinted 1986 (twice)

© Jeffrey Quill 1983
Foreword © Sir George Edwards 1983

Printed and bound in Great Britain by
The Guernsey Press Co. Ltd
Guernsey, Channel Islands

ISBN 0 09 937020 4

Much of this book is about the Spitfire, without doubt one of the greatest fighter aircraft of all time. But the Spitfire was a machine and so could not have the human qualities of courage, determination, tenacity and endurance. These were provided by the pilots who flew and fought in her and to them this book is dedicated.

J.K.Q.

Contents

Illustrations

Figures

Sources of Illustrations

Plates 1, 3, 22–4, 26–7, 35–6, 38, 44, 54–8, 60: Vickers-Armstrongs (Aircraft) Ltd; 2: Charles Brown; 4: Royal Air Force; 5, 9: Vickers Ltd; 6, 10, 12, 30; Supermarine; 7, 11: Dr K. G. Mitchell; 13: Gordon Swanborough; 14: *Flight International*; 15: *Portsmouth Evening News*; 16–18, 45–9: the Author; 19–21, 37, 39: A & AEE (Crown copyright reserved); 25: via Alfred Price; 28–9: Royal Navy (Crown copyright reserved); 31–2: via E. B. Morgan; 34: B. Shenstone; 40–2: Rolls-Royce Ltd; 43: A. Lumsden; 50: Sport & General; 51: D. R. Robertson; 52: Alex Henshaw; 53: Mrs Lesley Errington; 59: M. C. Searle. The source of Plate 8 is not known. Figures 1 and 2: via E. B. Morgan; Figures 3–6: Pilot Press.

Foreword

BY SIR GEORGE EDWARDS OM CBE FRS FEng

I have great pleasure in writing this Foreword to Jeffrey Quill's *Spitfire: A Test Pilot's Story*; I have known him personally over most of the time that it covers. Many of the other test pilots about whom he writes became close personal friends of mine and some of them, sadly, lost their lives test flying aeroplanes which we in the aircraft industry had designed to the best of our ability; they were proving, in the only way possible, that the aeroplane was safe for passengers to travel in, or was an efficient piece of equipment for men to fight in.

Amongst all the members of the team that designs an aeroplane, the pilots and the observers are the only ones who actually risk their lives in seeing the job through. In the same way that the designers of the 1930s did not have modern computers and huge wind tunnels to help them get it right, neither did the test pilots have simulators, such as the sophisticated Concorde simulator, to enable them to do something like a test flight before the aircraft itself ever left the ground. So far as they were concerned, their first intimation that it would fly at all was when they got it in the air, flew a circuit, and got it down again. Their principal aids were a stop-watch and a notebook strapped to the thigh.

Readers will enjoy this book because of the factual accounts it gives of the process of developing a great aircraft such as the Spitfire and because it places that firmly within the context of the global events surrounding it. It also deals with the beginnings of the transition from the relatively light-hearted days of test flying in the mid-1930s to the more scientific and formalised processes of the present time. I say 'relatively light-hearted' because, when the war came, it was on the shoulders of these young men that the main fighting effort depended, and as recent events in the Falklands have shown, the youth of this country, when called upon, are, as always, ready to rise to the occasion.

In those days, the best test pilots were not the straight forward 'press-on' types but those men who could combine a long and mature experience of coping with the unexpected with something of the dash of youth. The relationship which I had with the test pilots I always felt to be one of the most rewarding parts of my job; I have always regarded them as a breed apart. Jeffrey Quill was one of the most articulate test pilots I ever encountered. In recent years he has carried a responsible job in the Panavia Organisation involved in the Tornado programme, but this book is essentially about being a pilot. How well I remember the flat spin of the Wellesley. My old friend Mutt Summers did the first flight on the Spitfire, but the huge effort of subsequent testing fell fairly and squarely on Quill, and to him goes much of the credit for turning Mitchell's brilliant concept into a great fighting machine, so that the pilots who fought the Battle of Britain had an aeroplane as good as, or better than, the enemy's, and, later, for keeping it in the front line of battle throughout the war.

Young men who read this book will find much to excite them and those of us who are not so young will be reminded of some of the great and dangerous days through which we passed, and will finish it with an especial feeling of gratitude to those who, like Jeffrey Quill, made so many aeroplanes in the end perform as their designers had always hoped they would.

Preface

A full and detailed history of the Spitfire would be a massive undertaking and this book makes no attempt at that. It is an account of certain aspects of the story and for convenience I have made it autobiographical in form. Most books are subject to the constraints of overall length and much that I would have liked to include about events and especially about people has necessarily had to be omitted; even so, the essential story, as I saw it, is here.

When, in June 1936, Supermarine received an order from the Air Ministry for 310 Spitfires it was, by a large margin, the biggest production order that the company had ever received. By the time the last aeroplane had been delivered from the factories during 1948 no less than 22,759 Spitfires and Seafires had been built in – according to my reckoning – some 52 operational variants. The Spitfire was the only fighter on the Allied side which remained in full production from the very first day to the very last of the Second World War, and in fact it remained in front-line RAF service until 1951.

The full, complete history of this extraordinary aeroplane can only be an amalgam of many accounts written from many points of view, and based either upon the diverse knowledge and experience of individuals who were involved or put together by later historians who will have researched the various aspects. If this book makes some contribution to that amalgam I shall be more than satisfied.

Jeffrey Quill

November 1982

Acknowledgements

My warmest thanks are due to the people who have helped me in the preparation of this book: Mr Alec Lumsden for his valuable research, using both his own and external sources, and for his work on photographs and the index; Mr Peter Pimblett, who has drawn upon his extensive store of relevant historical information and knowledge and has also read through the entire typescript; Air Commodore R. Spiers, OBE FRAeS, Commandant of the Aeroplane & Armament Experimental Establishment, Boscombe Down, for great help received from members of his staff: Mr T. H. J. Heffernan, Mrs Joan Woods and Miss Alison Whatley; Messrs K. Meadows, D. Goode and B. Kervell of the Royal Aircraft Establishment, Farnborough; Mr Humphrey Wynn of the Air Historical Branch MOD; Mr E. Brook and Mr R. A. Forrester of Rolls-Royce Aero Engines Ltd; Mr J. Fowler of the Public Record Office at Kew; Mr Hugh Scrope and Mr B. Wexham of Vickers Ltd; Messrs Norman Barfield, E. B. Morgan and E. Fice of British Aerospace PLC; Mr J. R. Rasmussen, late of Supermarine; Mr J. M. Bruce of the Royal Air Force Museum at Hendon; and Mrs J. M. Cowland of the Meteorological Office, Bracknell.

Finally, I would like to thank Mrs Christine Ashworth who somehow deciphered my handwriting to produce the original typescript.

1

Fledgeling

During the First World War, when I was very small, an aeroplane once landed on the stretch of common between our house at Littlehampton in Sussex and the sea and after some delay took off again. We had a ringside seat for the take-off from our balcony. Sometime later another aircraft crashed in a field at Rustington and my elder brothers and I were taken to see it. These two incidents made a considerable impression on me.

Officers in uniform very often came to our house for lunch or tea and amongst them was a pilot in the Royal Flying Corps, Jack Hunter, whose family lived locally. He seemed to me a figure of immense glamour and I well remember how, in answer to the inevitable questions from well-meaning adults, I always replied that when I grew up I would join 'the Flying Corps'.

I had a book of pictures of aeroplanes which I studied avidly. Occasionally – great excitement – real aeroplanes would fly overhead and my brothers and I would watch them intently until they were out of sight. Next, I had a craze on model aeroplanes and quickly became hooked on the smell of the oiled silk with which their wings were covered and the lubricant used on the multiple elastic bands which constituted the power for the propellers.

But it was at school at Lancing that my interest in aviation became almost an obsession. When I was an 'under-school' (fag) I was appointed one of the two 'library under-schools', whose privilege it was to enter the library at any time whereas boys of the Lower School were normally allowed in only at strictly limited times of day. As a result I was able to spend much of my little spare time browsing through aviation publications such as *The Aeroplane*, then edited by C.G. Grey; *Flight*, edited by Stanley Spooner; the *Royal Air Force Quarterly*; the *Cranwell Gazette*; and *Jane's All the World's Aircraft*. Thus I learned a little about aeroplanes and became familiar with some of the well-known names in the aviation world such as Camm and Pierson, and Mitchell, Bulman, Sayer and Summers, and Uwins, but it was beyond my wildest dreams to think that they would one day be my friends and associates.

Lancing stands on the South Downs overlooking the small port of Shoreham and Shoreham aerodrome, which was then a small grass field with some old hangars and a wooden hut for the flying club. The club was run by Fred Miles, later to achieve fame as an aircraft designer in the firm of Phillips & Powis and later still in Miles Aircraft Ltd. The Flying Club offered instruction on Avro 504K aircraft fitted with Clerget rotary engines. The instructor was the legendary Captain Cecil Pashley who had been an instructor at Shoreham since before the war. 'Pash' did innumerable circuits and bumps with his various pupils which brought his Avro over the College only a few hundred feet high. Aircraft in the air were few and far between in those days, and as far as I was concerned a daily diet of aircraft at such close quarters was a feast. A master at Lancing, E.B. Gordon, used to organise each year a party of boys to go to the Royal Air Force Display at Hendon. The first one I attended was in 1927 and subsequently I went on each annual expedition until 1930. 'Gordo' took especial trouble over those of us he knew to be interested in aviation and the Royal Air Force. His brother, C.F. Gordon, always known as 'the Horse', was a Squadron Leader in the Royal Air Force and sometimes he used to fly down to the college in an Avro 504N (Lynx Avro) from the RAF Central Flying School and land on the Downs just above the College or sometimes on one of our vast playing fields – dodging goalposts as he did so. On one occasion when the Horse's Avro was on the ground at 'Boiler Hill', on the Downs just above the College, Fred Miles spotted it and landed one of his Avro 504Ks alongside to see what was going on.

By the time I had been at Lancing for two years I had resolved to go into the Royal Air Force and was thus spared the difficulties of deciding what to do on leaving. My only doubt was whether I would pass the rigorous medical examination. In an attempt to ensure this I took an enormous amount of physical exercise and slept in the freezing dormitories with a minimum of bedclothes in the quaint belief that this would make me physically tough.

My father had died the year before I arrived at Lancing and my mother was left with very slender financial resources and five children, of whom I was the youngest. For this reason I decided to apply for a Short-Service Commission rather than sit the examination for Cranwell, because as a short-service officer I would be self-financing from the outset.

So, armed with a letter of recommendation from my Headmaster, I duly presented myself at Adastral House in London for my interviews and medical examination. At this time I was mildly and kindly lectured by various uncles and family friends on my rashness in bypassing University. Did I realise, they said, that after five years I could well find myself out of a job with no degree and no sort of qualification for employment in the civil field? Furthermore, the country was in the throes of an economic crisis and aviation in any form was a highly speculative business. A job in Lazards, in the City, was open to me offered by my Uncle 'Bob' Kindersley, but my reaction to all these arguments was one of mild astonishment that anyone should worry about anything so remotely in the future as five years.

In due course I was informed by the Air Ministry that I had been accepted for a commission as an Acting Pilot Officer (on probation) and that I should report to the Royal Air Force Depot at Uxbridge on 9 October 1931, by which time I would be aged eighteen years seven months.

Our three weeks at Uxbridge were spent square-bashing under the supervision of a Warrant-Officer Mawby late of the Brigade of Guards, now transferred to the RAF, and in attending lectures from officers on the Depot staff, which were our first indoctrination into the ways of the Service. Uxbridge also gave us our first contact with a Royal Air Force Officers' Mess. Although the Uxbridge Mess lacked the intimacy and family atmosphere we were later to encounter in the messes of operational stations it was pleasant and comfortable. But we were required to be very quiet and self-effacing. At the Depot there was a continuous flow of officers of various ranks, many just returning from overseas postings. We, Acting Pilot Officers on probation, the lowest of the low, observed this traffic with a silent, deferential but half-amused eye.

The Commanding Officer of the Depot was a much-decorated Group Captain, F.L. Robinson. We saw little of him until one afternoon, in the middle of a lecture, he came unannounced into the room causing all present to spring to their feet and stand stiffly to attention. He motioned to us to sit and then proceeded to give us an apparently completely off-the-cuff talk on the Royal Air Force, its composition and history, its military roles, with special emphasis on its overseas tasks and finishing up with a crisp analysis of what would be expected of us as young officers in a Service in which we must consider ourselves extremely privileged to be allowed to serve.

The Headquarters of Fighting Area (which some years later became Fighter Command) was nearby in Hillingdon House and the Officers of this Headquarters used the Depot Mess. Most evenings a figure of stratospheric seniority, an Air Vice-Marshal no less, would stalk into the ante-room. This was the Air Officer Commanding Fighting Area, 'Ginger' Bowhill, a man of short stature but terrifying aspect due to his red hair and piercing blue eyes beneath bushy and prominent eyebrows.

It was only at the very end of our short course at Uxbridge that we were informed of our next destination. In those days there were four Flying Training Schools (FTS) for the training of short-service officers and of officers commissioned directly from the universities who were known as 'direct entry' officers. These were No. 2 FTS at Digby in Lincolnshire; No. 3 FTS at Grantham, also in Lincolnshire; No. 4 FTS at Abu Sueir in Egypt; and No. 5 FTS at Sealand near Chester. Of our course at Uxbridge ten were posted to Abu Sueir and the rest of us to No. 3 FTS at Grantham. There the courses lasted for an academic year and, as there were two entries per year, we spent about five months in the junior term and five months in the senior term. Although as short-service officers we were commissioned from the day we joined, the probationary nature of our commissions was strongly emphasised from the outset. We could summarily be awarded a 'bowler hat' for any failure to measure up to requirements and we were frequently reminded of this. We were treated as officer cadets, not as commissioned officers.

The routine at Grantham was PT at 7 a.m., working parade at 8.30, with the rest of the day divided between lectures, square-bashing and flying instruction. Our term was divided into two groups or squads; and while one was flying the other was receiving lectures, ground instruction, drill or some other form of activity considered good for our souls or our bodies. Wednesday afternoons were devoted to sport, which at FTS was compulsory.

There were three 'ab initio' training flights – one equipped with the Avro Tutor, a biplane of metal tubular construction with an Armstrong Siddeley Lynx engine; a second was equipped with Hawker Tomtits; and the third with De Havilland Tiger Moths. I was allocated to the Avro Tutor flight, which pleased me well because the Tutor seemed to me a man-sized aeroplane whereas I thought the Tiger Moth a toy by comparison, redolent of a civilian flying club.

My 'ab initio' instructor was Flying Officer Stevenson, a man of few words which is a great advantage in an instructor. He taught me well and soundly, giving neither praise nor blame, and he sent me solo after five hours twenty minutes' dual, apparently the shortest time for anyone on our term. Before a pupil could be sent on his first solo flight he had to undergo a test by the Flight Commander, who, in my case, was Flight Lieutenant H.M. ('Tishy') Groves, who approved me for solo after one circuit and bump. He climbed out of the front cockpit, stowed his straps, patted me on the shoulder and said 'Off you go' and off I went. I well remember the exhilaration, then, of finding myself alone in the air, the empty front cockpit ahead and the conscious effort to suppress my excitement in order to rehearse the basic instructions which had been dinned into me. I did a good landing, to my great relief, and the first major hurdle in my flying training was safely surmounted.

At this time the Station Commander at Grantham was Group Captain Bowen. He was a tall, distinguished, rather haughty-looking man. Shortly after my first solo I was walking through the camp with a group of other pupils when we encountered him coming the other way on the opposite side of the road. As we all saluted he called me sharply by name. I crossed the road, saluted him again and stood to attention, wondering what on earth I had done to incur his displeasure. Suddenly his face broke into a smile and he shook me warmly by the hand and congratulated me on my first solo flight. I subsequently discovered that he did this to everyone after their first solo!

Training continued according to a carefully arranged syllabus. Regulations required that no pupil could do more than two and a half hours' consecutive solo flying without a period of dual from his instructor. This was to guard against the accumulation of bad or potentially dangerous habits or over-confidence. The syllabus was comprehensive and included the technique of low flying (vital in those days because low flying was frequently forced upon one by bad weather), forced landings, air pilotage, airmanship, aerobatics, map reading, cross-country flying and 'pinpointing'. On the ground we were lectured on, and examined in, engines, airframes and rigging, armament, navigation, theory of flight, Air Force law, Air Force history, administration and, of course, there was plenty of square-bashing and rifle drill.

By the end of our junior term I had accumulated 57 hours 55 minutes in the air and I felt confident all round – probably over-confident. During the last few days of the term the weather turned very cold and we experienced for the first time the visual transformation of the terrain caused by heavy falls of snow – and the ease with which one could get lost in such a suddenly unfamiliar landscape. My last afternoon's flying in the junior term was devoted to practising inverted turns and inverted spins. I considered trying my hand at a bunt (an outside loop), which was strictly forbidden, but thought better of it. It would have been a pity to collect a 'bowler' on the last day of term.

Senior term status at Grantham provided little difference in the routine. One was conscious of taking a minuscule step upwards in seniority when a lot of fresh faces arrived with the new junior term, and some new university entrants joined us in the senior term, but the main excitement was the transition from elementary to advanced flying training, which was conducted in 'service types'. These were the Armstrong Whitworth Siskin IIIA single-seater fighter in 'C' Flight and the Armstrong Whitworth Atlas two-seater Army Co-operation aircraft in 'B' Flight. Both were powered with the Armstrong Siddeley Jaguar 14-cylinder twin-row radial of 450 bhp and both were still in frontline service.

I was appointed to the Siskin flight, commanded by Flight Lieutenant H.L.P. ('Pingo') Lester who had flown in the Royal Naval Air Service during the war; and my instructor was Flying Officer Kenneth Knocker*. Any subsequent success that I achieved as a pilot, and indeed my very survival, I attribute primarily to the quality of the teaching and encouragement I received from these two men, and the solid horse-sense about flying aeroplanes which they imparted.

The Siskin had for several years been the standard equipment of the RAF's fighter squadrons, all of which were at that time

---

* Killed in action, Bomber Command, 1942

deployed in the United Kingdom. It had now been replaced by Bristol Bulldogs and Hawker Furies but there were still a few Siskins left in the front line. The single-seater Siskin IIIA was an extremely good advanced trainer. It was large and heavy enough to make a pupil feel he was flying a real Service aeroplane and not something out of which all faults and vices had been designed in order to make it suitable for training. But it had the reputation of being difficult to land. In fact, the Siskin was not difficult to land but only unforgiving and intolerant of mishandling. It was a sesquiplane, which means that it was almost a parasol mono-plane, the very small lower wing being there as much for structural as for lifting purposes. This configuration also gave it a high centre of gravity. If the aircraft dropped a wing on landing, which it was likely to do if mishandled, it quickly reached a steep lateral angle before the small and short lower mainplane touched the ground and the aeroplane was then liable to cartwheel over on to its back. The trouble was that, at the three-point landing attitude, the wing went beyond its stalling incidence and the lateral stability broke down. The trick, therefore, was to touch down just short of the three-point attitude taking care to be dead into wind and with no excess speed whatsoever. This required practice. The man who had worked it all out was 'Pingo' Lester and a little instruction from him put most people right. If, during the time that the Siskin IIIA had been in front-line service, every squadron pilot had received the 'Pingo treatment' it might have saved the Air Force vast sums of money in damaged Siskins. Also a lot of 'Siskin noses' caused by pilots striking the face against the forward edge of the cockpit in such accidents.

The Siskin was a good aeroplane for aerobatics although its ailerons were heavy. I had a great deal of help from Kenneth Knocker in learning and practising aerobatics and as a result I won the Aerobatic Trophy – the Duggan Cup – which was competed for at the end of the senior term. (Many, many years later, when No. 3 FTS had moved to Leeming in Yorkshire, I was invited to a Guest Night and found the Duggan Cup with my name engraved upon it reposing opposite my place at dinner – an elegant and alert compliment from the Mess.)

In those early days of the 1930s, it was both tradition and policy in the Air Force that aircraft should be landed from a gliding approach with the engine fully throttled back. One took the power off at about 500–700 ft on the downwind or base leg of a left-hand circuit. The object was to aim to overshoot slightly and then, at the last moment, to side-slip in order to get rid of excess height before crossing the threshold of the aerodrome for touch-down. The whole operation had to be judged precisely. The technique of side-slipping, once mastered, gave one considerable flexibility on the approach and it was highly satisfactory to judge it well and finish up with an elegant three-point landing exactly on the intended spot. Incidentally, no fighter aircraft in those days had wheel brakes so it was, on those small grass aerodromes, important to be able to put the aircraft down exactly where one wanted. To be seen to misjudge an approach, undershoot and have to apply a burst of power to drag the aircraft over the boundary fence, was considered shameful and in some squadrons meant buying drinks all round in the Mess. The theory behind this practice of engine-off approaches was that only by the daily use of this skill could a pilot cope with a forced landing in a field in the event of engine failure. Against this, almost every foreign air force did power-on approaches as a matter of routine, and they argued that the British lost more pilots as a result of stalling and 'spinning in' from glide approaches than they lost due to engine failures. They were probably right. The RAF abandoned the practice when the more modern (and much more expensive) aeroplanes came along in the later 1930s.

Although at Grantham great emphasis was placed upon flying training and we, in our one (academic) year's course, accumulated more flying hours than the Cranwell cadets accumulated in close on two years, other aspects of our training were by no means skimped. Our passing-out parade demonstrated that we had become surprisingly good at drill and parade-ground ceremonial, nor were we backward in the ground subjects on which we had to sit passing-out examinations. Perhaps the significant number of short-service officers who subsequently gained permanent commissions and achieved senior rank in the Service illustrates the point.

By July the passing-out exams were upon us after which, if satisfactorily negotiated, we would be confirmed in rank, the words 'acting' and 'on probation' would disappear, and we would become genuine Pilot Officers. Our passing-out order and hence our places in the Air Force List would be established, our pilot

ratings awarded, and our postings to an op[...]
announced.

There were four possible pilot ratings: [...]
'Average', 'Above Average' and 'Exceptional [...]
received the rating of 'Exceptional' which w[...]
my log-book and signed by the Chief Flying I[...]
at that young, immature age, I am glad I [...]
recognise that I owed my 'Exceptional' rating primarily to my
two senior term instructors, Kenneth Knocker and 'Pingo'
Lester.

At that time the standard of flying training in the RAF was
justly considered the finest in the world. It had its origins in the
old Gosport system established by Lieutenant-Colonel R. Smith-
Barry's School of Special Flying during the First World War.
Prior to Smith-Barry, few flying instructors had any proper
understanding of what they were trying to teach. The result was
an appalling casualty rate amongst pupils, especially when converting to their operational aircraft. This tragic situation was
aggravated by the fact that few young men in those early days
drove cars or rode motor-bikes, and so had little basic knowledge
of mechanical things or their working. They were much more
familiar with horses.

By no means too soon, therefore, Smith-Barry established a
logical and formalised system of teaching which gave pupils a
proper understanding of the basic functioning of an aircraft in
the air. More important, his system produced properly trained
instructors and the Central Flying School or CFS, established
originally in 1912, was made responsible after the war, for
standardising and supervising the standards of flying training
throughout the Service as well as for training all instructors.

After leaving Grantham I flew intensively for sixteen years and
logged well over a hundred different aircraft types, many of them
high performance fighters, including jets. Throughout this time
I enjoyed a high level of confidence in my ability to handle
aircraft of widely different characteristics, and attribute this to
the quality of the instruction I received in the Royal Air Force.

Early in my career, I read a phrase which has stuck in my
memory. It said, 'aeroplanes are not in themselves inherently
dangerous but they are very unforgiving'. This fundamental
piece of wisdom taught me always to keep a very firm grip on

dation which arose in the air, so as never to be taken by
se and so never to have to ask any aeroplane for too much
iveness.

There was an agreeable tailpiece to my time at Grantham. When
term ended and everyone went on leave, there were two or three
Siskins in 'C' Flight which had only a few flying hours to go
before becoming due for major inspections. Obviously it was
desirable that these hours should be flown off so that the inspections could be carried out during the leave period. My friend
Quentin Ross and I volunteered to stay behind at Grantham and
fly off the surplus hours.

'Pingo' Lester arranged for us to authorise our own flights – a
rare privilege for such junior officers – and so we flew each day for
as long as we could. We were not authorised to land at other
aerodromes, except in emergency, so I planned a number of
triangular cross-country flights to practise my navigation and
map-reading. Our Siskins were not equipped with any form of
blind-flying instrument and our only training in cloud flying had
been a few flights 'under the hood' in a Moth fitted with a Reid &
Sigrist gyroscopic turn-and-bank indicator. I decided, in my
ignorance, that I should be able to climb a Siskin through a few
thousand feet of cloud using only the compass, altimeter, bubble
side-slip indicator and airspeed indicator, and I made several
attempts to do this with spectacular lack of success. It seems
incredible, when I recollect the times that I got completely out of
control and emerged from the cloud base at some grotesque
attitude and with rapidly rising airspeed, that I did not kill
myself. It was only, perhaps, when I was climbing through a
snow-filled cloud and suddenly observed the snow-flakes going
in altogether the wrong direction that I began to accept the truth
– namely, that blind flying without a gyroscopically controlled
instrument was not only impossible but highly dangerous.

Quentin Ross and I had received joining instructions from the
Adjutant of 17 (Fighter) Squadron, stationed at Upavon, Wiltshire, and accordingly we dismounted one fine day from a GWR
train at Pewsey where RAF transport in the form of a Trojan was
waiting to drive us to Upavon.

Upavon is on Salisbury Plain, on the road between Marlborough and Andover. It is on the crest of one of the gentle green

slopes which roll like waves southwards towards Salisbury itself. Ross and I arrived at about tea-time and decided to have a walk round the station. We headed for the hangars and out onto the aerodrome which was, of course, entirely of grass except for the tarmac apron in front of the hangars. I remember two things particularly: we started up two hares which scampered off southwards, and we could clearly see Netheravon and Boscombe Down in the distance beyond – aerodromes which, like Old Sarum, were steeped in RAF history.

I had a strong feeling of new adventure but felt all the nervous anxiety arising from an urgent need to succeed and the fear that I might somehow fail in a vital point of duty or be found wanting in any one of a hundred different ways. I went to bed that night, however, with a feeling of considerable excitement. It was not much more than a year since I had left school and I was, after all, now an officer in a Royal Air Force Fighter Squadron.

2

Royal Air Force

In 1932, the Royal Air Force – under the Chief of the Air Staff, Air Chief Marshal Sir John M. Salmond – had a strength of 29,500 officers and men, the bulk of whom were stationed overseas, in India, Iraq, Egypt, Sudan, Palestine, Transjordan, Gibraltar, Malta, Aden and Singapore. There was a total of 61 operational squadrons, excluding Fleet Air Arm units, which for operational purposes were mostly organised in 'Flights'. The squadrons were classified as Fighter (all deployed in the UK), Bomber, Bomber Transport, Army Co-operation, Coastal Reconnaissance (flying boats), Torpedo-Bomber and Fleet Spotter Reconnaissance and Communications. Every aeroplane in RAF service was a biplane, the High-Speed Flight at Calshot with its monoplane racing seaplanes having been disbanded after the successful winning of the Schneider Trophy in 1931.

The operational role of the Royal Air Force at home was the air defence of Great Britain against any possible attack. Thus the main operational Command at home was called ADGB (Air Defence of Great Britain) of which the Commander-in-Chief was Sir Geoffrey Salmond, Sir John's brother. ADGB Headquarters at Uxbridge administered a series of 'areas': Fighting Area, Wessex Bombing Area, Inland Area, and Coastal Area. The principal overseas commands and areas were Middle East, Transjordan and Palestine, Iraq, India, Mediterranean, Aden and Far East. Each command had its imperial role and its relationship with the other two Services in its area clearly defined. The Fleet Air Arm was a joint Service affair. The Navy, naturally, provided the aircraft carriers, the Air Force provided the aeroplanes, and the manning, both for air crew and ground crew, was on a 50/50 basis.

The highest performance operational aircraft then in service was the Hawker Fury biplane fighter of which there were three squadrons, Nos. 1, 25 and 43. It had a top speed of 207 mph at 14,000 ft. The world's air speed record stood at 407.5 mph, held by the British with the Supermarine S.6B seaplane, the aeroplane which had won the Schneider Trophy in 1931.

In February 1933 the RAF gained the world's non-stop long-distance record, set up by Squadron Leader O.R. Gayford and Flight Lieutenant G.E. Nicholetts with a specially built Fairey long-range monoplane on a flight from Cranwell to Walvis Bay, South-West Africa, a distance of 5,341 miles flown in 57 hours 24 minutes. The world's altitude record for aeroplanes was taken from the US Navy in August 1932 by a Vickers Vespa with a special Bristol Pegasus engine flown by Cyril Uwins (Bristol's Chief Test Pilot) to a height of 43,976 ft, only 14,000 ft below the absolute ceiling set by Professor Piccard in a balloon that same month.

As far as the air defence of Great Britain was concerned the potential enemy, in the absence of any credible threat from elsewhere, was deemed to be France. Belgium and The Netherlands were not considered to pose any danger; Germany was forbidden to have an air force under the Treaty of Versailles and the Soviet Union and the Eastern European countries, such as Poland and Czechoslovakia, were reckoned to be too far away; Italy and Spain were a threat only in the Mediterranean and thus were not the business of ADGB.

So the annual air exercises, in which the ADGB Fighting Area defensive arrangements were tested, were conducted on the assumption that attacks would come from France. Wessex Bombing Area, with its Virginias, Hinaidis and Sidestrands, and a couple of squadrons each of Fairey IIIFs and Harts, simulated such attacks. In Fighting Area, with our fourteen squadrons of fighters, we did our best to intercept the bombers and attack them, using camera guns. There was an elementary but well-thought-out system of fighter control based on operations rooms and plotting tables at all the main fighter stations and, of course, two-way R/T communications. These were really the prototypes of the similar but much more highly developed operations rooms used in Fighter Command in 1940, by which time radar was in action. In 1932–3 information for the plotters was extremely sketchy, based on Observer Corps (not yet 'Royal') reports and a certain amount of cheating arising from prior knowledge of the routes to be taken by the raiders. Therefore the information reaching us over the R/T in the air was even more sketchy. We

carried out our interceptions by day and (if we were lucky) by
night. If one came back with a good close-up camera-gun picture
of the tail gunner of a bomber that was very satisfactory, although
sometimes one got into trouble for going too close, for bomber
crews did not appreciate very close-up views of a Bulldog's nose
and guns. There was a certain air of unreality about this whole
business but for young fighter pilots it was all very amusing and
great fun.

At this time, there was a movement within the League of
Nations at Geneva which sought to promote an international
agreement to 'outlaw' the bomber aircraft; and there were some
people who wanted to abolish all Air Forces entirely. They
seemed to have the cosy idea that with a stroke of the pen one
could un-invent the aeroplane. We used to listen, with somewhat
sardonic detachment, to reports on the wireless of the speeches of
politicians who felt it was their moral duty to abolish us; for we
realised that their attitudes stemmed largely from electoral and
budgetary considerations. (I often reflected on all this when I was
once again serving in a RAF fighter squadron in the summer of
1940.)

On 27 September 1932 Quentin Ross and I reported to the
adjutant of 17 Squadron, Flying Officer Bob Preller. He was
wearing the greenish khaki uniform of the South African Air
Force, although by this time he was commissioned in the Royal
Air Force, having transferred from the SAAF. After the custom-
ary courtesies we were given a run-down on the squadron and its
personnel and activities. Ross was appointed to 'B' Flight commanded by Flight Lieutenant Borthwick-Clarke and I to 'C'
Flight commanded by Flight Lieutenant B.B. Caswell. The
Squadron, in fact, was temporarily under the command of
Caswell as it was awaiting the arrival of its new CO, Squadron
Leader F.J. Vincent DFC, whose Service career had started in the
Royal Marines during the First World War. When shortly afterwards Vincent did arrive to take over the Squadron he soon made
it clear that he expected the highest standards of behaviour and
discipline and would tolerate nothing less. My experience of him
was that he was a hard but meticulously fair man in all his
dealings with those under his Command and he soon earned
everyone's respect and co-operation. Indeed the Air Force in

general at that time would have been better off with more officers of the calibre of F.J. Vincent.

On 28 September I was taken for a flight in a dual Siskin by Flight Lieutenant Reggie Pyne for purposes of familiarisation with the aerodrome, which was small and undulating and thus provided interesting possibilities for aircraft devoid of either flaps (hardly heard of in those days) or wheel brakes. Immediately after this I did my first flight in a Bulldog, K2138. This was a somewhat different aeroplane from the Siskin, the only other fighter I had flown. Whereas, in the latter, one sat in a comfortable but upright position with the rudder pedals set fairly low, in the Bulldog one's feet were much higher and the body therefore more bent in the middle, which proved to be a source of discomfort at the base of the spine on long flights. The cockpit was much higher relative to the centre line of the fuselage so that one's head was almost in line with the trailing edge of the upper mainplane, enabling one to look both over and under it. There was thus a slight feeling of riding *on* the aeroplane rather than in it. The line of the fuselage abaft the cockpit was lower than that ahead of it which provided a very good rearwards view. With the adjustable seat in the uppermost position the shoulders came well above the cockpit coaming – draughty, but providing a very good all-round view and a feeling of being in control of events.

The aircraft was of fabricated metal tubular construction and the cockpit was roomier and better laid out than that of a Siskin. The two Vickers .303 machine-guns were mounted low inside the cockpit, one on each side and at about hip height. The breeches were actually inside the cockpit and thus easily accessible for clearing stoppages, but the barrels protruded through external channels in the forward fuselage and fired through the propeller disc. The controls for the Constantinesco hydraulic interrupter gear, which prevented the bullets from hitting the wooden propeller, were mounted centrally on the upper dashboard and readily visible and accessible. The interrupter gear required a certain amount of setting up, bleeding air out of the system before use, for example, but once set up it worked well.

Unlike the Siskin the Bulldog did not carry fuel in the fuselage. It was in tanks at the root end of each upper mainplane and piped down to a small collector box just aft of the engine. There were individual on/off cocks situated one each side of the dashboard and the feed to the collector box was by gravity. A contents gauge was situated at the base of each tank clearly visible from the cockpit. The Bulldog's fuel system thus had the merit of extreme simplicity which was a great deal more than could be said of the Siskin. Nevertheless, even with the Bulldog's apparently 'pilot-proof' system, we had one accident on the station due to mis-handling of the fuel – something I thought well-nigh impossible until it happened.

It seems incredible, in retrospect, that only seven years before the Second World War we were still flying aeroplanes which were little more than derivatives of the RFC fighters of the First World War. Like the Camel and the Snipe we fired two .303 Vickers machine-guns; we used the same Constantinesco inter-rupter gear to protect our wooden propellers; admittedly our airframes were constructed of metal rather than wood but they were still fabric-covered braced structures. We had good and reliable supercharged engines and undoubtedly our airframe structures were more scientifically stressed and much safer. We had, however, like the SE5A and the Camel, no flaps, no wheel brakes and no cockpit heating. Amazingly we had no oxygen (although some squadrons did) and so our 'Battle climbs' were limited to 16,000 ft. Although we had radio telephony there were no direction-finding ground stations so R/T was used only for air-to-air and air-to-ground communication purposes – the latter having an important part to play in the then elementary but developing system of fighter control or semi-ground-controlled interception.

My first impressions of flying the Bulldog were that its greater all-up weight, compared with the Siskin, was immediately apparent, but its aileron control was much lighter and more responsive, due to its Frise ailerons which had been developed by Bristol. Its nine-cylinder Jupiter radial engine was somewhat rougher, as might be expected, than the 14-cylinder twin-row radial of the Siskin. It was noticeably but not spectacularly faster than the Siskin and on this, my first flight in a Bulldog, my log-book tells me that I remained airborne for 40 minutes and did 'landings', 'turns' and 'gliding turns'. Gliding turns had a real significance in those days. It was standard practice in the Air Force to carry out engine-off approaches and landings except when landing in formation; this involved a series of gliding runs which had to be executed with precision and accurate speed control if the ever-present danger of stalling into an incipient spin was to be avoided. Thus the ability to carry out steep gliding turns naturally, instinctively, and accurately was one of the first things to be mastered when familiarising oneself with a new type of aircraft.

After that first flight in a Bulldog, I taxied in, slipped off my Sutton harness and parachute harness, and hoisted my backside on to the fuselage behind the cockpit with my feet on the seat (the first necessary stage in leaving the aircraft). This gave a complete view of the surface of the upper mainplane with its gleaming silver dope finish and the double black zigzag stripes of 17 Squadron running spanwise between the large red, white and blue RAF roundels at each wing tip. I reflected upon what beautiful things aeroplanes were when you were really close to them and felt a surge of excitement and pride on being a member of this squadron.

Two days later I made a flight of one hour, recorded as a 'tour of the local area'. The tour took in Netheravon, Old Sarum, Boscombe Down, High Post (a small civilian field with a flying club), Stonehenge and Andover. Upavon was on the northern edge of Salisbury Plain; the river Avon ran southwards to Christchurch and Poole Harbour, and Salisbury Cathedral spire was a significant landmark on the way. The northern edge of the plain ran westwards towards Westbury and eastwards to Tidworth and Andover. Marlborough and Savernake Forest lay to the north with the promontory of Oare Hill as an obvious bad weather hazard to be carefully noted. Indeed some while later Paul Gomez, a pilot in 'C' Flight, hit it while descending through cloud and lost his left foot as a result. His Bulldog ploughed through a line of trees at fairly high speed and was well and truly wrapped up. I was in charge of the party of airmen dispatched to recover the wreckage, with a very capable Sergeant called Gommo, and a cold and miserably wet job it was. I remember my astonishment and relief that Paul – by then safely in Savernake Hospital – could have survived such a crash and I took a crumb of private comfort from this.

The next few months were spent on the individual and flight training programmes. I concentrated upon getting as much time in the air in the Bulldog as I could, practising formation flying, acting as target for interceptions, making camera-gun attacks on other aircraft using one or other of the official Fighting Area Attack patterns which were classified by number, e.g. FA Attack No. 1A, etc. These always struck me at the time as being potentially suicidal if the target aircraft had had a competent rear gunner!

We attacked ground targets with 20-lb practice bombs and carried out air-to-ground firing with live ammunition on the ranges at Lydd or Dungeness. For this we used to fly to Hawkinge. We carried out routine 'Battle flight climbs' against some suitable target when 'C' Flight was 'duty flight', and we did a good many 'cross-country' flights to other stations, the primary purpose of which was usually to have lunch with one's friends. Fighting Area comprised 14 squadrons based on eight aerodromes, so we tended to know each other well and to do much mutual visiting. It was all 'good for training'. We also did much night flying.

About every two weeks my log had an entry 'slow flying and spins', each initialled in red ink by my flight commander. This was a regulation, and a good one, to ensure that every pilot was constantly in practice at flying near the stall and at recovering from spins.

The complex aerodynamics of the spin, from which followed the technique of recovery, were first postulated at Farnborough where Dr F.A. Lindemann (later Lord Cherwell) played an important role. In August 1916 the chief test pilot at Farnborough, Major F.W. Goodden, had demonstrated recovery from spins, both right and left, in an FE8 and in June and July 1917 Lindemann himself carried out some successful spin recovery tests on a BE2C at Farnborough. The spin had been something of a bogey to the RFC squadrons during the war and in 1932 some of this neurosis still survived. In fact, the Bulldog IIA, as we flew it in 1932, had a viceless spin and would respond to the correct recovery procedure instantly. I once completed 50 turns in a Bulldog for the hell of it but, naturally enough, made no mention of this illicit operation in my log-book. The real significance of the spin at that time was that an aeroplane would lurch into a spin if stalled with any degree of yaw or sideslip in its flight path and it would then perform roughly a complete turn of an incipient spin and a few hundred feet would be lost in the course of this even when recovery action was taken at once. If, therefore, the aircraft was inadvertently stalled during a gliding turn in the course of an approach to land and there was not enough height to recover from the incipient spin, you were dead. This was what was called 'spinning in'. Although some aeroplanes were more prone to this type of accident than others it was basically caused by careless flying.

I also spent a great deal of time practising aerobatics. After fulfilling the official purpose of a flight, e.g. gunnery or interception, there was usually enough fuel left to indulge in ten minutes' aerobatics before entering the circuit to land. I enjoyed aerobatics but also realised that, unless they were practised assiduously to the point where one was familiar with every conceivable combination of speed and attitude of which the aircraft was capable, one was not master of the aeroplane. Therefore a day would come when the aeroplane decided that it was in charge instead of its pilot and that would be the last day. I never had cause to modify that view, and I kept my aerobatics well honed up to the day of my last flight as a pilot.

At Upavon there were, of course, days of frustration and tedium but our daily life was mostly very agreeable. The day started with Colour Hoisting parade, which was in effect a station working parade with squadrons marching off to their respective hangars. Flying then started as soon as possible and continued during the afternoon when, in normal circumstances, we knocked off at 4.30 p.m. The rest of the day was free for recreation, except on the four nights a week when the officers dined in Mess. Dinner in the Mess was in effect a parade and one presented oneself in the ante-room at 7.30 duly attired in Mess dress. After dinner we would play billiards or snooker or cards or read, or in the summer make a quick change and knock a golf ball around on our nine-hole course. Many people used to complain about dining in the Mess so often. Certainly it inhibited one's extra-mural activities a bit, but, living as we were in a rather isolated camp, I personally felt that it was a good discipline and made life orderly and agreeable.

Our batmen were not airmen but civilians who wore the blue uniform and Crown badges of the civil service, and were mostly retired NCOs from one of the three Services. I was lucky to have a splendid and rather elderly retired Sergeant of the Royal Horse

Artillery called Newton. He looked after me like a father. I was a
congenitally bad morning riser; Newton would have me out of
bed, shaved and dressed and propelled out of my room, buttons
gleaming, in time for morning parade even if I was barely conscious.

In the evenings I would sometimes get back to my room from
playing squash or golf at about 7.20 with no more than ten
minutes in which to change into Mess kit and get over to the main
Mess building for dinner. Newton would by this time have
created a sort of invisible man inside my Mess kit for whom I
could be substituted in the minimum time. Having struggled into
my shirt, collar and tie I would then step into my boots, pull
the trousers up, slip the braces over my shoulders whereupon
Newton would be hovering behind me ready to slip on my
waistcoat and jacket in a single deft operation. I would then start
to run and such minor matters as doing up fly-buttons and
straightening the tie were attended to, as it were, at the gallop. I
was never late, for which I had Newton to thank. Had I been late
for a parade or in the slightest degree improperly dressed,
Newton would have regarded it as a reflection upon himself.

There were, generally, very few married officers and practically none amongst the junior ranks, for marriage allowance was
not payable to officers below the age of thirty. Some did marry
below that age but not being officially on the married establishment they had to get permission to live out of the Mess (which
was not invariably granted) and had to finance their nuptial bliss
without the aid of the Air Ministry allowance. This was generally
referred to as 'living in sin'. The result was that virtually all young
officers were bachelors and we all lived together (and very well) in
the Mess, got to know each other well, flew together, played
sports together, shared our station duties, generally kept each
other out of trouble and enjoyed ourselves enormously.

The main events remaining to complete the Squadron's training
year were: the rehearsals for and participation in the 1933 Royal
Air Force Display at Hendon; the two weeks at the Air Firing
practice camp at Sutton Bridge in Lincolnshire; and the annual
Air Exercises to test the Air Defences of Great Britain.

We started rehearsing our 'turn' for Hendon in April 1933. We
were to carry out a low flying attack at squadron strength (nine

aircraft) against a transport column. The scenario, as described in the official programme, was as follows:

3.32 EVENT 4
LOW FLYING ATTACK

Officer Commanding No. 17 (Fighter) Squadron has been ordered to carry out an offensive patrol. The leader, observing an enemy convoy, decides to attack it with machine-gun fire by individual aircraft, followed by flight attacks. The varying stages of the attack will be broadcast.

Low-flying aircraft offer to rifles and machine-guns on the ground the easiest target when flying away from them. Fire from convergent directions is, therefore, adopted with the object of maintaining continuous attacks on the target from rapidly-changing directions. Whilst one aircraft is leaving the target, the next is making its attack and covering the retirement of the previous aircraft.

Squadron	Commanding Officer	Aircraft	Engine
No. 17 (F) Squadron	Squadron Leader F.J. VINCENT, DFC	Bulldog	Jupiter

We were to use the technique of low-level converging bombing which was designed to exploit the fact (as explained in the blurb) that an aircraft attacking a ground target was more vulnerable to ground fire when leaving the target rather than when approaching it. Thus simultaneous attacks by aircraft converging from different directions would, it was hoped, confuse and terrify the gunners defending the target.

Our show started by approaching the target area at about 1,000 ft in echelon to the right. On arrival at the target the leader peeled off to the left and dived down at the target, followed closely by the rest of us in line astern. All having fired a burst at the target, we in 'C' Flight (Caswell, Holland, Sergeant Little and myself) detached ourselves from the rest of the Squadron and carried out a converging bombing sequence which was complicated but, if done well, spectacular. Starting with an aircraft at each point of an imaginary circle surrounding the target we executed almost simultaneous attacks from four different directions, each aircraft timing his dive so as to pass closely behind the tail of the aircraft passing over the target from his right to left. Each then pulled up into a left-hand climbing turn so as to begin the next dive one quadrant (90°) to the left of the point at which he had started and so on until with the fourth dive the circle had been completed. Gunners positioned at the target thus had four aircraft attacking them almost simultaneously from four different directions and by the time the sequence was completed sixteen attacks had been made altogether. It required split-second timing; if someone was late, or early, with their dive the situation became chaotic – analogous to a mistake when dancing a Scottish reel – but at rather too high a speed for comfort.

We rehearsed the show over and over again at Upavon and then had to go and do it at Northolt so that it could be witnessed by the AOC and finally we had to do it at Andover for the Commander-in-Chief, ADGB, before going to Hendon.

It was at Andover, by which time we had the show pretty well perfect, that something went seriously wrong. After one of my dives I had reached the top of the subsequent steep left-hand climbing turn before diving again when Sergeant Little's Bulldog suddenly flashed over the top of my upper mainplane; he was so close that I clearly heard his engine above the noise and clatter of my own and I do not believe we could have had a nearer miss. I realised that I could not expect many more escapes like that, but I never knew what went wrong and I was exactly within my flight pattern. I was too startled to be angry and left it to Caswell, the Flight Commander, to sort it out afterwards. I never heard another word about it, but the sound of Little's engine so close over my head stayed with me a long time.

Our neighbours at Upavon were 3 Squadron, also equipped with Bulldog IIAs and, as its number implies, one of the oldest squadrons in the RAF, dating back to the Royal Flying Corps of the pre-1914–18 period. They also were rehearsing a show for Hendon with a flight of three Bulldogs led by Flight Lieutenant B.W. Knox with Flying Officers D.P. Boitel-Gill and Bill Clark as his numbers two and three. They were to attack a Sidestrand bomber using one of the Official Fighting Area attack procedures by way of demonstration to an unsuspecting public. The scenario called for one of them, Bill Clark, to be 'hit' by the Sidestrand's rear gunner whereupon he was to press a button to trail artificial smoke and perform a series of manoeuvres to simulate a shot-down aircraft and finally to disappear behind some convenient piece of landscape out of sight of the spec-

tators. Bill Clark's method of simulating an aircraft coming
down out of control was to execute a series of lazy stall turns,
losing height after each one until he was low enough to disappear behind some suitable topographical feature. One day
Bill Clark misjudged his last stall turn, took it too slow at the
top, took too long a drop out of it and was unable to pull out of
the subsequent dive. He hit the top of one of the slopes between
Upavon and Netheravon and was killed instantly. It was a
sobering spectacle for those of us who were watching and cast a
gloom over the whole station, for he was much liked.

Two days before the display, we flew to Hendon in squadron
formation and parked our aircraft ready for the final rehearsal
the following day, Friday, which went without a hitch. We had
to cruise around north London in a holding pattern while
awaiting our turn and I remember admiring how Vincent
brought us in absolutely on the dot of time. Our target was a
convoy of vehicles under the command of the resourceful Flight
Sergeant Hards. A number of devices such as 'thunderflashes'
had been positioned round the target and during our attack
Hards and his men were to rush back and forth touching them
off to simulate the bursts of the anti-personnel bombs with
which we were (theoretically) armed.

We awoke on the Saturday to find very low cloud and steady
rain. The Hendon show had enjoyed several successive years of
good weather and had never been rained off but today looked
like being the first occasion. At the aerodrome we found an
atmosphere of soggy depression, as our airmen stood dejectedly
around and our aeroplanes glistened and dripped in the wet. As
the morning wore on the rain began to ease, the cloud to lift a
little and become a little more ragged at the base, but it was still
clear that our converging bombing act was likely to spend most
of its time in cloud and we should probably end up attacking
Hendon Town Hall in error!

Shortly before the programme was due to start all participating
aircrew were summoned to a briefing by Air Vice-Marshal
'Ginger' Bowhill, Officer in Charge of the 1933 RAF Display.
We stood in a semicircle in the open and he addressed us. He told
us that the meteorological forecast indicated at best a slow
improvement in the weather but it was in any case going to be
bad. He had two choices – to cancel the programme or to carry on

with it. He had decided to carry on with it. I looked at the cloud base and thought to myself, 'My God – the old boy isn't half taking a chance.' He looked at us from beneath his bushy and fiery red eyebrows. 'Gentlemen,' he continued, 'the day is in your hands. I can only wish you luck,' and with that he turned and stumped off. It was an extremely courageous decision; he would certainly carry the can if there were a disaster in front of the public.

The public stands and enclosures were already filling up. We went back to our aircraft and the Squadron came to life as the airmen got busy preparing the aircraft, doing the D/Is (daily inspection) and running the engines. We were not due to take off until 3 p.m. The cloud base began to lift agonisingly slowly, but when we taxied out it still looked grim and I wondered how Vincent was ever going to get us into a position whence we could see the target and start our show; I also wondered how we in 'C' Flight were ever going to get through our converging bombing act. We took off and scudded around in and out of the cloud base, got into our echelon to starboard and kept disappearing in and out of cloud. We were flying in our breeches and puttees underneath our overalls and I remember sweating profusely in the humid atmosphere. Vincent led us over the target and we started our first attack (nine aircraft in line-astern) and then we in 'C' Flight broke away to start the converging bombing sequence. At each point when we pulled up between dives we disappeared into the cloud base; as we re-emerged on the way down it was a matter of intense interest to see whether one was correctly aligned with the target and could see the other aircraft through the murk. Miraculously it all worked perfectly; we reformed with the rest of the Squadron without a hitch and Vincent brought us in to land in three Vic formations of three. As so often happens in England, towards the late afternoon the weather brightened up considerably as the front passed over and the programme was completed without incident.

Some of us drove down to the Royal Air Force Club in London that evening which was, as always on the evening of the Hendon Display, extremely crowded, full of participant aircrew and very noisy. The following day we made our way to Hendon in order to fly, again in squadron formation, to Sutton Bridge for our annual practice camp. Having seen us off, the NCOs and airmen followed by road. Sutton Bridge, the air firing practice camp near King's Lynn, was a grass airfield situated on the edge of the Fen country with somewhat primitive hutted accommodation combined with a certain amount of canvas. There was a distinctly camp-like atmosphere about the place and if the weather was bad it could be cold, damp and most uncomfortable. Usually two fighter squadrons were in residence at any one time.

Although we did a certain amount of firing against ground targets in the normal course of our squadron training at our home bases, it was only during our two weeks at Sutton Bridge that we were able to fire our guns in the air against towed targets. The 'tug' aircraft were converted Fairey IIIF light bomber/general-purpose aircraft and they had a power-driven winch fitted in their large rear cockpit which also carried a winch operator. The targets were either a flat elongated flag or a circular cross-section drogue and they trailed at the end of several hundred feet of cable which was winched out by the tug aircraft after take-off. The weighted flag or drogue trailed at a level well below the towing aircraft and could, at least in theory, be attacked by a fighter with live ammunition without any danger of the tug being hit; sometimes the tug pilots needed a little convincing of this, but there were comprehensive systems of red and green signal lights controlling the attacking aircraft. A shower of red Verey lights would greet any fighter getting its sights too close.

The tugs trundled backwards and forwards along a line over the Wash and the bullets from the attacking aircraft finished up in the sea or the saltings. The job of being a tug pilot was one of unspeakable tedium interspersed with moments of extreme alarm. Indeed, a posting to Sutton Bridge as a target-towing pilot was one of the most formidable disciplinary threats available to the authorities at that time. In the squadrons the tug pilots used to be regarded with a faintly condescending pity and remarks such as 'What did you do, old boy, to get yourself into this pickle?' were not infrequently heard in the Mess.

That year I carried out 19 air-firing sorties. These were mostly against flag targets which were dropped on the airfield after the sortie and the bullet strikes were counted and one's 'score' assessed. The holes in the 'flag' were then hurriedly marked and it was used again on a later sortie. The operation ran on a competitive basis and at the end of the year there was a shoot-off between the top scoring pilots of each squadron for the Fighting Area championship. We had Aldis telescopic sights which were an improvement on the old ring and bead from the First World War, but if a gun stopped you were supposed to be able to clear the stoppage in the air. If you failed to do this you just lost the remaining unspent ammunition in that gun for scoring purposes. As the guns were perpetually stopping and were often difficult to clear it seemed a hard world. We carried a special clearance tool on a length of cord round our necks and, of course, the breeches of the guns were actually inside the cockpit alongside one's thighs. The guns made a great deal of noise and clatter, creating an abominable stink in the cockpit, and while they were firing the cocking handles thrashed back and forth at a great rate. If you got a simple 'No. 1' stoppage, you could reach down and grab the cocking handle and yank it back and away the gun would go again. On one occasion I heard one of my guns stop and immediately reached for the cocking handle without releasing the firing button; unfortunately I chose the wrong gun and received the hardest rap over the knuckles I ever had in my life.

I found that I was a poor shot which rather surprised and dismayed me because I was quite good with a 12-bore and my father had been a first-class shot. Not until more than half-way through our all-too-short time at Sutton Bridge did I begin to latch on to the technique or the knack of attacking towed targets. The first point was to remember that nobody was shooting back and therefore there was no hurry, so the approach to the flag should be slow, deliberate and not rushed because the lower the relative airspeed the longer the effective burst that could be fired. The second point to remember was to keep the engine revs low because of the nature of the Constantinesco interrupter gear, and the third was to judge the approach angle to the target very precisely, and to get in really close. On one occasion I got in too close to the flag and hit the weighted leading edge spar of the flag with my upper wing tip as I was breaking away. This damaged my wing tip and took a little bit of explaining away afterwards. On one's first practice camp it took time to work out the techniques for oneself, and the competitive nature of the enterprise meant that those pilots who had previously mastered the techniques were not going to pass the information on to the others. I left Sutton Bridge with a poor overall score but fairly clear in my mind about the techniques; a revelation which had come too late but made me determined to get a really good score next year.

I flew back from Sutton Bridge on my own via Northolt where I stayed the night. Returning to Upavon the following morning, 10 July, I ran into bad weather; the cloud base got lower and lower, the rain increased and I had to depart from my direct track to avoid high ground until I was unable to read my map because my full attention was devoted to dodging solid obstacles. When I was almost clipping the tree tops I said 'enough is enough' and landed hurriedly in a field which I chose because it was on an upward slope. I just managed to stop before colliding with the far hedge. The rain was pouring down in bucketsful and having shut down the engine I got out and ran to the edge of the field where there was a main road on the other side of which was a fairly large institutional looking building. This turned out to be Savernake Hospital. Here I was dried off, given cups of cocoa and generally cosseted by the nurses. In some trepidation I telephoned my Flight Commander to confess that I had flown into bad weather and finished up in a field, albeit the right way up and undamaged. Caswell then bowled the expected fast balls at me: Why had I taken off in face of a bad Met forecast? Having done such an idiotic thing why had I not turned back to Northolt while the going was good instead of pressing on until it was too late? Did I realise that I had needlessly endangered one of His Majesty's aircraft and caused the Squadron more trouble than I was worth? Finally, having perpetrated such enormities, why had I not had the elementary good sense to break my bloody neck when such a splendid opportunity had presented itself?

Having respectfully acquiesced in these wise and penetrating remarks, I asked permission to take off again when the weather cleared.

'If you think you can manage to find your way back to Upavon without the necessity of an intermediate stop in the Outer Hebrides, or perhaps the State of Luxembourg, you may,' said Caswell. I said I thought I could.

'Yes, sir,' I said, 'my compressed air cylinder is fully charged and I'm sure I can start up on internals.'

'No, sir, there is no damage to civilian property.'

'Yes, sir, I have noted that I will have the privilege of acting as Station Orderly Officer for the next three week-ends.'

I bade farewell to my kind and cheerful hostesses, started up the Bulldog and saw the white-clad figures waving from the front door as I circled the hospital before setting course for Upavon.

Almost immediately the Air Exercises were upon us. These followed much the same pattern each year with only marginal changes to the scenario. REDLAND (no political significance) was at war with BLUELAND. REDLAND's bomber force was to attack targets in BLUELAND, usually confined within certain general areas specified in the operations order which was issued in great detail and at considerable length beforehand. BLUELAND's fighter force was to intercept the bombers in the course of their dastardly surprise attack upon the old country. Camera guns would be used by both attackers and defenders and at the end of it all the score would be totted up, the lessons learned both operationally and organisationally would be recorded, issued to suitable recipients under 'secret' cover, filed away and no doubt forgotten. However each year some lessons were learned and recorded and slowly and painfully there evolved the basis of a viable fighter control system for Air Defence which was later to pay a vital dividend.

This year, 1933, coincided with the rise of Hitler to political power in Germany. At this time a great deal of high-powered thought and effort was, although we were not aware of it, being devoted to the apparently intractable problems of identifying, locating and tracking incoming bomber aircraft so that an effective means for their interception and destruction by fighter aircraft could be established. All we knew about were the attempts to track incoming aircraft by acoustic means through 'sound mirrors'. For this to work it was necessary, amongst other things, that the acoustic tracking stations should be able to differentiate between friendly and hostile aircraft and thus it was necessary to establish the 'sound signature' of all home-based aircraft so that in wartime all others could be assumed to be hostile.

One of our periodic chores in 17 Squadron had been to fly to Biggin Hill and patrol up and down a predetermined line at various heights and engine RPM for the benefit of the sound locators and for the recording of our 'sound signatures'. At least that is what we were told, but it seems more likely that, at this stage, the sound locators were really using us to see whether they could track us at all and if so with what degree of accuracy.

While the year 1933 can probably be identified as the time when the problems of Air Defence were beginning to be addressed with some degree of urgency due to the trend of events in Germany, we in 17 and 3 Squadrons, living and flying and training at Upavon in the pleasant countryside of Wiltshire, were still (patently) deployed, together with the rest of Fighting Area, against a possible threat from France. We were the most westerly Fighter Squadrons in the country; most of the remainder were ringed around London, except for Tangmere and Hawkinge on the south coast. We were deployed at Upavon no doubt to spring to the defence of the Midlands and the strategically vital ports of Southampton and Bristol. However within a year there was a redeployment of some of the Squadrons of Fighting Area and 17 and 3 Squadrons were moved to Kenley in Surrey. Thus the system was to become orientated towards Germany.

Number 17 Squadron operated at squadron strength throughout the three days and nights of the 1933 Exercises. We had an elementary operations room at Upavon with a plotting table and direct telephone lines to ADGB and to Observer Corps posts. We had R/T communication with the operations room from the air but there were no radio direction-finding facilities at all. Once we were airborne the only information available to the Ops Room of our position was that supplied by us presuming that we ourselves knew where we were (which was by no means always the case). Information of the 'enemy' positions came from the Observer Corps stations, manned entirely by volunteers. Inputs were from sound locators and their own aural or visual observations plus, I always suspected, some prior knowledge from Group Headquarters or some other celestial source, of the planned approach tracks of the raids. The raiders were a mixed force of Vickers Virginias, Handley-Page Hinaidis, Boulton Paul Sidestrands and Hawker Hart day bombers. In spite of the heavy odds against an interception it was surprising in fact how often we succeeded. Possibly this was partly due to the fact that the raiders themselves were as keen for an interception as we were so that their gunners could retaliate with their camera guns as we attacked them. While we claimed to have annihilated them they no doubt claimed to have done the same to us, so everybody was happy.

We used the standard RAF quarter-inch maps, but for exchanging positional information with the operations room the grid system was quite impractical with a folded map held in one gloved hand inside the cold and draughty cockpit of a fighter of those days. Instead there was a certain number of key towns or other landmarks which were underlined on our maps and marked on the operations table and we used those and only those as reference points. 'Position fifteen, one five, miles S.E. of Hungerford' for instance. This, as I have said, was in the happy event that we ourselves actually knew where we were!

The Air Exercises provided a pleasant break in the peacetime routine. There was an atmosphere of purposeful activity throughout the station. We were up at all hours of the day and night at various stages of readiness. Flare paths were out each night and all sorts of normally chairborne Station Officers had the even tenor of their lives disturbed by periods of duty in the operations room usually at the most ungodly hours. For pilots it was generally fun, if occasionally a bit of a bind. The people who were most relieved, however, when the exercises were over were the Mess servants who had to produce meals at all hours of the day and night. Successive annual Air Exercises during the 1930s, amusingly unrealistic and decidedly ludicrous though they often seemed, undoubtedly flagged up, for those who had eyes to see, the vital problems which had to be solved if we were ever to defend our country against a determined air attack.

Basically these were the problems of locating, identifying and tracking incoming enemy bomber aircraft, of 'controlling' and vectoring our own fighter aircraft on to the bombers, and of recovering them safely and quickly to base. Wireless direction-finding stations were on the way, but the real solution lay in the hands of the scientists who, aware that sound location would not provide a satisfactory answer, were already within something like a year of devoting serious attention towards a much more sophisticated and effective solution – Radar. It was also clear that a vast improvement and expansion of the whole communication network would be needed to back up a new Air Defence system and that this must be allied to a great improvement in the ability of the RAF to operate in bad weather. Civil aviation was beginning to show the way in this respect but hitherto the Air Force had been slow to follow suit. Few pilots were trained in cloud flying, all bad weather flying was discouraged and the attitude throughout the Service was 'if you can't see, stay on the ground'. That this simply was not good enough was painfully obvious to me at the time.

Also needed was a quantum jump in the performance of our fighter aircraft. The large biplane Handley-Page Heyford bomber with twin Rolls-Royce Kestrels, just due to enter service, could very nearly outpace a Bulldog and the only fighter with any reasonable performance was the Hawker Fury and this was of very short range and endurance. Finally, and above all, a huge expansion of the numbers of squadrons available for Air Defence was essential. The strength of Fighting Area was still substantially smaller than that planned as long ago as 1923; this was of course of serious concern to the Air Staff but the required funds could not then be procured from a Parliament which was still much preoccupied with disarmament conferences and the League of Nations. Fortunately, however, there were a number of senior and mid-rank officers, some scientists and engineers, some communications experts, some aircraft designers and industrialists and even some politicians who had the eyes to see and the courage and determination to act.

3

Met Flight

During 1933 some prototypes, which had been under evaluation at the Aeroplane & Armament Experimental Establishment (A&AEE) at Martlesham Heath, were sent to 17 Squadron for 'Service trials'. These were the Armstrong Whitworth AW XVI, the Gloster SS 19B and the Bristol Bulldog Mk IIIA. All were competing for the RAF order eventually won by the SS 19B which went into production as the Gauntlet I. The 'Service trials' we conducted had, I believe, no impact whatever upon the final result because the decision had probably already been taken by the Air Ministry. They were sent to us more with a view to gaining some experience of operating the aeroplanes within a regular squadron environment and with regular squadron pilots and ground crews.

Within the Squadron the SS 19B was certainly the favoured aeroplane both as far as performance and handling were concerned. This no doubt accounts for the fact that, as a junior Flying Officer, I managed to get my hands on it only once whereas I flew the AW XVI and the Bulldog IIIA R-7 often. The AW XVI was quite an exciting aeroplane to fly but its performance was not up to that of the SS 19B. The Bulldog IIIA was heavier and more cumbersome than our Bulldog IIA and the only noticeable improvement was that it had wheel brakes and cockpit heating, the latter of which was extremely welcome; we all disliked dressing up like polar bears in winter.

During August 'C' Flight was sent on temporary attachment to an advanced landing ground at Weston Zoyland in Somerset for the purpose of collaborating with an Army anti-aircraft unit. Caswell must have been on leave because Borthwick-Clarke, who normally commanded 'B' Flight, took Laurie Holland and me on this attachment as his numbers two and three. B-C, as he was known in the Squadron, had not long before been involved in a collision in the air during formation flying and had baled out of his Bulldog and been quite badly injured in the process. It was said that thereafter he did not care for his numbers two and three to formate on him too closely. As soon as we were airborne, therefore, Laurie and I tucked our wingtips really close in to B-C just for the hell of it; 'We'll show him how we do it in "C" Flight' no doubt we said to ourselves, but B-C showed not the slightest concern. When we arrived at Weston Zoyland, still in the tightest possible formation, he led us in a low pass over the aerodrome and we were both expecting to receive the signal to 'break' preparatory to landing individually in sequence. But to our astonishment B-C led us round the circuit and started shaping up for a formation landing. A formation landing always required a great deal more space because the approach had to be flatter and faster; I looked at the very small aerodrome ahead, Laurie and I exchanged grimaces from our respective cockpits and I thought, 'Hell – this is going to be as tight as can be – what *is* the man doing?' B-C then proceeded to lead us in at a very much lower speed than was normally considered safe for a formation approach, causing Laurie and me to juggle our Bulldogs uncomfortably close to the stall whilst frantically trying to keep station. He then dropped us neatly in over the airfield boundary and we eventually stopped, but with very little room to spare, and Laurie and I were both sweating more than somewhat by the time we succeeded in pulling up. We taxied in, aligned our aircraft neatly on the tarmac and the three of us walked together to the Watch Office. We muttered some words of polite praise to B-C for having brought us into such a small aerodrome in formation; he smiled broadly to himself but spoke never a word. Laurie and I felt decidedly chastened.

Back at Upavon in early September we were immediately involved in the Army manoeuvres on Salisbury Plain. 'A' Flight was sent on detachment to operate from a small landing ground called Imber Clump. This was a clump of trees standing on reasonably smooth ground from which it was possible to operate aircraft, but in no way could it be called an aerodrome. We lived under canvas for the few days we were there. The Army also had a small unit with its transport hidden within the clump and we used their tented Mess facilities.

The Bulldog Flight comprised Sergeant Little, one or two others and myself under the command of Reggie Pyne ('A' Flight Commander), Caswell having by then been posted. In the late

afternoon of 22 September, a day on which we did a great deal
of flying, Reggie Pyne took off with a Vic of three Bulldogs,
Sergeant Little on his right and me on his left. Little flew off very
wide to Reggie's right and just as we became airborne he went
slap into a low haystack which was to the right of the take-off
area. Reggie and I landed at once. Little's Bulldog was completely destroyed and we had great difficulty in getting him out of
it. He was still alive but obviously only just, and he died in the
ambulance on the way to hospital. Reggie Pyne was naturally
very distressed, but examination of the wheel tracks clearly
established the fact that Little had taken off far too wide and, of
course, as he was watching his leader during take-off he had
failed to see the low obstruction straight ahead of him. This cast a
gloom over our usually festive evenings with the Army officers in
their Mess tent. The next day the 'crash party', coming from
Upavon to gather up the remains of Little's Bulldog, became
thoroughly lost in the general confusion of Army transport on the
by-roads leading to Imber and I was sent out to find them from
the air and drop a message to tell them where to go. This probably
caused even greater confusion but eventually they arrived. In due
course we flew back to our base at Upavon, less the unfortunate
Sergeant Little, and resumed our training routine.

Following Caswell's posting we had a new Flight Commander
named Moreton, recently promoted to Flight Lieutenant and
very much of the post-war generation. In November he told me
about an Air Ministry letter which Vincent had received asking
for recommendations for Flying Officers suitable for posting to
the Meteorological Flight at Duxford in Cambridgeshire.

The 'Met Flight' was a very small and specialised unit which
existed for recording upper air temperatures and other weather
information to help the Meteorological Office in London to
prepare its daily forecasts.

For a good while now I had been irritated and frustrated by
Service attitudes towards flying in bad weather; and was fed up
with being kept on the ground in weather conditions in which I
knew I could fly. The Met Flight – by definition a unit which
specialised in flying in the worst of weather – seemed to offer the
chance, therefore, of a release from this. Also I felt that, as I had
done a complete year of the annual training sequence in a Fighter

Squadron, all that would happen next year would be to go through the whole business all over again without much extending my experience. I had come to the Squadron from FTS with the pilot rating of 'Exceptional', very young and full of enthusiasm; both Vincent and Caswell had obviously taken the view that I needed to be firmly disciplined and restrained if I was not to kill myself and possibly someone else due to over-confidence and over-enthusiasm. Looking back on it, they were certainly right and probably I owe my life to their restraining influence, but at the time I was chafing at the bit and felt the need for change. So with Moreton's help I put in an application to join the Met Flight – drawing attention to the fact that the Chief Flying Instructor at Grantham had, in my passing-out report, mentioned an aptitude for flying in bad weather. Vincent forwarded the application and the posting duly came through.

One more thing remained to be done at Upavon. The Central Flying School 'travelling circus', giving instruction in blind flying under the hood, arrived with their Avro 504Ns and there was just time for me to get this course in before I left for Duxford. Instrument flying in the Air Force was then in its very early stages, and was considered to be something slightly magical.

Although most pilots believed that they flew aeroplanes by feel or 'by the seat of the pants' as the saying was, this was in fact only true to a very limited extent. Obviously 'feel' was a factor which came into the equation but the fundamental fact was – and still is – that if a pilot is robbed of all visual reference to the outside world, as happens when flying in thick cloud, he soon becomes disoriented and dangerously out of control. Furthermore, experience had shown that in blind conditions a pilot's sense of feel could be actively misleading and simply compound the problem. Simplistic attempts to solve this problem by the adaptation of spirit levels or bob weights had all failed and eventually it was realised that the only answer was to provide an artificial reference to the earth's surface by means of a gyroscopically stabilised instrument in the cockpit.

Various attempts to develop such an instrument had been made over the years and the Air Force had finally adopted the Reid & Sigrist turn-and-bank indicator. This was not an artificial horizon (this came later) but it indicated rates of turn and rates of sideslip and it needed proper interpretation by the pilot which required special training and some skill. The Reid & Sigrist had the immense advantage that whatever the pilot did with the aeroplane – and sometimes some very odd things were done – the gyros never toppled, so the instrument never became inoperative. The gyros were driven by suction produced by a Venturi tube mounted in the slipstream and the worst thing that could happen was for this to become iced up. If that happened in thick cloud you were in big trouble, but the Venturis were usually mounted within the warm slipstream behind the cylinders of an air-cooled engine, and later on the gyros were driven electrically. Early experimental work on gyro-stabilised instruments for blind flying had been done in the USA and in Britain in the 1920s, but it had been a long time before such an instrument could be adopted as standard for RAF aeroplanes and for the training in their use to become established.

The Central Flying School had developed for the RAF the standard methods of operation and training for the Reid & Sigrist instrument and were regarded very much as the experts in the matter. Hence the 'travelling circus' which went round visiting operational stations and giving short courses in blind flying. They brought their own Avro 504Ns equipped with folding canvas hoods which closed over the rear cockpit thus simulating blind conditions for the pupil, the instructor or safety pilot sitting in the front to cope with the situation if the pupil got out of control.

As usual when a new technique is introduced, a certain amount of false magic and mumbo-jumbo had worked its way into the system. The standard CFS method of blind flying was based upon doing 'flat' (i.e. unbanked) turns which were considered safer in cloud and were supposed to simplify the interpretation of the instrument. It seemed to me that a flat turn was an abomination and a ridiculous concept because it could not be done in formation and was quite unsuitable for passenger aircraft. However whilst on the CFS course it was prudent to do what the man in the front cockpit said.

I soon realised that it must be more than coincidence that an Avro 504N (the 'standard' aeroplane at CFS) would do flat turns almost on its own. As soon as I was in the Met Flight and regularly climbing and descending through as much as 25,000 ft of often ice-laden cloud in a fighter aircraft it became instinctive to carry out normal turns and with that sort of practice I found I could fly on the Reid & Sigrist instrument just as accurately as in blue sky conditions. In fact I could almost do blind aerobatics. I became more than ever fortified in my view that the reason the RAF was at that time so backward in bad-weather flying was simply that not enough pilots did enough of it and so the general level of proficiency was low. However, I was glad of my instrument-flying course, during which I did 6 hours 35 minutes under the hood and was passed out by the Chief Flying Instructor at CFS, Squadron Leader R. Harrison.

There remained little more to be done before leaving Upavon and 17 Squadron. I would certainly miss the fun and activity of life in a Fighter Squadron; but I had made my decision and one afternoon I flew to Duxford with 'Steve' (Squadron Leader A.C. Stevens), the Commanding Officer of 3 Squadron, to make my number with the Met Flight.

The Cambridgeshire countryside was very different from and in many ways more attractive than that around Upavon, and we were only about twelve miles from Cambridge itself.

Because the Cambridge University Air Squadron did its flying training at Duxford we had close links with the University which I enjoyed as I was very much of an age with the undergraduate members of the CUAS who spent a good deal of time at Duxford. From what I had heard of the Meteorological Flight I was aware that this posting was a challenging one. It would involve a great deal of flying in extremely bad weather with no 'aids' as we know them today.

Duxford housed 19 (Fighter) Squadron, equipped with Bulldogs. There was also a large Station Flight with the principal function of providing the Flying Training for the University Air Squadron. It was equipped with Avro 504Ns, which were soon to be replaced by Avro Tutors (on which I had learned to fly at Grantham) and there were about eight instructors in all. Also coming under the Station Flight for administrative and disciplinary purposes was the Met Flight. There was also a Hawker Hart allocated for the use of Professor B. Melvill Jones, who was head of the Aeronautics Department of Cambridge University which itself was a sub-department of the University Department of Engineering. The aircraft allocated to this research unit were in effect part of the CUAS, which had been created by the Air Ministry in 1925 'in order to give students of Cambridge University an opportunity to learn to fly and to become familiar with the circumstances surrounding flying . . . It was hoped also that the Squadron would be able to carry out some research in aeronautics in co-operation with the University'.* Various aircraft had from time to time been allocated to Melvill Jones for basic research purposes but at this particular time it was a Hawker Hart on which a section of wing had been specially prepared for investigation into the 'boundary layer' of the airflow. This aeroplane was flown by a former RFC and RAF pilot, Flight Lieutenant Alec Haslam, then a full-time member of Melvill Jones' department.

The Met Flight shared a hangar with the CUAS and we had our own flight office. The nature of the work was specialised and we flew in weather conditions which would not for a moment have been authorised in a normal service unit, and also at unusual times of day.

The Flight consisted of two Flying Officers as pilots, one Flight Sergeant, a Corporal and several airmen, fitters, riggers and electricians.

An officer's posting to the Met Flight normally lasted two years and was staggered so that for the first year he was the number two pilot and the second year the Flight Commander. When I joined, Flying Officer Eric Noddings was just leaving and Flying Officer G.N. Snarey became Flight Commander. A year later I took the Flight over and was joined by Flying Officer R.C. Reynell, an Australian who became a very good friend.

Our aircraft were Armstrong Whitworth Siskin IIIAs with Armstrong Siddeley Jaguar IVc supercharged 14-cylinder radial engines. The single-seat cockpit of the Siskin was open and as in all RAF aeroplanes at that time there was no cockpit heating of any sort. We wore electrically heated suits which plugged into a socket in the cockpit by a sort of umbilical cord. The boots and gloves plugged individually into the suit.

These suits, developed at the Royal Aircraft Establishment at Farnborough, were still somewhat experimental but made life

---

* Quoted from Sir William Farren CBE MBE FRS in Cambridge University Engineering Dept. report.

tolerable at 25,000 ft in an open and unheated cockpit. On the whole they were reliable but sometimes a boot, or the finger of a glove, would go 'off line' resulting in a painful time spent after landing in thawing out the affected member.

There was one occasion when the kapok lining of George Snarey's suit caught fire and began to smoulder. Fortunately he was able to land in a field and strip it off before he too began to smoulder.

The role of the Flight was to climb twice daily to between 18,000 and 25,000 ft and to record temperature and humidity readings at every 50 millibars of altitude, the heights of the base and top of all cloud formations, exact types and classification of cloud (of which there are very many) and any special meteorological conditions such as temperature inversions, areas of fog on the ground, haze tops and so on.

The morning climb was airborne promptly at 0700 in the summer and 0800 in the winter. There was considerable urgency for the morning figures which were signalled or telephoned through to the Met Office in London. The telephone number (Holborn 3434) is still engraved on my memory. In order to save time we usually went only to 18,000 ft in the morning and if we were unable to get back to Duxford due to bad weather, which was very often the case, we would land in a field near a house and telephone the observations to the Air Ministry. The afternoon climb took off at 1300 and as there was less urgency for the figures we usually went to 25,000 ft or a bit more if we could and recorded the heights and amount of high cloud such as cirrus, cirrostratus and cirrocumulus. Our supercharged Siskins, stripped of guns, ammunition and radio, were quite light and performed well. We carried no radio because in those days there were no direction-finding stations on the ground so R/T could do nothing for us navigationally nor as a let-down aid, so we preferred to dispense with the weight of radio sets and once airborne we were very much on our own.

We carried a strut-mounted psychrometer for recording temperatures wet and dry bulb, a very large and sensitive altimeter graduated in millibars instead of feet and a Reid & Sigrist turn-and-bank indicator the gyros of which were driven by a strut-mounted Venturi. Our cockpit instrumentation was normal. The basic aim, and the principal problem, was to maintain the maximum frequency and regularity of the climbs whatever the weather.

So we flew in all weathers, and authorised our own flights. In conditions of very low cloud we climbed through it, levelling off for two minutes or so every 50 millibars to record the temperatures. We maintained a series of reciprocal courses up and down what we believed to be the wind direction and we aimed to let down and break cloud over the Fen district which was below sea-level. Surprisingly, we nearly always managed to hit it off. If the wind was very strong the cloud base was usually broken and ragged making the final stages of the let-down less hazardous so it did not matter if we missed the Fen district. In very strong winds one sometimes broke cloud over the sea which was always rather a daunting experience; it happened to me more than once, but steering a course somewhat north of west always resulted in eventual repatriation. The worst hazards were firstly the very wet and solid low stratus cloud with its base almost at ground-level and which often went up to 15,000 ft or so. In such conditions it was absolutely vital to let down and break cloud over the low-lying Fen district. This presented a nice problem of D/R navigation particularly as we had no knowledge of the upper winds. I got it wrong only once in these conditions, with results described later in this chapter. The second hazard was radiation fog in the early mornings and in high-pressure conditions. This, at certain times of the year, was very widespread and rendered visibility at ground-level zero. Such fog, however, usually only went up to about 600 or 1,000 ft at which point one burst out into brilliant sunshine. The problem, therefore, was how to take off and how to get down again.

We had a chalk line cut in the grass of the aerodrome pointing directly outwards from the tarmac. There was never any wind in those zero-zero conditions so one positioned the aircraft at the inner end of the fog line, leant one's head out of the side of the cockpit, opened the throttle and followed the line. To start with the Reid & Sigrist instrument, being Venturi driven, was inoperative but as the aircraft reached flying speed it began to come to life, and one climbed through the fog, waiting to burst out into the sunshine and continue with the climb and then think about how to get down again.

Frequently the fog was extremely widespread but sometimes

high ground, such as the Chilterns, would be sticking up through it like islands in the sea. There could be no question of landing back at Duxford except sometimes in the summer when the fog would at times begin to burn off while one was airborne, so we landed in any suitable field that was visible on high ground, but mostly we went to Tangmere. It was a strange thing but there could be radiation fog covering almost the whole country, but it would butt up against the north face of the South Downs and the narrow coastal strip where Tangmere lay would be clear. We had a system whereby half an hour before take-off when Duxford was under thick fog, telephone calls would be made to Tangmere, Wittering and North Coates to ascertain their actual weather. Tangmere was nearly always clear and many were the good breakfasts I enjoyed in that pleasant Mess.

There were, of course, many occasions in the winter when the weather did not fall into such tidy classifications and was just plain miserable – low cloud, driving rain, unpredictable upper winds or sometimes freezing fog at low level merging into thousands of feet of cloud.

Funnily enough, ice did not cause us too much trouble. The Siskin being a braced biplane had thin wings. I remember collecting fantastic amounts of ice on wing leading edges, struts, flying wires and wind screen and it used to break off in great chunks every so often. It caused a great deal of vibration but never once do I remember being seriously bothered by lift or control problems. It certainly looked very daunting at times but one learned to keep one's spirits up and not worry about it. The RAF in those days was very far from being an all-weather air force. In the Met Flight we developed our own all-weather techniques and very effectively in the circumstances. The other technique at which we became expert was that of landing our aircraft in small fields in unfavourable conditions when we could not get back to base. We became expert at the selection of suitable fields, judging the state of their surfaces which of course varied greatly with the time of year, assessing gradients, and in particular noting the proximity of houses with telephone wires.

We occasionally had to land back at Duxford in gale force winds. For this we organised two lines of airmen on the airfield and would do a 'wheel' landing keeping the tail up to the last moment. The airmen would grab our lower wing tips as we stopped, and see that we did not get blown over on our way to the hangar.

My first year's flying in the Met Flight was reasonably uneventful, and we achieved something over 95 per cent of our scheduled climbs, the few missed being due to really appalling weather. Of a total of 258 Met climbs which I personally carried out in 1934 there were 14 failures to get back to base resulting in forced landings either at other aerodromes or in fields. All these were accomplished without too much problem except for one which nearly landed me in big trouble. This arose from a dance given by the Oxford University Air Squadron to which my friend, Tom Barker at Balliol, had invited me, with instructions to bring a partner. I invited Margie Childerstone who lived in London. The question arose – and it was a point upon which her father made searching inquiries – as to how I was going to get Margie from London W2 to Oxford and back all in one evening. Simple I replied. I would drive my car from Duxford to London, pick up Margie and drive her to Oxford where we would change in Tom Barker's rooms. After the dance I would deliver her safely back home to London, and then drive myself back to Duxford in time for duty the following morning.

Initially all went well; my ancient Morris Cowley had bowled along in fine style and, right on schedule, Margie and I emerged from Tommy's rooms in Oxford, she in a beautiful evening dress and I in my tails. After a gay and festive evening – but by now substantially behind schedule – Margie and I, she still sparkling with fun and I by no means sober, set forth confidently for London. After a few miles it became painfully clear that the Morris Cowley was running short of water and that unless it was very quickly given a drink an awkward, not to say expensive, disaster would ensue. There were no garages open at that hour in the morning but finally I located a well in a roadside garden and after some problems in reaching the water, during which Margie became convinced I would fall down the well, the Morris Cowley was revived with sweet well water and we resumed our journey. All this had caused considerable delay and I had to be back at Duxford in time to do the 0700 hours Met climb and we were still a good way from London. In due course I delivered Margie to the bosom of her family, safe and unsullied, and then drove hell for leather – if such an expression is appropriate to a 1928 Morris

Cowley – for Duxford.

On the final straight between Royston and Duxford I looked at my watch and began to consider the situation. If I were to go straight to my quarters, discard my tails and get into my uniform, then go to the hangar and get into my extensive flying kit I surely would not be airborne sharp at 0700. On the other hand were I to drive straight to the hangar and don my electrically heated suit over my tails (and who was to know?) I would just about make it. I began to cock an experienced eye at the state of the weather which had been looking progressively more unfriendly since I left London. If I arrived back at Duxford after the climb, I could get straight out of the aeroplane into my car, drive to my room, discard my flying gear and my tails in one operation, bath and shave and appear at breakfast in the Mess looking every inch the smart young officer so much favoured by the authorities. On the other hand, I thought, if the weather were to deteriorate much more there was a very strong chance that I would finish up weatherbound at some strange RAF station and the prospect of stripping off my electrically heated suit and reporting to higher (and strange) authority clad in my crumpled white tie and tails from the night before seemed unlikely to be good for my career.

So I settled for a late take-off; and thank the Lord as it turned out. The cloud was very low and the wind and rain were whistling round the hangars as I climbed into the Siskin. 'Why', I thought to myself, 'does this sort of thing have to happen the morning after the OUAS dance?' I took off and settled into the climb trying to hold the Siskin as steady as I could whilst measuring the temperatures at each successive 50 millibars. Eventually the climb was finished and I started the let-down and although I knew the cloud base was very low I expected the base to be broken and ragged due to the high wind so I was not unduly anxious. As it turned out, conditions were much worse than I had expected; I broke cloud uncomfortably close to the ground and it did not seem likely that I would manage to get back to Duxford for amongst other things I was by now very, very tired. So I started looking for a suitably large field in which to land. Quite suddenly I saw Henlow aerodrome through the driving rain and with a sigh of relief I circled to the downwind side, turned into wind and approached for a landing. I was being bounced about a good deal in the turbulent air and at touch-down the Siskin decided to behave at its most Siskinish; a wing went down and cut into the ground and, with a 'crump' and an elegant cartwheel accompanied by a shower of earth kicked up by the propeller, I was over on my back.

I was not hurt except for shoulders bruised by the Sutton harness but I was whisked off by ambulance to the sick quarters as regulations demanded. It was a bit early in the morning for the MO and I passed the time chatting to the orderlies. Eventually the MO arrived and having examined me all over he said, with a distinct tone of professional frustration, 'You don't seem to be injured at all.' I said that this had already occurred to me and perhaps therefore the ambulance crew would be good enough to drive me to the Mess as I felt very much in need of a cup of good, strong, black coffee.

The subsequent inquiry into this incident passed off rather more easily than I had dared to hope. It was noted that the weather had been extremely bad and the landing conditions at Henlow abominable, especially for a Siskin.

To have taken off in the conditions prevailing at Duxford was judged reasonable in view of the special tasks of the Met Flight; in short, it was an accident in the true sense of the word and no blame should be attached to the pilot.

Fortunately no research was carried out into my activities during the preceding 12 hours and it was, presumably, assumed that I had been safely tucked up in bed. The contrary evidence which could have been supplied by the sentry whose duty it was to call me at 6 a.m. and had found an empty and unslept-in bed was never sought.

In November 1934 George Snarey was posted and I took over the Flight, and Flying Officer R.C. Reynell arrived from 43 Squadron at Tangmere. Dick Reynell and I got on very well together at Duxford. After a time we did some research into the records and found that the Met Flight had never in its history achieved 100 per cent regularity in its scheduled climbs over a full year. We decided to put that right. This meant flying the climb twice every day (0700 and 1300) except Sundays, without missing a single one for a whole year. Since our only navigational aids were a compass and a watch, and our cloud-flying instrument was the Venturi-driven 'primary' (Reid & Sigrist turn-and-bank indicator) it was rather a tall order but we mutually decided to have a go. The Met Flight had a wide degree of discretion on flight authorisation in view of its special tasks, and Dick Reynell and I stretched those powers to the limit!

There is no doubt that in setting out to achieve our self-imposed task of a full year without missing a climb, we took the most colossal risks. I think we nearly turned our CO's hair grey and I have always been grateful to Johnny Chick for trusting us the way he did. We never, of course, told him what our real aiming mark was, and we had to keep assuring him that our flights in zero-zero conditions were 'a piece of cake'. Whether he believed us or not he never inhibited us although he occasionally used to threaten to put one or the other of us under arrest.

During 1935 when we were fairly well on the way to our goal, Dick Reynell, whose family owned extensive vineyards in Australia, suddenly had to go home for private reasons. I was dismayed because I had no idea whom I should get in his place. Dick and I understood each other perfectly and each knew the other would not let him down by missing a climb. I remember many a dark and cold winter morning in appalling weather when I climbed into my Siskin and said to myself, 'This is completely bloody daft – but I must go' and I am sure that as many times as this happened to me it happened also to Dick.

In Dick's place there arrived Flying Officer Ken Stoddart who, with his uncle, a retired Air Commodore, had just competed in the MacRobertson Air Race to Australia. It did not take long for me to realise that I could not have dreamed of a better replacement for Dick Reynell and Ken became completely dedicated to achieving our objective of 100 per cent climbs over a year. (Ken was killed in 1937 and Dick, later, in the Battle of Britain.)

During that year, Johnny Chick was posted and a new Commanding Officer arrived, Squadron Leader Tankerville ('Tanks') Chamberlayne. I was nervous that he might clip our wings a bit, because we certainly used to put our Commanding Officer at considerable risk. Had one of us been killed, there would have been some very searching questions asked from on high. But 'Tanks' also supported us splendidly and we finally achieved our one year without missing a climb. When I left the flight on 31 December 1935, 'Tanks' gave me the pilot rating of

'Exceptional' in my log-book and recommended me for the Air Force Cross.

Our uninterrupted run of 100 per cent climb regularity was finally broken after about 13 months by me. It was the day before Christmas Eve 1935 and I took off from Duxford at 0800 hours in thick fog. However it was not the comforting pure white radiation fog out of which one usually burst at 1,000 ft or so into bright sunshine but it was dark and ominous and obviously merging into thousands of feet of cloud; furthermore it was abominably cold and there was snow on the ground. I had known before I took off that there was no hope of getting back to Duxford and the telephoned 'actuals' from Wittering and Tangmere precluded any hope of getting into either of them. However I was now committed, there was no turning back, so I concentrated on finishing the climb and decided to worry about how to get down again when the time came. In the meantime I headed southwards hoping that the conditions might ease. As it happened, when I had let down to about 700 ft in broken and layered cloud I could see that, while the ground was still covered in fog, there were occasional thinner patches through which the ground was just discernible vertically downwards although horizontal visibility would be zero. I was just reflecting that if I had not been born so stupid I would not now be in this mess, when vertically beneath me I could just discern Hatfield, which was a great piece of luck.

I carefully located myself vertically over the top and started to descend on an accurate course to half my height and then did a 'button hook' turn on to reciprocal and continued my descent praying that I should be able to pick up Hatfield in the very restricted visibility at ground-level. Fortunately I hit it off exactly and saw Hatfield in time to make a hurried approach and get down on its snow-covered surface. Hatfield was a grass aerodrome then, very new, and at its perimeter was the newly built factory of De Havillands and also the DH School of Flying which was a civil school. Everything looked very much closed down for Christmas so I taxied to the school building, shut down the engine and found some signs of human life and a telephone. I telephoned the Met figures through to the Air Ministry and, realising that I would have to do the afternoon climb from Hatfield (Ken Stoddart was on leave), I started to consider the problem of starting the engine when the time came in about $3\frac{1}{2}$ hours' time. There was no 'Hucks' (a vehicle with a mechanical device for swinging propellers) at a civil aerodrome such as Hatfield, so I would have to depend upon my small compressed air bottle in the aircraft to get a start on internal resources. To be certain of this it was advisable to have an external compressor on a trolley driven by a two-stroke engine to boost up the aircraft's compressed air system. I telephoned North Weald to ask that a lorry be dispatched to Hatfield with a compressor or alternatively a 'hucks' starter plus a couple of airmen. The station was already closed for Christmas leave and I got a dusty answer; as I did, also, from Duxford for the same reason, so I was on my own with my internal compressed air bottle, and the Siskin was standing out there in the freezing cold. So when 1300 hours came and I was all dressed up for the afternoon climb, I could not start the engine. After some 13 months of 100 per cent regularity, therefore, the climb was missed and as it was the last scheduled climb before the Christmas break I felt very annoyed and frustrated. But at least we in the Met Flight, that is to say Dick Reynell, Ken Stoddart and I, had done something which had never been done before.

Admittedly we had written off or damaged one or two aircraft in the process but we were the last and only operators of Siskins in the Air Force and no doubt there were people at Command Headquarters at Uxbridge who considered it a cause for celebration every time a Siskin was written off charge. Apart from the earlier Henlow incident, I had personally written off another Siskin on 14 March 1935 at a place called Babraham not far from Six Mile Bottom. I had taken off with some misgivings in conditions of extremely low and very solid stratus cloud, almost 'on the deck' at Duxford, and with practically no surface wind. I carefully flew a pattern during the climb designed to bring me out over the Fen district after letting down but this time it did not work and obviously the upper winds must have accounted for this. I was letting down very gingerly, using a bit of engine in a nose-up attitude with about 70 mph indicated on the clock and with my altimeter creeping down to a distressingly low figure. At last I could see I was about to break out of the cloud when I became aware of a sudden green tinge in the light and with a loud 'crump' I hit the ground in a perfect three-point attitude; immediately I saw ahead of me a large and rather high hedge. The

Siskin had bounced back into the air, shaking and vibrating after its rude and unscheduled contact with terra firma and I caught it with a burst of engine and floated it over the hedge, cut the throttle and touched down in the next field. Immediately showers of earth flew into the air, the aircraft went onto its nose and turned smartly over on to its back. This time I received the classic 'Siskin' blow across the bridge of the nose from the cockpit coaming and as it was not long since broken bone had been removed from my nose in Uxbridge Hospital following a boxing mishap, it was never quite the same again. Fortunately the centre section struts did not collapse and I scrambled out of the cockpit as quickly as I could in that awkward inverted position, egged on by the fact that I could smell a good deal of fuel swilling about and, in common with most aviators in such a predicament, my efforts were stimulated by the ever-present terror of fire.

I found that I had crashed quite close to a country lane and there was a small house nearby which had a telephone. I dictated the Met figures to Air Ministry and then rang up Duxford informing them of the accident and requesting a crash party. I then walked back to examine the damage to the Siskin. Clearly, on the original impact one of the main undercarriage tubular struts had failed and a wheel had thus been bent over at right angles. The next touch-down had been in the next field and the damaged undercarriage had dug into the ground and turned me over. I walked back into the field where I had originally touched and there were two deep gouges in the earth from the first impact, which had clearly broken the undercarriage and from which I had bounced back into the air and motored myself over the hedge. I was considerably shaken by this accident; in such conditions of very low stratus I had always managed to break cloud in the low-lying areas of the Fen district, but missing it and actually hitting the ground just at the moment of breaking cloud seemed to be a little beyond a joke. I also began to consider how I was going to report all this. If I reported the matter exactly as it was someone would take fright (reasonably enough) either at Duxford or HQ Fighting Area and start laying down formal weather minima for the Met Flight and away would go our chances of completing a year without missing a climb – and it would be my fault. I looked at the high and spiky hedge with saplings growing out of it which separated the crashed Siskin from the point of original impact. With any luck no one would think of looking in that first field and so find the deep gouge marks. So when the Station Warrant-Officer (Tech) arrived with the crash party later in the morning he inspected the failed undercarriage tube. I admitted that I had touched down pretty hard as I dropped the aircraft in over that high hedge, although I feigned surprise that the undercarriage leg had failed in the circumstances. The SWO (Tech) seemed more concerned about my by now bruised and swollen face than about the Siskin's undercarriage and muttered something about metal fatigue failures and the number of hours these old Siskins had accumulated, and how it was a bloody miracle that they flew at all. He must have reported accordingly because to my great relief the matter passed off without more than the routine reports being required.

As the morning wore on the cloud lifted and the sun broke through sporadically and a small crowd of local villagers and farmworkers collected around the crash. Then the proceedings were further enlivened by Harry Broadhurst arriving overhead with his Flight of three Gauntlets resplendent in the blue and white chequered markings of 19 Squadron. They circled round in tight formation and 'buzzed' my crashed Siskin with me standing beside it, several times, to the delight of the small crowd.

I, perhaps with a more discerning eye, did not fail to notice a few unmistakable hand signals from the leading Gauntlet each time it passed very low overhead. I got the message. It arose from the fact that some weeks earlier I had taken off on a morning Met climb in thick early morning fog which had partially 'burnt off' during the climb and I had landed back at Duxford at about 9 a.m. not without difficulty because the fog was extremely patchy and very thick in places. As I taxied in and switched off I was told that Squadron Leader Cassidy and Flight Lieutenant Broadhurst in their Gauntlets were overdue and believed to be down in a field somewhere near Cambridge and would I try to locate them and report? I immediately took off again and started to search. As the Gauntlet was then the newest fighter and the pride of the Air Force, I was worried and hoped that nothing serious had happened. Then I saw them; just south of Cambridge, in perfect formation, upside down in a field of soft plough. Cassidy had taken them off from Duxford as the fog had begun to burn off but it had closed in again and he was unable to get back and, running short of fuel, he led them into this large field which nine times out of ten would have been all right. But the surface was soft, the Gauntlet had streamlined 'spats' enclosing its wheels, these had become choked with mud, the wheels had locked, and towards the end of their run the aircraft had turned slowly and tidily over onto their backs. So what could I do? I flew low over them, recognised Broady standing beside his Gauntlet with about three pounds of mud on each boot, stretched my ungloved hand over the side of my cockpit and signalled a greeting which was well understood throughout the Royal Air Force.

Now, standing beside my wrecked Siskin at Babraham, I was getting it back again – and in formation.

During the London 'season' of 1935 I received many invitations to deb dances and dinner parties beforehand. I could leave the Station at 4.30, motor to the RAF Club in London, get there in time to bath and change into tails and arrive in time for dinner at the appointed hour. When the dance was over, or sometimes before, a sortie to a night club would often ensue if one's partner had been able to square her parents beforehand, and occasionally if she had not which invariably led to subsequent explanations and apologies. So I did many a dawn drive from London to Duxford to arrive in time for the 0700 Met climb and my old Morris Cowley never let me down. (Later I replaced it with a 3-litre Bentley of happy memory.)

Sir Philip Sassoon, the Under-Secretary of State for Air, Member of Parliament for Hythe in Kent and man of very great wealth and possession, had always taken a great interest in the Met Flight. He had a DH Leopard Moth of his own and made frequent visits to Royal Air Force Stations when he prided himself on never forgetting the names of Officers or NCOs who were presented to him. I was first introduced to him when I was a Pilot Officer in 17 Squadron, lined up for inspection in front of my Bulldog with my fitter and rigger. Then nearly two years later he turned up at Duxford and as my then CO, Beardsworth, was about to introduce me, Sassoon interrupted him in his clipped and incisive voice with 'Yes, I know Quill, we met at Upavon – how are you, my dear fellow?' This, of course, had happened to many other people but nevertheless the effect upon one's ego was stimulating to say the least. Later on when I got to know Sassoon better he told me that he worked to a system but worked hard at it. In the aeroplane on his way to a Station, his staff provided him with a complete list of names which he studied carefully and this usually enabled him to recognise the names of those whom he had met before. From his own memory he could often put a face to them and remember where he had met them, but if not back numbers of the Air Force List were hurriedly consulted. There were innumerable stories about Philip's remarkable memory for names and it was said that on one visit a Station Commander got stuck over the name of one of his own Officers and, with a broad smile, Philip provided it for him.

During the summer of 1935, I received a summons to spend a weekend at Philip's house at Port Lympne above Romney Marsh. These gatherings were famous for Philip brought all sorts of people together – politicians, writers, usually a smattering of Air Force Officers – and often his sister Hannah was there to act as hostess. Life was extremely relaxing and luxurious and Philip organised the entertainment of his guests in a quiet but authoritative manner. Each day's activities would be discussed at dinner the night before. So and so will play golf – the car will leave at 9.30. Another party will go to Canterbury to see the latest restorations to the Cathedral – the car will leave at 10 (woe betide anyone who is late). The cars were usually Rolls-Royces each with Philip's silver cobra coiled with head poised to strike, in place of the silver Spirit of Ecstasy normal for such cars. Although there was a superb pool in the garden, Philip believed there was great merit in sea bathing and at dinner one night a party, including me, was detailed to go next morning to the beach near Hythe – the car would leave at 9.30. After dinner Osbert Sitwell drew me aside.

'Do you like sea bathing?' he asked.

'Only if the weather is very hot,' I said.

'It won't be. It will be hideously cold,' he said. 'Let's refuse to go.'

'Do we dare?' I asked.

'Yes,' he said and we did.

So when the party of impressed men went down to the beach to bathe, Osbert Sitwell and I spent the morning sitting in the garden, reading the papers and talking; and a very stimulating morning it was. At Port Lympne that same weekend were Nigel Norman (the founder of Airwork at Heston), Sir Alfred Beit, Philip's sister Hannah and a few others, and Noel Coward came over for tea. Number 601 Squadron, Auxiliary Air Force, of which Philip was honorary Air Commodore, was in summer camp at the aerodrome at Lympne and several of them came to dinner.

Already, now, the political situation in Germany was casting an ugly shadow. British rearmament and the expansion of the fighting services had become a major political issue but it was only 17 years since the end of the First World War and millions of people still put their faith in the Locarno Agreement, collective security, the League of Nations and disarmament. The various 'peace' movements had a strong emotional pull. As a result the concept of rearmament was horrific and unacceptable to the country at large; and the Government knew it, having in 1933 lost a famous by-election in East Fulham on a wave of pacifist fervour.

4

Change of Direction

In March 1934 the Air Estimates made provision for four new
squadrons for the RAF but by July the Prime Minister, Stanley
Baldwin, announced a new five-year programme by which the
Air Force would be increased by 41 squadrons or about 860
aircraft (including those already announced in the March estimates). Winston Churchill, then in the political wilderness, had
been loudly and boldly sounding warnings about British in-
adequacy in the air compared to the resurgence of aeronautical
effort in Germany. Now at last the penny seemed to have
dropped.

To us in the Royal Air Force, for so long the ugly duckling of
the fighting Services, this modest expansion plan seemed the
beginning of a new lease of life. At last the major role we knew we
had to play in the country's security was recognised by the
Government even if not yet accepted by the country as a whole.

In March 1935 the Government received a severe shock when
Hitler told Sir John Simon, the Foreign Secretary, on a visit to
Berlin, that the German Air Force was already as strong as the
Royal Air Force and that his objective was parity with France.
After investigating this claim Simon wrote a long letter to the
Prime Minister on 10 April giving figures for German Air Force
and industry expansion, and ended thus: 'The conclusion which
might have to be drawn from the above figures, if they are
correct, is that this country is seriously open to the threat of
sudden attack by a continental power in a degree to which it has
not been exposed for hundreds of years.' So although the Government was aware of the threat, and although some, but by no
means all, of the national press made much of it there was a
marked reluctance within the country to face unpalatable facts.

In April 1935, my friend from 17 Squadron days, the South
African Bob Preller, conceived the idea of hiring some private
aeroplanes from a firm at Heston called Air Hire Ltd and touring
the Continent. He roped me in as well as two other Flying

Officers called Paddon, and John Mynors. Under Bob Preller's overall organisation we hired a Puss Moth to be flown by me, a Leopard Moth to be flown by Paddon and a four-seater Avro Commodore to be flown by Bob himself. The idea was to find seven passengers to come with us on a cost-sharing basis and tour Germany and some of the main capitals of Europe, the whole trip lasting from 19 to 24 April. As it turned out our passengers were all girls except for Mynors and one of the minor miracles of the operation was how Bob Preller managed to talk their respective mothers into allowing them to come. Nevertheless, whatever may have been their misgivings they seem to have overcome them and I took off from Heston on 19 April in Puss Moth G-ACIV with Ann Chaplin and an attractive South African girl and set course for Saarbrucken, 3 hours 20 minutes flying time away. Paddon followed with his passengers in the Leopard but Bob Preller, delayed by a technical snag, said he would join us in Munich. Saarbrucken had been much in the news arising from Hitler's agitation for the return of the Saar to German sovereignty, which had finally been settled in his favour by a plebiscite in January 1935. I was half expecting the airfield to be full of booted and strutting Nazis but in fact it was a small aerodrome with a wooden terminal and club building and a pleasant restaurant where we drank some beer in the sun, ate lunch, saw the aircraft safely refuelled and proceeded on our way to Munich in the afternoon. With two girls and three suitcases in the back I noticed that the longitudinal control of the aeroplane was now extremely sensitive and I had to concentrate hard on the flying to avoid giving my fair passengers a switchback sort of ride. Although I did not know it, it was my first experience of flying an aeroplane with inadequate longitudinal stability margins due to the centre of gravity being too far aft. Some years later this problem in more extreme forms was to become part of my daily life.

We landed at Oberwiesenfeld, then a fair-sized grass aerodrome on the outskirts of Munich and used by Lufthansa and the local flying clubs. That evening we visited the Hofbrauhaus, a huge bierkeller where Bavarian beer was dispensed in enormous steins carried by powerful, buxom women who seemed able to carry about five in each hand. It was all very large, very festive and very noisy and we drank a good deal of the beer accompanied by a variety of suitable food. I remember being greatly impressed by the way our slender and delicate-looking girls polished off steins of beer as if they were cups of tea. We found to our relief that our special tourist cheques (introduced by Hitler) gave so favourable a rate of exchange that such an evening cost remarkably little. We spent the following morning seeing something of Munich before going back to the aerodrome to prepare the aircraft for the flight to Vienna. I had trouble starting my Gipsy engine and, suspecting a carburation problem, sought the assistance of Lufthansa. A mechanic arrived wheeling a small trolley with a cylinder of gas from which extended a long tube which he inserted into the air intake of the Gipsy engine. We turned the propeller over a few times to suck in some of the gas, the tube was removed and the engine started at the first swing. I discovered it was carbide gas. I doubted whether it was good for the pistons but it was effective.

In Vienna we rode up to the aerodrome in two horse-drawn Victorias. On the way to Berlin we landed at Dresden to refuel. Berlin itself accorded with our expectations – somehow it seemed more 'German' than Munich – and the officials at Tempelhof were precise, openly efficient and brusque and although, as English private aviators and tourists, we were treated with meticulous courtesy there was an atmosphere we had not noticed in Bavaria nor in Dresden. Our passports revealed that we were Royal Air Force officers but we were asked no questions about the purpose of our visit. Next day we saw some of the sights of Berlin but personally I was more interested in watching the Germans themselves and wondering what was really going on in that country and whether one day we were going to have to fight them all over again. I had never been to Germany before and so could not compare it with a previous visit, but there was a great feeling of vitality and energy about the place and a certain menace. At the aerodromes, especially at Dresden, there were aircraft of many differing types, some with a decidedly paramilitary aspect. The flying clubs were active and full of bustling, purposeful-looking people, pupils and instructors, all dressed in professional-looking sporting garb, which contrasted with the more amateur, relaxed and casual atmosphere of the English flying clubs. I wish I could say that I left Berlin convinced of German aggressive intentions and that our country was in mortal peril but such was not the case; nonetheless I did gain an uncomfortable and uneasy impression and I had the feeling that in Britain we were somehow being left behind in a race that had no rules.

When I got back to Duxford at the end of my leave, 'Tanks' Chamberlayne said to me, 'Hell, – have you just been flying round Germany?'

'Yes, sir,' I said.

'Well, you should have gone to the Intelligence people for a briefing before you left – you'd better get down and see them right away – I'll fix it up.'

So next day I found myself being interviewed in the Air Ministry by a Wing Commander and a Squadron Leader who dressed me down for not coming to see them before I left. They said they could have briefed me about what to look out for and what to do, but as it was I had probably failed to bring home any information of any use whatever. I apologised but explained that in the first place I had no idea they existed and in the second place I thought that that sort of intelligence was gathered by people in false beards and shabby raincoats and not by officers on leave. They made me promise that if I did go again I would see them in good time beforehand.

Towards the end of 1935 I was reading the papers one day in the ante-room at Duxford when Pat King, a Flight Lieutenant on the Station, said to me, 'By the way, Quill, I saw Mutt Summers over the weekend and he told me he was looking for a young pilot who might join Vickers and become his assistant test pilot there. I took the liberty of mentioning your name.'

I said, 'Oh! Well, as a matter of fact I'm not due to leave the Service for another ten months. I've been posted to Martlesham from January so I presume I'm to be offered a permanent commission or at least a medium-service commission. They're unlikely to send me to a place like Martlesham just for a few months. So I'm afraid I wouldn't be interested in going to Vickers at this particular moment. Thanks, all the same, for mentioning my name.'

'Well,' said Pat King, 'I've told you about it. If you're interested give Mutt a ring and fly down to Brooklands to see him – otherwise forget it.'

My immediate reaction was to forget it. I wanted to stay in the Royal Air Force and felt, now that the expansion programme was under way, that I had a good chance of being selected for a permanent commission. I had not perpetrated any glaring misdemeanours; my flying record was tolerably good and I had accumulated a good deal more than the average number of hours in the air. Why should I want to become a civilian test pilot, however interesting it might sound? No – my future lay in the RAF, I said to myself.

Flight Lieutenant 'Shorty' Horry, the adjutant at Duxford, had been a test pilot at Martlesham and we often used to talk about it. He knew most of the leading test pilots in the aircraft industry, and when I told him I had decided not to follow up the Vickers job, he pointed out that this was a great chance and that I was gambling everything on getting a permanent commission of which there was no certainty.

'And suppose you do get one,' he argued, 'it will be fine while the flap lasts and the expansion carries on, but as soon as they sort this thing out politically they'll cut the money and slam on the brakes and there'll be a God-awful promotion blockage. Look at me – I fought in the war and I'm still only a Flight Lieutenant.'

Thus doubts began to assail me. I thought of an uncle who had served in the First World War and was still a Captain in the DCLI. Could it also happen in the RAF?

In spite of the situation in Germany and the commotion over Mussolini in Abyssinia, I tended to feel, like 'Shorty', that there would be some kind of political solution, that the 'flap' would die down and that his gloomy predictions about a promotion block might well turn out to be right. Furthermore *The Times* very much played down the threat from Hitler's Germany and was strongly supporting the policy of appeasement (an attitude which, to its discredit, it maintained almost up to the outbreak of war). Had I been sure of a permanent commission there would have been no question of even thinking about a job in the industry; but I could not be.

I contacted Mutt Summers at Vickers and flew to Brooklands on 1 November. Mutt told me what the job was – to help him with a heavy programme of experimental prototype flying both at Weybridge and at Supermarine at Southampton which was brewing up as a result of the expansion programme; if I was

interested I would have to fly down again for an interview with
Sir Robert McLean, the Chairman. When I told him that my
short-service commission did not expire until October 1936 he
said the job would not wait; I would have to apply for early release
or forget it. I thought I would go ahead with the interview with
Sir Robert and, in the unlikely event that I was offered the job,
would then have to make my decision. I remember vaguely
hoping that I would not be offered the job, thus relieving me of
the problem.

I flew to Brooklands again therefore on 18 November and
lunched with Mutt Summers and Sir Robert, followed by a short
interview with the latter. The result was that I was offered the job
of Assistant to the Chief Test Pilot at a salary of £500 a year
conditional on my applying for immediate release from the Royal
Air Force. I asked for two weeks to decide. I flew my Siskin back
to Duxford in a state of great uncertainty and wished that the
whole damn business had not cropped up.

The next two weeks I spent in a turmoil of indecision. The
truth was that I did not wish to leave the Royal Air Force, but Sir
Robert had looked me in the eye and said, 'I cannot remember an
occasion when I have been able to offer such a young man so great
an opportunity as I am offering you today.' I went to my CO,
'Tanks' Chamberlayne, and asked him if he had any means of
knowing whether I was on the list for a permanent commission.
He rang up a friend in 'P' staff at Air Ministry, but such information could not be divulged. I wrote to Sir Philip Sassoon and had
a charming and courteous reply but was none the wiser.

So I had to make up my own mind. A lot of medium-service
(ten-year) commissions were being awarded at the time but that
was not what I wanted. With the utmost reluctance I concluded
that reliance upon the award of a permanent commission was too
big a gamble and I telephoned Mutt Summers and said I was
applying for early release – could I please have something in
writing to substantiate my application?

So on 28 December 1935 I carried out a routine Met climb in
Siskin J8882, which was my last sortie in the Met Flight and
indeed the last flight of my short-service commission. On the last
day of the year, having said my goodbyes, I piled my modest
luggage into the back of my old 3-litre Bentley and headed off
from Duxford towards London with very mixed feelings.

It was no good pretending that I was not quite excited at joining the rather exclusive band of test pilots in the British aircraft industry, but I had the gravest misgivings about leaving the Air Force; I had felt absolutely a part of it from the day I joined and I had always had an inner certainty that I was destined to stay in it. I had become accustomed to the life and loved it and found it hard to visualise any other. As my old Bentley went burbling along through Royston and Stevenage on the way to London, with the distinctive throaty exhaust note emanating from its low-revving engine, I felt very much alone – almost like a little boy running away from home and wondering what the future would hold. I remembered the strong feeling of home-coming and warmth which I had always experienced as I drove in through the Guard Room gates of a Royal Air Force station when returning from leave. I was always acutely conscious of crossing a threshold between the outside world, uncertain, only half-familiar, potentially unfriendly and inhabited by a different breed of people, into a familiar world which I thoroughly understood, which was well ordered and in which the aims and obligations and duties were clear and not in question. That I would not again experience this warm feeling of belonging to the Service filled me with depression and a certain amount of apprehension. Suddenly I realised I was on my own.

I also began to think of Vickers. That firm, long established, had produced a number of very successful aeroplanes, yet they seemed to me to have been stolid, not very inspired and perhaps rather mundane or 'work-horse' in their general characteristics. But Mutt Summers had told me of a new high-performance fighter which was soon due to emerge from Supermarine at Southampton, designed by the famous R.J. Mitchell, and also that there was a new fighter coming out from Vickers at Weybridge and that I should be needed to help with the testing of both these aircraft. This thought cheered me up considerably.

5

Birth of 'the Fighter'

Vickers (Aviation) Ltd, when I joined it in January 1936, was a wholly owned subsidiary of Vickers Ltd, then one of Britain's great industrial companies whose activities covered a wide field of general engineering, shipbuilding, both commercial and naval, and, through Vickers-Armstrongs Ltd, the manufacture of armaments. The Aviation Company, under Sir Robert McLean, answered directly to the Vickers Board and operated with a high degree of autonomy.

At that time the British aircraft industry comprised 16 firms which had Air Ministry-approved aircraft design, development and manufacturing capability; and there were four approved firms which designed, developed and produced aero engines. The shape and size of the industry of the inter-war period was the result of broad Government or Air Ministry policy which, viewed in retrospect, had been wise and farseeing; in essence the policy had been to maintain a small number of firms of all-round capability to form a base for rapid expansion in an emergency. The post-First World War industry could not have survived, however, if the Royal Air Force had not been formed in April 1918 as an independent Service, for it was wise enough to realise that an effective aircraft industry to back it up was an essential requirement for its own survival in the face of the energetic post-war attempts which were made to strangle it. The RAF therefore did its best to keep the industry alive with the limited resources at its disposal.

The fact that during the 1920s there were perhaps too many aircraft firms scrambling for too few Government orders had the effect, however, of stimulating a strongly competitive spirit within the industry. This commercial competition was further stimulated by the need for the industry's design departments to keep their heads in front of their competitors in solving the many technical problems which aircraft presented in those early days. It also stimulated the search for export orders as an aid to survival. There was at first no coherent Government policy for civil aviation, a concept which most people in positions of power regarded as a sort of Wellsian nightmare. Flying was for young daredevils or for the military and certainly not for fare-paying passengers except possibly in large airships of the Zeppelin type. Thus those who had, in the 1920s, started to pioneer commercial air transport by aeroplane, as Vickers (Aviation) Ltd did with the Vimy Commercial (a Rex Pierson design), did so on the basis of 'hunch' and not in response to any Government encouragement or to any commercial market forecasts. It was a hitherto non-existent market which had to be created by demonstration and example out of nothing. When Winston Churchill, as Secretary of State for War and Air in 1920, remarked that 'civil aviation must fly by itself; the Government cannot keep it in the air,' he neatly expressed the attitude of the time.

In January 1936 Vickers (Aviation) Ltd at Weybridge was effectively dominated by a small but powerful group of men. These were Sir Robert McLean, the Chairman; Maxwell-Muller, the General Manager; Archie Knight, the Works Manager (a character almost straight out of a nineteenth-century novel); Rex Pierson, the Chief Designer; Barnes Wallis, who was developing advanced ideas into the design of aircraft structures; and Mutt Summers, the Chief Test Pilot.

Mutt was my boss and a strange, somewhat contradictory character with whom I got on well and who exercised great influence within the company. He was a very able pilot who had become a shrewd judge of an aeroplane and was very much a child of his own aviation generation. He had held a short-service commission in the RAF and, like me, had learned to fly at a very early age. In fact I think he was only about eight years older than I was but he had crammed a tremendous amount into those years. He had taken over as Chief Test Pilot at Weybridge when 'Tiny' Scholefield had been killed in 1928. This was at the time when prototype aircraft were produced very quickly, sometimes two in one year. Mutt therefore accumulated a huge amount of experience through the first flights and early development testing of a wide variety of aeroplanes. This was also a time when test flying was very much a qualitative business. The techniques of measuring aircraft performance (e.g. speeds, rates of climb, range and endurance) in the air were fairly well established, and with suitable instrumentation could be done accurately but required methodical flying by the pilot. On the other hand the techniques of measuring and quantifying flight-handling characteristics were almost non-existent and depended almost entirely upon the test pilot's individual assessment and opinion. The chief test pilot in the company therefore needed to have a highly developed type of horse-sense in judging the qualities of an aeroplane. Also he had to win the personal confidence of the Chief Designer and be able to transmit his own judgement to the designers in practical terms on which they could work. Mutt had certainly established this sort of relationship with Rex Pierson who always paid a great deal of attention to what he said. Sir Robert McLean also was much influenced by Mutt; this fact, which was apparent to everyone, put Mutt in a strong position within the company.

There were two other test pilots at Weybridge: 'Sonny' Banting and Ronnie Louis, but they were confined primarily to the routine testing of production aeroplanes and they were answerable in the main to the Works hierarchy, under Archie Knight and Maxwell-Muller. Mutt Summers regarded himself (in my opinion, rightly) essentially as part of the design and development process with an audible voice in the area of future design policy, while the Works pilots saw themselves as part of the manufacturing process – a sort of airborne extension of the inspection department. Mutt was the more sophisticated man both in his approach to the job and his outlook towards the general aviation scene, and in the matter of his outside contacts.

Thus there was an evident division in the system. I was to be assistant to Mutt Summers and was to concentrate upon what might be described as design testing. My chain of responsibility ran through Mutt to Rex Pierson and ultimately to McLean and I was not directly answerable to Knight or Maxwell-Muller. This situation highlighted two totally disparate approaches to the role of the test pilot in industry, and it was an issue which, on an industry-wide basis, was to take some years to resolve. In other words, where did the test pilot really fit into the hierarchy?

After Mutt, or through Mutt, the man with whom I came most into contact was Rex Pierson, the Chief Designer. Rex was a very large man in every way. He was enormously tall and very heavily built, moved rapidly and energetically, almost creating a draught as he went by and generally giving an impression of great power and authority. He treated me most kindly at all times, and especially when I was new to life in an aircraft company and somewhat overawed by the high-powered discussions which would take place from time to time in the Chief Designer's office. Rex Pierson's suite of offices was in one corner of the large drawing office in which some 150 draughtsmen, section leaders and supervisors worked at serried rows of drawing boards. It was on the top floor of a building which housed part of the metallurgical test department, with a canteen down below. The Chief Draughtsman, Paul Wyand, presided at his desk on a raised dais overlooking the whole area and next to him sat Bewsher, a senior designer, a cheerful and droll fellow who looked very much like Grock, the immortal Swiss clown, and was often called by that nickname. He was in charge of the detailed design of the new Vickers Venom fighter on which I was to do a great deal of the flying. When I had much trouble with fires in the exhaust system of the Venom, which at times looked extremely daunting in the air, Bewsher's mirth was unbounded, but he always took prompt and effective action.

A year before I arrived at Vickers in 1936 a young man joined the design department who was destined, in the future, to have a profound effect not only upon the firm but upon British Aviation as a whole. His name was George Edwards.

Immediately outside Rex's office was a bench of three drawing boards and another small office. At these boards worked Rex's immediate technical staff, comprising Arnold Wright, an expert on propellers and performance calculations; Anthony Bray, who was a bright mathematician and had been invalided out of the Air Force after a crash in a Bulldog; a man called Wheatley; and Bob Handasyde. Bob was a flight test observer and a specialist in flight performance who planned the flight test programmes and did odd bits of design work under Pierson's eye. In the small adjacent office worked John Radcliffe who was Pierson's technical assistant. I used to spend a good deal of time with Bob, Arnold Wright and John Radcliffe, picked their brains as much as I could and learnt a lot from them technically. Bob flew with me on test flights in Vildebeests, Harts, Wellesleys and Wellingtons.

Rex Pierson's office door was always open and his voice could be heard booming away over the telephone or talking to one of his constant stream of visitors. Every now and then he would burst from his office like a whirlwind, bound for the board of some unsuspecting draughtsman for whom the sky would suddenly darken and the earth begin to shake as Rex's huge form bore down upon him to examine with a critical eye some feature of a drawing.

In another room in the Designer's Office sat the now-legendary Barnes Wallis, who had the position of Chief Designer, Structures. 'Wally', as we called him, had been an airship man at Vickers Barrow, before being brought by Sir Robert McLean to apply his ingenious and novel ideas to the structural design of aeroplanes down to Weybridge. When developing his highly successful R100 airship Wally had solved a knotty structural problem associated with gas-bag containment by the use of geodesics and this became the basis of an entirely new approach to aeroplane structures. His first geodetic structure was applied to the fuselage of a biplane bomber built to an Air Ministry specification which flew in 1935. Then, as a private venture, Vickers built a monoplane version, but with an entirely geodetic structure, to the same specification (G.4/31). This was so much more efficient than the biplane that an Air Ministry order for 150 of the biplanes was cancelled and replaced with an order for the monoplane. When I arrived at Weybridge the prototype G.4/31 (K7556) was no longer a private venture, having received Air Ministry financial support for its continued development. It was in the factory being repaired after a belly landing due to an undercarriage hang-up and was having a number of modifications embodied to bring it up to official specification standard. There was still a great deal of development testing to be done before it emerged in production as the Wellesley and I was lucky enough to do the bulk of that testing in the ensuing months, with Bob Handasyde as my observer and mentor. During this work on the prototype Wellesley I came in contact with Wallis a great deal. Austere and difficult at times, even a bit bloody-minded, through it all shone a sort of natural charm which was captivating and one was constantly aware of a great deal of internal fire.

Sir Robert McLean, late of the Indian State Railways, was the undisputed boss at Weybridge and Supermarine and he made sure that everybody knew it. He was small, a bit dour, although not without a sense of humour. I never found him easy to get on with, as people like Rex Pierson, R.J. Mitchell and Wally were easy. J.D. Scott, in his history of Vickers, described McLean's attitude towards his position as head of the Aviation Companies – which, of course, were wholly owned subsidiaries of Vickers Ltd – as follows: 'McLean's responsibility was directly to the Board of Vickers and his attitude to it was vice-regal. This attitude Lawrence* understood and accepted; there was, after all, pro-consular blood in his own veins. Men cast in a less august mould were, however, apt to find McLean's uncommunicative in-dependence trying or even unnerving.' In fact McLean's pro-consular approach to his position was not limited to the Board of Vickers but extended very much towards the Air Ministry and to the Air Staff who were his most important customers.

In my position of assistant experimental test pilot my minor contacts with McLean began to assume the aspect of a series of head-on collisions. By 1937 I was convinced that war was inevit-able and was beginning to regret leaving the Air Force, so I applied to join 600 Squadron Auxiliary Air Force at Hendon, was accepted by them but it was vetoed by McLean, very much to my annoyance and disappointment. Then, with my friend John Hopcraft, who had obtained the sponsorship of Colonel W.C. Devereux (Chairman of High Duty Alloys), I was entered to fly Comet G-ACSS in the 1938 Kings Cup Air Race; again McLean vetoed it. Then David Atcherley and I arranged to fly a private aircraft to the Soviet Union and we had obtained a promise of help from Maisky, the Soviet Ambassador in London; unfortun-ately something of this venture leaked into the gossip column of a London evening newspaper and yet again the McLean veto descended upon my neck.

McLean made regular visits to Supermarine and there would be informal gatherings round some drawing board in the project office usually with Mitchell, the Chief Designer, and Alan Clifton, Chief of the Technical office, Mutt Summers, myself and various other people, sometimes from Vickers' London Office. These discussions would be dominated by McLean and Mitchell and, as both men were listeners rather than talkers, the proceedings occasionally tended to drag on a bit. But it was

* General Sir Herbert Lawrence, Chairman of Vickers Ltd.

impossible not to admire and respect McLean with his clear-headedness and uncompromising authority. He guided the destinies of the company with a firm and sure hand, even though he was building up a tide of antagonism against himself both within the Air Ministry and within the main Board of Vickers.

I had not been at Weybridge for more than two weeks before Mutt drove me down for my first visit to Supermarine. The Supermarine Works were at Woolston, on the outskirts of Southampton, where they had been since 1913 and a slipway ran from the erecting shop into the River Itchen down which the flying boats were launched. The administrative offices at that time were very basic and the Drawing Office and Technical Offices were in a large wooden loft over the Works. The General Manager was Trevor Westbrook, a young and exceedingly force-ful character – some people used to say a tyrant – who had his offices in the Works so that he could emerge straight on to the shop floor at a moment's notice. He had been trained at Wey-bridge under Archie Knight, and McLean had appointed him at the age of twenty-eight to ginger up the production arrangements at Supermarine. One of the first jobs he had to do was build two S.6Bs for the 1931 Schneider Trophy within little more than six months and this he achieved.

My first encounter with Trevor came during that first visit to Supermarine when Mutt Summers suggested I should have a look at the aerodrome at Eastleigh and at the erecting shop there. He said that Mr Gingell, the foreman of the Works transport section, would arrange for me to be taken there by car. So I sought out Mr Gingell and asked for a car and a driver and he replied in a very friendly manner that I would have to ask Mr Westbrook. 'Who', I asked, 'is Mr Westbrook?' This seemed to surprise Gingell and deprive him of further speech. He led me without a word into the Works and pointed to an office door close to the machine shop; I noticed that he had turned slightly pale. I entered and was confronted by a dark-haired man in his thirties sitting at a very cluttered and untidy desk with at least three telephones on it.

'I need a car to go to Eastleigh, please. I'm told I should ask you,' I said.

He replied, very gruffly, 'There's a lorry going up in half an hour – you can go in the cab with the driver' and looked down again at the papers on his desk. I reflected for a moment and decided that this sort of thing from an evidently middling official in the Works was not good enough and that I should not accept it.

'I have been told that I should go by car. Therefore I have no intention of travelling in the cab of a lorry, nor of waiting for half an hour, as I'm in a hurry. Please authorise a car.'

Westbrook threw his pencil down on the desk, leaned back in his chair and looked hard at me with his very dark and piercing eyes.

'Who the bloody hell are you?' he asked.

I told him and he continued to stare at me for a few moments and I stared steadfastly back.

'OK,' he said. 'If you want a car you'd better have one. Tell Gingell I said so.'

'Thank you very much,' I said. 'I'm sorry to have bothered you.' As I left his office I heard him mutter to himself, 'Cheeky bugger.'

On the way back to Weybridge I asked Mutt if he knew a fellow at the Works called Westbrook. 'I should say I do,' said Mutt, 'he's the General Manager of the Company – why?' 'Oh nothing,' I replied, feeling slightly unwell.

When I related this story later to people at Supermarine it was received with an awed incredulity, rather as if I was telling of slapping a lion on the rump during a chance encounter in the jungle. However, after that episode I always got on extremely well with Trevor both at Supermarine and later at Weybridge. He was ruthless, demanded high standards and would not tolerate slackness. He tended, at least in his younger days, to bully those who were afraid of him but if you stood up to him he respected you and he always treated me fairly. He achieved a great deal and, in my view, deserved well of his country.

Apart from that somewhat abrasive first encounter with Trevor the main events which stick in my memory from that first visit to Supermarine were my meeting with the then already legendary R.J. Mitchell, and my first sight of the prototype F.37/34, partially built and standing on trestles in the erecting shop at Woolston. 'R.J.', as he was always known, was sandy-haired, of slightly florid complexion, and a man of few words. Not that he was taciturn. He and Mutt seemed to get on well together although I cannot remember anything in detail of that first conversation during which I kept silent anyway. I met some members of Mitchell's staff during that visit, including Alan Clifton, Beverley Shenstone, Arthur Shirvall and Ernest Mansbridge, and after these introductions Mitchell took Mutt and me down to the shop to look at 'the Fighter' as it was called. It looked long and sleek from what one could see of it, for it was surrounded by the confusion and equipage of manufacture and assembly; but even to my inexperienced eye it was obviously reaching somewhere near completion, and I knew that, before long, the wings would be removed and it would be trucked up to Eastleigh for re-assembly and preparation for the first test flight.

During that first visit I also met George Pickering, who had come to the notice of Mitchell and Westbrook while serving as an RAF test pilot at the Marine Aircraft Experimental Establishment Felixstowe and they had offered him a job as test pilot at Supermarine as there was quite a heavy flying-boat programme impending there based on Seagulls, Walruses, Scapas, and Stranraers. George was a very practical and down-to-earth man, both as to his general character and his approach to flying and he was prone to call a spade a spade with no sort of equivocation. At a time when some test pilots tended to adopt a somewhat prima donna-ish attitude if they thought they could get away with it, George's attitude, even if sometimes a little over-expressed, was refreshing and healthy. He was a few years older than me with a flying-boat rather than a Fighter background and he was also some two years senior to me in the company. There were, I suppose, all the ingredients for a state of veiled rivalry to spring up between us but this never happened and we became very good friends.

In general George was the acknowledged and undisputed expert on the marine side at Supermarine and I, in spite of my young age, was generally accepted as the 'Fighter boy'; but neither of us attempted to form any sort of a 'closed shop'. There had always been a certain mystique surrounding flying boats, but George Pickering, like the true expert that he was, would have none of this. As opportunities arose he taught me to fly them, concentrating on the essentials and dismissing the trivia. I was lucky to have my first introduction to flying boats from such a man.

Until flying started on 'the Fighter' there was nothing for me to do at Supermarine. All the action with which I was involved was at Weybridge for the time being. There I was installed in a small office and I lived in a hotel at Walton-on-Thames. In production at Weybridge were dual Hart Trainers (a contract obtained by Vickers through under-quoting Hawkers); a few Valentias, a derivative of the old Victoria troop carrier but with Pegasus engines; Vildebeests; and Vincents, and I did production testing on all these types. But I would often fly down to Supermarine to get to know the people there and would usually spend the evening with George.

In February, the first of a batch of Valentias emerged from the Works. In this lumbering old stager – a sort of aeronautical dinosaur from the 1920s – the pilots sat, side-by-side, in a large open cockpit in the nose of the bulbous fuselage the rear portion of which was designed to carry 22 fully equipped infantry troops. The control response of the Valentia, like that of the Virginia, was slow and dignified in the extreme, particularly at the higher weights and in turbulent air. The massive biplane structure, with its forest of interplane struts, flying wires and landing wires and its two engines poised midway between upper and lower mainplanes, had a span of 87 ft which seemed very large indeed. The approach for landing was at about 70 mph 'on the clock' and in bumpy conditions the aircraft would occasionally take a great lurch to one side, whereupon the wheel would be wound over fully in the opposite direction as one awaited events. Slowly and cumbrously the aircraft would regain an even keel and after much thrashing about of the rudder it was possible to keep the aircraft pointing in the desired direction. After the small and lively fighters to which I was accustomed, and which I loved so much, it was a fascinating experience. One of that batch of Valentias, destined for service overseas, was equipped with an amplifier and powerful loudspeaker directed downwards through the floor of the cabin. This was to enable local political officers in the tribal areas of Iraq to address a recalcitrant village or tribal settlement in their own language from a few hundred feet instead of dropping a few punitive bombs. Such a thunderous voice from heaven, previously rigged up in a Victoria, had proved extremely effective. For me there was a strong temptation to switch it on during a test flight and address some remarks to the citizens of Walton-on-Thames, but this I managed to suppress.

Next was the re-emergence of the prototype G.4/31 monoplane K7556 which had been damaged when Mutt made a belly-landing with a hung-up undercarriage. The monoplane G.4/31, the first aeroplane of entirely geodetic construction, was a very clean monoplane with a long slender wing having a span of 75 ft and an aspect ratio of 7. It was destined, during its subsequent Royal Air Force career, to gain the world non-stop long-distance record of 7157.7 miles with a flight from Ismailia in Egypt to Darwin in Australia.

On 5 February 1936, we took delivery of a brand-new Miles Falcon G-ADTD with Gipsy VI engine, from Phillips & Powis. I flew it on a 15-minute provisional acceptance flight. The Falcon was a three-seater low-wing monoplane with an interesting reverse-slope windscreen. After that first acceptance flight the Falcon went into the Works for a thorough technical check-over by the Works inspection department and then I flew it again with Bob Handasyde in the back in order to check its performance against the 'brochure' claims, all the instruments having been thoroughly calibrated. We took off diagonally across Brooklands and at about 500 ft the engine quietly but decisively faded away to zero power. I quickly checked all fuel cocks and switches and everything seemed in order so the engine had simply decided to die. It was a case of getting down on one of the narrow tree-lined fairways of St George's Hill (difficult enough with a golf ball but even more problematical with a powerless aeroplane) or of breaking the golden rule turning downwind back to the aerodrome. I decided this was an occasion for breaking the rule and, pushing the nose down, I turned very gingerly left-handed and just scraped in over the members' banking of the race track to the eerie silence of a dead propeller and the sound of heavy breathing from Bob Handasyde in the back. The reason for the power failure was discovered to be an accumulation of some form of gunge in the fuel filters which had its origin in the type of flexible tubing used for the fuel supply. A different brand of flexible tubing was duly substituted and I flew the Falcon as a communications aeroplane for many years thereafter without a cough or a splutter from its excellent Gipsy VI engine.

On 6 March I flew the Falcon from Brooklands to Martlesham

to take Mutt Summers from there to Eastleigh. Popular folklore has it that the first flight of the Spitfire was on 5 March 1936 but I flew Mutt to Eastleigh for the particular purpose of making that first flight on 6 March. Also on that day I gave a 10-minute joyride in the Falcon at Eastleigh to Major H.J. Payn, who was R.J. Mitchell's technical assistant, and Stuart Scott-Hall, the Air Ministry resident technical officer at Supermarine, both of whom were present to witness the prototype Spitfire's first flight, as Plate 7 testifies. 'The Fighter' was in its Works finish, that is to say it was unpainted except for priming coats. It was fitted with a special fine-pitch propeller to ensure a safe take-off run and to minimise swing due to propeller torque during take-off (a characteristic of which Supermarine had much hard experience from the Schneider seaplanes) while the aeroplane itself was well below maximum take-off weight with no guns or ammunition installed.

There was a light wind blowing across the aerodrome which meant that Mutt had to take the short run and he taxied towards one of the four large Chance lights which (in those days) were situated round the perimeter, turned into wind and opened the throttle. The aeroplane was airborne after a very short run and climbed away comfortably. Mutt did not retract the under-carriage on that first flight – deliberately, of course – but cruised fairly gently around for some minutes, checked the lowering of the flaps and the slow flying and stalling characteristics, and then brought K5054 in to land. Although he had less room than he would probably have liked, he put the aeroplane down on three points without too much 'float', in which he was certainly aided by the fine-pitch setting of the propeller. He taxied towards the hangar and the point where we in the group of Supermarine spectators were standing. This included R.J. Mitchell, Alan Clifton, Beverley Shenstone, Alf Faddy, Ernest Mansbridge, 'Agony' Payn, Stuart Scott-Hall and Ken Scales, the foreman in charge of the aeroplane. There must also have been quite a few other people there but there was certainly not a crowd. It was very much a Supermarine 'family affair'.

When Mutt shut down the engine and everybody crowded round the cockpit, with R.J. foremost, Mutt pulled off his helmet and said firmly, 'I don't want anything touched.' This was destined to become a widely misinterpreted remark. What he meant was that there were no snags which required correction or adjustment before he flew the aircraft again. The remark has crept into folklore implying that the aeroplane was perfect in every respect from the moment of its first flight, an obviously absurd and impracticable idea. After the 15-minute first flight the aircraft was still largely untested and unproven, having done one take-off and one landing. Mutt was far too experienced a hand to make any such sweeping statement at that stage in the game.

However, it was a highly successful and encouraging first flight and Mutt Summers, with his experience of flying a great variety of prototype aircraft, was a highly shrewd judge of an aeroplane. By now I knew him well enough to see that he was obviously elated. Certainly to those of us watching from the ground 'the Fighter' in the air took on a very thoroughbred and elegant appearance, a strong but indefinable characteristic which was to remain with it throughout its long, varied and brilliantly successful life as a fighting aeroplane. Later that afternoon I flew Mutt back to Brooklands in the Falcon and we put the aircraft away and walked across to have a drink in Bob Lambert's well-known and congenial Brooklands Flying Club bar. Mutt was pleased, obviously, to have one more successful first flight tucked under his belt, and I felt excited about this long, sleek and elegant machine which I knew that soon I would fly. A hundred yards from where Mutt and I were leaning against the bar was the hangar in which was standing K5083, the prototype Hurricane, which had made its first flight in the hands of George Bulman some four months previously.

So the two new fighter aircraft – destined four years later to save our country in time of war – had now both flown in prototype form. Neither was yet anywhere near being a practical fighting machine nor was either yet ordered in quantity by the Royal Air Force, so much work still remained to be done. Ironically perhaps, the very next day, 7 March, Hitler's troops re-entered the demilitarised zone of the Rhineland in direct defiance of the Versailles Treaty. France and Britain, paralysed by political indecision, did nothing. Had they reacted with even the slightest resolution or show of military force the German Army was under orders to withdraw immediately, but that, of course, was not known then. Thus the last chance of effectively and cheaply blocking Hitler's expansionist ambitions was lost and the Spitfire was born into the inevitability of war.

6

K5054

Two days later Bob Handasyde and I set off in my old 3-litre Bentley, with parachutes, overalls, helmets and other gear stowed in the back, to drive from Brooklands to Martlesham to start the full load trials on the G.4/31 prototype (soon to become the Wellesley) and to complete the contractors' trials in accordance with official requirements.

The official test requirements were stringent and very detailed and I had studied them long and earnestly. I was acutely conscious of the responsibility for doing these trials at Martlesham whilst Mutt was standing by K5054 for his next flight down at Southampton. It was necessary before each flight to transpose carefully a lot of the requirements on to paper on a knee-pad to serve as an *aide-mémoire* in the air and on which to record the results.

So on 10 March I took off in K7556 from Martlesham with Bob Handasyde in the back and with a full load of fuel and ballast to represent the payload. We started the specified slow flying and stalling tests, 'behaviour near the stall', and these had to be carried out both wheels up and wheels down. I completed the wheels-up sequence and then selected undercarriage 'down' but one leg hung up and I was left with one green light and one red. 'God dammit,' I thought, 'not again – just my luck.'

With the huge span of the G.4/31 I began to consider the likely damage of a landing on one leg and a wing tip as against a straight belly-landing with both legs retracted and decided the latter would probably be the better course. In any event the aircraft would be quite badly damaged so it would be sensible to fly back to Brooklands and do the deed there, right outside the Works, rather than miles away at Martlesham. As I had plenty of fuel in the tanks I passed a note to Bob and set course for Brooklands. Passing round the northern perimeter of London we encountered low cloud and fog and although I got as far as Staines reservoir I could not get any further. Reluctantly I turned back towards

Martlesham, knowing that the crash landing there would greatly complicate the repair job and cause it to take much longer.

On arrival at Martlesham, after some three hours in the air, I selected undercarriage 'down' and, lo and behold, the recalcitrant leg came down but not completely so that I did not have a green light indicating that the 'down' locks were engaged. However I could see the leg was almost in the fully down position and reckoned it probably would stand up to a careful landing. So it proved; and the trouble was discovered later to be due to a broken ballrace.

On 26 March, Mutt told me to get ready to fly the Spitfire. R.J. was at Eastleigh at the time and so was Ernie Mansbridge, who was the member of the technical office whose job it was to organise flight test schedules and special instrumentation, and to arrange for the calculations necessary to correct and record performance figures obtained in the air. In short, Mansbridge was the technician on the ground who directly complemented the pilot in the air. Also there was Alf Faddy who, under Joe Smith, had been largely responsible for the detail design of the structure and was thus deeply interested in the engineering and functional aspects of the test flying, and of course Ken Scales who was 'nanny' to the prototype and practically never let it out of his sight except, unavoidably, when it was flying.

So, I climbed into the cockpit and Ken Scales, standing on the port wing root, helped me fasten my parachute and the Sutton harness and then closed the little access door at shoulder height on the left-hand side of the cockpit. The cockpit was narrow but not cramped. I sat in a natural and comfortable attitude, the rudder pedals were adjustable, the throttle and mixture controls were placed comfortably for the left hand, the seat was easily adjustable up or down. The retractable undercarriage selector lever and hydraulic hand pump were situated to the right of the seat. The instrument panel was tidy, symmetric and logically laid out. The windscreen was of curved perspex which gave a good deal of optical distortion but it had a clear view glass panel (not yet armoured) for vision dead ahead in the line of the gunsight. The sliding canopy was straight sided and operated directly by hand with a latch which engaged the top of the windscreen. With the seat in the fully up position there was very little headroom, but at once I felt good in that cockpit.

I primed the Merlin engine carefully and it started first time. I began taxiing out to the north-east end of the airfield which, of course, was entirely of grass. Never before had I flown a fighter with such a very long nose; with the aircraft in its ground attitude vision directly ahead was completely obscured so I taxied slowly on a zigzag course in order to ensure a clear path ahead. The great two-bladed wooden propeller, by this time of maximum coarse pitch, seemed to turn over very slowly and from the stub exhausts, one for each of the 12 cylinders, came a good powerful crackle whenever a small burst of power was applied for taxiing followed by a lot of popping in the exhausts as the throttle was closed again. On arrival at the edge of the field I turned the aircraft 45° off the wind and did my cockpit checks which, at that stage, really consisted only of fuel cocks, trimmer and flap settings, radiator shutter, tightening the throttle friction grip and a quick check over the engine instruments. With a last look round for other aircraft I turned into wind and opened the throttle.

With that big fixed-pitch propeller able to provide only very low revs during take-off, the acceleration was sluggish and full right rudder was required to hold the aeroplane straight. The torque reaction tended to roll the aircraft on its narrow under-carriage but soon we were airborne and climbing away. At once it was necessary to re-set the rudder trimmer and then to deal with the undercarriage retraction and the canopy. This presented a minor problem insofar as the undercarriage had to be raised with a hydraulic hand pump, so it was necessary to transfer the left hand from the throttle to the stick and operate the hand pump with the right. This was difficult to do without inducing a longitudinal oscillation of the whole aircraft.

However, once fully airborne and 'tidied up' the aircraft began to slip along as if on skates with the speed mounting up steadily and an immediate impression of effortless performance was accentuated by the low revs of the propeller at that low altitude. The aeroplane just seemed to chunter along at an outstandingly higher cruising speed than I had ever experienced before, with the engine turning over very easily and in this respect it was somewhat reminiscent of my old Bentley cruising in top gear. I climbed up to a few thousand feet and carried out some steep turns and some gentle rolls and found the aeroplane light and lively but with a tendency to shear about a bit directionally. I put it into a gentle dive and it accelerated with effortless ease and then I came back to rejoin the circuit for landing. The flaps, which I had already tried out in the air, came down on the prototype to only 60° which was the maximum lift, but not maximum drag, position so the glide angle on the approach was very flat and the attitude markedly 'nose up'. This feature was accentuated by the fact that the big wooden propeller ticked over extremely slowly and produced no noticeable drag or deceleration. The approach, with the use of a little power and very 'nose-up', meant the view straight ahead was almost non-existent as one got close to the ground, so I approached the airfield in a gentle left-hand turn, canopy open, and head tilted to look round the left-hand side of the windscreen. Mutt had warned me about this so I was able to get myself on the right line at the outset. As I chopped the throttle on passing over the boundary hedge the deceleration was hardly discernible and the aeroplane showed no desire to touch down – it evidently enjoyed flying – but finally it settled gently on three points and it wasn't until after the touch-down that the mild aerodynamic buffeting associated with the stalling of the wing became apparent. 'Here', I thought to myself, 'is a real lady.'

I decided that I must do another take-off and another landing, so I taxied back again to the edge of the field and opened up. Shortly before becoming airborne I realised that I had forgotten to retract the flaps. It was too late to cancel the take-off so I pressed on and we became airborne without trouble albeit with a bit of buffeting. At about 200 ft I raised the flaps and the aeroplane sank a few feet and then climbed away normally. I flew round for a while and came in for a second landing, this time with full confidence and was delighted to make another perfect 'three-pointer'. I noticed how the stick hardly moved during the flare-out for landing, which really seemed to be a case of finger-tip control for the aircraft seemed almost to land itself.

I felt rather foolish about having done my second take-off with the flaps down and I apologised to R.J. who said, 'Don't worry. We needed to try that sooner or later anyway – now you've done it so we can forget it.' The next day, 27 March, I flew K5054 twice more doing performance measurement (level speed runs) and recording cooling figures and the effect on speed of various settings of the ducted radiator. That same day I took R.J. Mitchell and Jimmy Ellor of Rolls-Royce for a flight in the Falcon to circle over the RMS *Queen Mary* which was anchored in Cowes Roads waiting to enter Southampton on her way from the Clyde for her maiden voyage to New York. We flew low over this great ship which had a crowd of yachts and small craft milling around her. *Queen Mary* and the Spitfire, both brand new, seemed to me in their different ways to be symbolic of an enterprising, exciting and challenging future.

After those flights, K5054 disappeared into the Works for various outstanding jobs to be done and it did not fly again for six weeks. During that interval I spent much time at Martlesham continuing the tests on the Wellesley prototype. On 11 May I flew K5054 on level-speed performance measurements at altitude, checking lateral stability characteristics at the stall and ground handling and air handling at the forward limit of the centre of gravity. Then, later on that afternoon, Mutt Summers flew K5054 on a handling check and I flew the Falcon with R.J. in the back accompanied by John Yoxall, the chief photographer of *Flight* magazine, to take the first air-to-air photographic sortie of K5054.

It was at about this time that the G.4/31 and the F.37/34 acquired their official names: Wellesley and Spitfire. The first use of the name Wellesley appears in my log on 3 April and the use of the name Spitfire (as opposed to 'Supermarine Fighter') on 11 May.

It is said that Sir Robert McLean proposed the name Spitfire and the Air Staff agreed to it. The name had previously been used unofficially for the F.7/30 gull-winged steam-cooled fighter designed by Mitchell and first flown on 19 February 1934. It was an ill-starred project of extremely disappointing performance which never got beyond the prototype stage. The failure of this aeroplane had been a sore point with Mitchell, who had tended to blame the restrictive nature of the Operational Requirement laid down by the Air Ministry, but the F.7/30 episode had the positive and significant result of inspiring Mitchell to start an altogether new design project. The result was K5054. When the name of his failed aeroplane was revived and applied to his beautiful new creation Mitchell was far from being enchanted. He was, too, by this time, a much sicker man than any of us realised and he could sometimes become rather tetchy. When told that henceforth K5054 was to be known as Spitfire he barked, '. . . sort of bloody silly name they would give it.'

The immediate task, however, was to get the Spitfire to Martlesham for its official trials upon which the whole future of the aeroplane depended. By the time I first flew the aeroplane on 26 March Mutt had done only a few spot checks of speed performance and nothing on climb or ceiling. He had concentrated only on establishing that the basic flying qualities and other functional aspects were reasonably satisfactory. His cursory speed checks had not been encouraging and a thorough performance check was now required. I did two flights on 27 March devoted to recording accurate sets of level speeds above and below the full throttle height, which was just below 17,000 ft.

I also recorded information on the ducted radiator system. This had been designed as a result of basic research work done at the Royal Aircraft Establishment (RAE) by Dr Meredith and had been a major factor in reducing the cooling drag which would otherwise have constituted a most serious 'barrier' to the performance of both the Spitfire and the Hurricane. The early recording of data on its functioning was therefore a matter of great importance. Meredith's work at Farnborough was an excellent example of how basic research at the RAE could make a vital contribution to ad hoc design work carried out by industry. This was exactly how the system was meant to work.

The result of the set of level speeds I recorded on that day was extremely disappointing, showing a top speed in the region of only 335 mph. This was a source of great worry to Mitchell because it was little more than the bush telegraph system was telling us about the top speed of Sydney Camm's Hurricane, already several months ahead of us in development. Mitchell was well aware that the Air Staff were hoping for a much better performance from the Spitfire and that, unless it had a substantial advantage in speed over the Hurricane, a production order would not be considered justifiable. Also, Mitchell had always afforded the first priority, in the design of the Spitfire, to the achievement of maximum performance, and several sacrifices of other characteristics, such as pilot's view and ease of production, had been made in pursuit of this. In deciding upon a wing of unusually low thickness/chord ratio he had gone against all contemporary aerodynamic opinion and fashion and here now was Camm's Hurricane, with a very thick wing, fabric covering and a humped back fuselage (affording excellent pilot's view) and with exactly the same power, going almost as fast as Mitchell's sleek metal-skinned thin-winged Spitfire. There was no question, therefore, of the aeroplane going to Martlesham until a much better performance had been achieved. A number of refinements were made in the hope of discovering sources of unsuspected drag and the efficiency of the aerodynamic design of the fixed-pitch wooden propeller came under suspicion. The Supermarine propeller designers considered that at full speed and revs the helical speed of the propeller tips were such that they might be running into compressibility (e.g. Mach number) problems so they designed a propeller with tip sections to alleviate this possibility. While this propeller was being manufactured we tested some other propellers but none of them produced any very significant improvement.

Then on 5 May I flew with the new Supermarine propeller and carried out a full set of level speed tests. Alfred Price quotes Ernest Mansbridge: 'Jeffrey went off and did a set of level speeds with it. When he came down he handed me the test card with a big grin and said, "I think we've got something here." And we had – we'd got 13 mph. After correcting the figures we made the maximum speed 348 mph, which we were very pleased with.' Mitchell's objective had been 350 mph but he considered 348 mph good enough. Apart from solving the performance problem it was of course essential to ensure that the handling and stability qualities of the aeroplane were fully acceptable before sending it to Martlesham and also that the general functional and strength characteristics had been proven. This is what occupied the rest of the limited flying available to us before the aircraft was dispatched to A & AEE. On one of his early flights George Pickering had encountered some incipient rudder overbalance and it was decided then and there to reduce the area of the rudder horn balance. Thereafter the directional stability characteristics were reasonably acceptable.

Determination of the centre of gravity limits was the next job. The forward limit was determined by ground handling and braking considerations, but the aft-limit by longitudinal stability characteristics in flight. I flew K5054 at an extended aft limit

1 Jeffrey Quill, *c.* 1943

2 J.K.Q. (*left*) and Dick Reynell (*right*) with M Flight Siskin, Duxford 1934

3 George Pickering (*left*) and J.K.Q. at Eastleigh, 1938

4 Bulldogs of 17 (Fighter) Squadron taking off from Upavon, 1933

5 The Vickers Valentia, which could carry 22 fully equipped troops

6 K5054 photographed just before its first flight. It was not painted until sometime later

7 Immediately after the first flight of K5054. *left–right*: Mutt Summers, H.J.Payn, R.J.Mitchell, S.Scott-Hall, J.K.Q.

8 J.K.Q. landing the Venom prototype at the SBAC Show, Hatfield, 1936

9 Wellesley prototype K7556 taking off for demonstration on 18 July 1937

10 K5054 at Eastleigh, 1936. R.J.Mitchell's Rolls-Royce car in the background

11 The only known photograph of R.J.Mitchell with the Spitfire, taken by his son

12 The high-speed development Spitfire N.17 with 'Schneiderised' Merlin
    engine of over 2,000 bhp, Eastleigh, 1939

13 The first real stage of development, 1940: the Spitfire Mk III with Merlin
    XX engine and wing span reduced by 6 ft

14 J.K.Q. taxiing for first night-flying trials of K5054, Eastleigh, 1938. This aeroplane was eventually destroyed in a crash at Farnborough on 2 September 1939; the pilot, F/Lt White, was killed

15 King George VI inspected the Spitfire in 1939; here talking with J.K.Q. (*left*), George Pickering and Alex Dunbar

16 65 Squadron. Paddy Finucane and Sam Saunders, Manston, August 1940

17 Hangar at Manston after dive-bombing attack, 12 August 1940

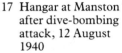

18 'B' Flight 65 Squadron, Rochford, August 1940. Photograph includes Dave Glaser, Sgt McPherson, Gordon Olive, Wigg, Lee Pyman and J.K.Q. (*on right, sitting on wing*)

19 Spitfire Mk IX with 30-gallon slipper tank

20 Spitfire Mk VB with 90-gallon slipper tank and tropical air intake

21 Spitfire Mk VC with 170-gallon ferry tank; this tank was not used on operations but for ferry purposes only

22 The first Griffon Spitfire, DP845 ('My favourite aeroplane'), which led to a series of Griffon-engined Spitfire derivatives

23 The prototype F.Mk XX, with the big two-stage Rolls-Royce RG 2.5M engine; still with small tail surfaces and extended wing tips which, happily, were eliminated later

24 The F.Mk VI high-altitude interceptor—the first operational fighter
aircraft to be equipped with a pressurised cabin. It was produced to meet
the threat from Luftwaffe high-altitude bombers

25 The pressurised cabin of the F.Mk VII (Merlin 64 engine).
The hood was clamped down after the pilot entered the cockpit, but was
jettisonable in emergency. A 2-lb pressure differential was maintained
through the height range

centre of gravity loading on 13 May and the aircraft was violently unstable. So we moved the centre of gravity progressively forward by a process of ballasting until we reached a position where, on a purely qualitative assessment, the longitudinal stability characteristics seemed reasonably acceptable. In those days, since there was no reliable or accurate method of measuring control forces (stick forces) or elevator angles the only quantitative way of measuring stability in the air was by recording 'phugoids'. This was done by disturbing the aircraft longitudinally from a trimmed condition of flight and then leaving it to its own devices and recording, by stopwatch and airspeed indicator reading, how and if the disturbance damped out or whether it increased in amplitude or even diverged. If the disturbance damped itself out and the aircraft returned to its original condition of trimmed flight, the stability was positive but if the disturbance increased in amplitude or diverged then the aeroplane was to a greater or lesser degree unstable.

At the aft limit loading which we eventually settled on at that time, the phugoids which I recorded showed the aeroplane to be just unstable but not seriously so. At its normal service loading, however, the stability was just positive and I thought this acceptable, but I asked Mutt Summers for his opinion and he agreed it as suitable for delivery to Martlesham. However, all this showed that the longitudinal stability of the Spitfire was very marginal and that the acceptable range of centre of gravity movement in flight was very small. This was, in fact, indicating a problem which was to be with us in one form or another throughout the long development life of the aeroplane.

Lateral stability at the stall (in accordance with ADM 293) also had to be checked and this was done on an opportunity basis during flights primarily devoted to performance measurement.

On 14 May I did the first dives to the design maximum permissible indicated airspeed of 380 mph IAS (indicated airspeed). These dives were done at a height at which the corrected true airspeed worked out at 465 mph. During the second dive the port undercarriage fairing tore away with a loud bang and damaged the underside of the fuselage. In those dives I observed that the aileron control was becoming rather heavy but not excessively so. On the first production versions of the Spitfire (1938) the maximum permissible indicated airspeed in a dive was increased by nearly 100 mph to 470 mph IAS, and this was when the aileron problems came to light. (See Chapter 15.)

Cooling suitability tests for glycol and oil systems had to be done before delivery and these required some special instrumentation and special flights. Spinning tests, however, were deferred until later, after the aeroplane had returned from its first sessions at Martlesham, because the model tests which had been carried out in the free spinning tunnel at the RAE had indicated very poor recovery characteristics. Obviously nobody wished to risk losing the aeroplane at this stage in the game. The pressures, both from the Air Ministry and from within Vickers, to get the aeroplane delivered as soon as possible to Martlesham were enormous, but the overriding consideration in Mitchell's mind had been to get the maximum possible speed performance and he would not let it go until he was satisfied. In retrospect, perhaps the most surprising feature of that early phase of tests was the very small amount of flying that was possible. This was due primarily to the aeroplane spending a lot of time in the Works on engine and propeller changes and modifications, and alterations of various kinds.

K5054 was flown to Martlesham on 26 May 1936 by Mutt Summers and handed over to Squadron Leader Anderson, CO of 'A' Flight A & AEE. At that time the normal all-up weight of the aeroplane was 5,819 lb with the centre of gravity at .321 of the mean wing chord. The three RAF pilots primarily involved in these early Martlesham trials were Flight Lieutenant H. Edwardes-Jones*, Sergeant S. Wroath† and Flight Lieutenant Simonds.§

The trials carried out at Martlesham established a top speed of 349 mph for the aircraft against our measured result of 348 mph. Such a close result was satisfactory for us and the discrepancy of 1 mph was probably accounted for by minor differences in instrument error. They also gave a service ceiling of 35,400 ft and a take-off run of 235 yds in a 5-knot wind.

The Martlesham report on K5054 was issued piecemeal, in a series of interim documents. It had a basic reference number

---

* Later Air Chief Marshal Sir Humphrey Edwardes-Jones.
† Later Group Captain S. Wroath, CBE AFC. Twice Commandant of the Empire Test Pilots School.
§ Killed at Martlesham in 1937.

followed by Interim 1, Interim 2, etc. Interim 1, issued in July 1936, dealt only with performance figures and gave no information on handling characteristics except for some phugoid plots reproduced without comment.

It can be concluded from this that the Air Staff were at that point interested only in the aircraft's performance for they would go ahead with it only if it offered a substantial improvement over the Hurricane. This is borne out by Sir Humphrey Edwardes-Jones who has said that, when the aeroplane was delivered to 'A' Squadron in 1936, he was telephoned by the Air Ministry and told to fly it at once and report on one immediate question: was the aeroplane capable of being flown safely by ordinary squadron pilots? Fortunately for us all he replied that in his opinion the answer was 'yes'. A production order for 310 aircraft was placed on 3 June 1936, before any formal report on K5054 had been issued by A & AEE, although no doubt the Air Staff had kept themselves informed on a daily basis by telephone. Such was the official urgency and desire for Mitchell's aeroplane. A contract for 600 Hurricanes from Hawkers was signed on the same day.

When the first Martlesham handling report was issued there were remarkably few criticisms and such as there were tended to be of relatively trivial nature. The wing stiffness of the prototype limited it to a maximum permissible diving speed of only 380 mph indicated airspeed. The A & AEE report stated: 'The aeroplane was dived to 380 mph ASI and up to that speed the ailerons were not unduly heavy and gave adequate response.'

On the subject of longitudinal stability the report stated: 'Longitudinally the aeroplane is neutrally stable with engine on and stable in the glide. The aeroplane is unstable in the glide with flaps and undercarriage down. In general the stability characteristics are satisfactory for a fighting aeroplane and give a reasonable compromise between controllability and steadiness as a gun platform.'

Martlesham criticisms were limited at this stage to the suggestion that, since the elevator control was very powerful and effective, perhaps too much so in the landing case, a reduction in the gear ratio between control column and elevator could be an advantage. Also the visual distortion caused by the moulded perspex windscreen was criticised and it was suggested that the windscreen might be made of flat glass panels even if this caused a small increase in drag. (In fact this was not done until 1940, when I returned from a short tour of operations in 65 Squadron and made very strong representations to Supermarine.) Changes to the stick/elevator gearing were in fact tried later on and found to be unsatisfactory and were abandoned. Production aircraft reverted to the original gearing.

K5054 went to Martlesham this first time with neither guns nor ammunition tanks fitted. This was because so few Browning guns were then available in Britain that there had been none to spare for the Spitfire prototype. No radio was installed nor anything that could really be described as operational equipment for a fighter. It was a single-seater flying machine of extremely good performance, very sweet to fly and with no vices. But it was very far from being a fighter aeroplane and therefore the production order was placed by the Air Ministry entirely on the basis of its potential. This represented a value judgement by the Air Council based upon the advice of the Air Staff in London and the RAF pilots at Martlesham who flew the aeroplane and recognised it for what it was – a thoroughbred. It was also an indication of the utmost confidence in R.J. Mitchell.

There was still, however, a long and difficult road ahead before a quantity-produced and fully effective fighting machine was to emerge from the Supermarine factory.

On 10 February 1936 the Air Minister, Lord Swinton, had submitted to the Cabinet proposals whereby the existing expansion Scheme C should be increased to provide a front-line strength for the Metropolitan Air Force of 124 Squadrons, or 1,736 front-line aircraft, by 1939. This was agreed by the Cabinet on 26 February 1936 and was known as Scheme F. Under this scheme reserves were to comprise two-and-a-quarter times the front-line strength and it was under Scheme F (which of course was not wholly devoted to Fighters) that the Air Ministry ordered 600 Hurricanes and 310 Spitfires. That these two orders were placed simultaneously makes it clear that, once Scheme F had been authorised by the Government, the Air Staff moved as fast as possible to order the most modern types. It was just as well they did because the problems of getting the Spitfire (and Hurricane) into production proved to be very great indeed.

7

RJM – and more about K5054

From this time in June 1936 until 1938, when I moved down to Supermarine full-time, I continued flying the prototype Spitfire as and when it was serviceable, by commuting in the Falcon from Brooklands to Eastleigh. I would sandwich my Spitfire flying with work at Weybridge mostly on Wellesleys (by now in production) or the little Venom single-seat eight-gun fighter.

As far as the development work on the Spitfire was concerned, although I had direct access to R.J. Mitchell and to Alan Clifton and other members of the Technical and Drawing offices at Supermarine, I worked as much as possible through Ernie Mansbridge on flight performance matters and through Alf Faddy on the 'nuts and bolts', or functional engineering matters. There were times when Mutt Summers flew the aircraft, and there were times when George Pickering flew it and I was glad of this because I was constantly looking for a second opinion or support for my own impressions; but on the whole I did most of the flying. I was only too aware of my youth and 'newness' in the company and sometimes felt the need of a little bolstering-up, which George would always provide.

Mitchell was a frequent visitor to the aerodrome at Eastleigh. Mansbridge was under orders to inform him immediately by telephone when the aeroplane was about to fly and so when I used to circuit the aerodrome prior to landing I would very often look down and see R.J.'s Rolls-Royce car (which had been given to him by Rolls-Royce Ltd after the successful 1931 Schneider Trophy contest) parked on the tarmac.

After any test flight Ken Scales was always the first to climb onto the wing root to help me out of the cockpit, anxious to know if all was well with his charge. Ernie Mansbridge would be there waiting for the figures and results of the test and anyone else who had questions to ask. Then R.J. would appear, hands in pockets, ostensibly listening casually to what was going on. If there were no snags and it was just a case of refuelling for the next sortie, he would often invite me to go and sit with him in his car while waiting for the aircraft to be ready again and this was when he would ask a lot of searching questions or discuss various aspects of the Spitfire. These conversations would sometimes range over a wide variety of topics. I was not a trained engineer, only a well-trained pilot, and I was very conscious of this fact and therefore tended, in those early days, to be overawed by the technical status and expertise so clearly evident in the design staff of Supermarine and Weybridge. Indeed I was well on the way towards acquiring a complex about this. Those talks with R.J. in the privacy of his car, casual and informal as they often were, restored my confidence and led me to see that, however learned and abstruse the methods and processes whereby scientists and technicians reached their conclusions, the conclusions themselves were capable of being expressed in straightforward terms intelligible to all reasonable men at least insofar as practical matters are concerned. There was a sort of direct and shining commonsense which illuminated R.J.'s approach to all problems. He made me see that the most valuable contribution which I could make was to concentrate upon becoming a better and better pilot and to try to absorb a natural understanding of the problems of engineers and designers by maintaining close personal contacts with them and doing my best to interpret pilots' problems to them, and vice versa.

One day he said to me, 'Jeffrey, if anyone tries to tell you something about an aeroplane which is so damn complicated that you can't understand it you can take it from me it's all balls.'

He may have been overstating the case a bit, but it did wonders for my morale, and he showed me the way that I should go to become a good test pilot. Those quiet talks with R.J. Mitchell are a memory I have always treasured.

Although I claim no clairvoyance I had a steadily growing feeling that this aeroplane was of immense importance and so I sometimes felt weighed down by a sense of awful responsibility. Suppose I got something desperately wrong or, horror of horrors, suppose I crashed it? There was at least one occasion during those early days when I might well have done so. It was on 18 June 1936 that Sir Robert McLean had arranged a great jamboree at Eastleigh when all the Vickers Aviation products were to be on show to the British Press. The reporters and Air Correspondents were brought from London by special train; a sort of champagne express. The star turns amongst the landplanes to be shown were the prototypes of the Wellington, the Wellesley, the Spitfire and the Venom; and amongst the flying boats the Walrus, the Scapa and the Stranraer. This was quite a turn-out for a single company. Mutt was to fly the Wellington and the Venom, I was to fly the Wellesley and the Spitfire, George Pickering the Stranraer, 'Agony' Payn the Walrus, and Ronnie Louis the Scapa. Mutt had done the first flight on the Venom at Brooklands only a day or two beforehand but on the morning of this show the weather was bad and he did not bring it to Eastleigh. In any case it was a bit too brand new for demonstration purposes.

At the last minute the Spitfire, which I had collected from Martlesham the previous day, was found to have an oil leak from its engine but in spite of much engine running on the ground we could not locate the leak. Mitchell and Bill Lappin of Rolls-Royce, Ken Scales and the resident Rolls-Royce mechanic and I had a sort of drum-head conference on the airfield – to fly or not to fly? The whole British Press, well primed by an expensive and no doubt liquid luncheon on the train and who had not previously clapped eyes on the Spitfire, were awaiting a demonstration. Bill Lappin, a wise old bird, was against flying. I argued that we had a tank full of oil (eight gallons) and it would only be a five-minute flight anyway – so what if it threw a bit of oil around inside the cowling? R.J. Mitchell, as usual, listened carefully to everyone and said very little until, after an agonising pause, he turned to me and said, 'Get in and fly it', and turned on his heel and walked away with Bill Lappin.

I took off from the south-west end of the aerodrome, parallel to the apron. When I was well and truly committed, a whole group of press photographers suddenly ran out onto the field ahead of me in order to get pictures as I became airborne. I was worried because they were much too close for comfort particularly as I already had full right rudder on to keep the aircraft straight against the torque of the big wooden propeller. As I became airborne one of them was very close indeed to my port wingtip. As soon as I was safely airborne I started to pump up the undercarriage and took a very quick downward glance at the oil pressure gauge and to my horror saw it dropping rapidly down to zero. I knew one thing for certain and that was that no high-powered aero engine would run for long on zero oil pressure before it started seizing up or throwing connecting rods through the crankcase, and here was I at about 100 ft at full power with no oil pressure and the Eastleigh railways works dead ahead of me. I used what kinetic energy I had to gain a few hundred feet of height and at once took off as much power as I dared, returned the undercarriage selector lever to 'down' and started to creep round in a low and slow left-hand turn. I prayed that I could get myself into a position from which I could land back on the aerodrome before any expensive or terminal noises came from the engine. As soon as I could I chopped the throttle and sideslipped in to land but I was too slow for safety and had to give one last burst of engine to which, thank God, it responded and then I heard the blessed rumble of wheels on the grass.

I taxied in, full of bitter disappointment as I had practised a sparkling demonstration of this little aeroplane of which we at Supermarine were by now becoming so very proud. But even that very short and abortive first public demonstration had made an impression on the Press. 'The fastest military aircraft in the world' was *The Times* headline over its report.

At the end of it all I felt a very friendly disposition towards the new Merlin engine. It started for me a process of confidence in that remarkable piece of machinery which was to grow ever stronger as my hours in the air with it increased and as progressively I demanded more and more from it in the way of continuous running at full power in the course of rigorous performance testing. I learned to be meticulous in the matter of correct engine handling at all times and although I never hesitated to run it to the absolute limit of its capabilities I was careful never to exceed those limits except when unavoidable. In return the Merlin hardly ever let me down and such total power failures as I experienced – and over the years inevitably there were many – were due as often as not to extraneous causes rather than to anything fundamental to the engine. The Merlin really was the pilot's friend.

So the Spitfire survived that contretemps of 18 June and after the fitting of a new engine was duly returned to Martlesham on about 24 June to continue its trials. In the meantime I got on with flying the little Venom (F.5/34) at Weybridge and at the SBAC

Show at Hatfield on 29 June (see Chapter 9). Mutt Summers flew
the Spitfire and the Wellington in that Hatfield show which was
the first SBAC show not to have taken place at Hendon on the
Monday following the Royal Air Force display. On 1 August I
collected K5054 from Martlesham to have its armament, gunsight and radio installed at the Works with various other modifications to raise the prototype a little nearer to the standard
required for production. The wings of the prototype Spitfire had
been built without the armament installed at all so there was a
good deal of work required. This work, together with the other
jobs to be done, took until 3 December to complete, much longer
than predicted. The guns delivered to the Works for this installation were those which had already been used for the Hurricane,
which was evidence of the continuing shortage of Browning guns
at that time.

When K5054 finally did emerge from the Works it had a
slightly modified version of the Merlin engine, the Merlin F, of
1050 bhp, eight Browning guns installed in the wings and the
GD5 reflector sight mounted in the cockpit. At last it was something like a fighter, or so we thought, and I remember a feeling of
irritation that the gun-firing trials were to be done at Martlesham
and not at the firm, for I longed to experience from the cockpit
the sound of those eight Brownings blasting away. However,
there were other things to be done, including performance
measurements with the new Merlin engine and oil-cooling
checks, trials with a four-bladed wooden propeller and then the
first spinning trials. On 4 December, in the course of a series of
level-speed runs up and down the south coast at high altitude
over cloud, I got further to the east than I had intended and ran
short of fuel so I had to land at Tangmere, which was the home of
1 and 43 Squadrons, equipped with Hawker Furies, a lovely little
biplane fighter. I taxied in to the tarmac and shut down the
engine and a crowd of pilots and airmen immediately gathered
round to examine this strange new beast. I took off my helmet
and began to shed my Sutton harness and parachute straps when
a strange crescendo of sound came from the rear fuselage which
considerably startled me – a sort of high-frequency hammering
noise, rather as sometimes happens in ancient domestic hot water
systems. I leant out of the cockpit and looked towards the tail in
some alarm and there I saw a crowd of airmen all tapping on the

metal fuselage with their knuckles. It was the first time they had ever encountered a metal-skinned aeroplane!

There were a number of convivial souls at Tangmere such as Prosser Hanks and Fred Rosier and I decided that it would be sensible to stay the night and get a Supermarine ground crew over in the morning to look over the aeroplane which had had a hard day's flying. And so the Spitfire spent its first-ever night on a Royal Air Force Fighter station and where better than Tangmere?

I flew back to Eastleigh the next morning and gave Tangmere a good beat-up on departure. Although my g* threshold was probably somewhat impaired I hoped I gave those two distinguished fighter squadrons a foretaste of things to come.

Then came the first spinning trials. The RAE at Farnborough, on the basis of the model tests they had done in their vertical spinning tunnel, had been decidedly gloomy about the Spitfire's spin-recovery characteristics. This was why spinning tests had been deferred until after the aeroplane's first series of trials at Martlesham. It was also why we had rigged up a spin-recovery parachute – an idea which was very experimental in those days. It consisted of a small parachute, about 2 ft in diameter when deployed, attached to a cable of which the other end was fixed to a ring bolt on the fuselage just ahead of the fin. If the aircraft would not recover from the spin by normal use of the controls this parachute would then be streamed to give the tail such a yank that recovery would be assured. Then I should pull a trigger in the cockpit which would operate a release mechanism on the ring bolt and the parachute would float away. The installation of this device was somewhat crude; the folded parachute was stowed in a small plywood box inside the cockpit. The cable passed out of the cockpit and externally down the starboard side of the fuselage attached at intervals by sticky tape, the rear end being attached to the ring bolt by the fin. If I had to use it the idea was that I should seize a fistful of parachute from its little box and throw it over the side of the cockpit where it would catch the wind and deploy, ripping the fixings of the cable. It was obviously important not to get the cable round one's neck!

The first spins were done with the centre of gravity at the

* 1 g equals one times gravity. At 3 g, for instance, a pilot is three times his weight.

forward limit – theoretically the most favourable configuration for recovery. I entered the first spin at about 20,000 ft from a strangely silent stall with the big two-bladed propeller ticking over very, very slowly. At the first turn the aircraft went very nearly over onto its back and then settled into a rough and uneven spin with a tremendous amount of longitudinal pitching and some lateral rocking. The movement was so violent that at one time I thought it was going to throw itself out of the spin which would certainly have been a novel experience. After a few turns I applied opposite rudder and eased the stick gently forward and it recovered almost at once. I climbed up again for another spin in the opposite direction with very much the same result although the spin was slightly more smooth and gentle to the left than to the right. The requirement was to demonstrate recovery from an eight-turn spin in each direction and this I did, on that same sortie, and recovery presented not the slightest problem. However, I was very surprised by the amount of longitudinal pitching in the course of each rotation for at one point in the turn the nose seemed to be pointing almost vertically downwards and at another point it had reared up above the horizon. Furthermore the rate of rotation varied from fast to slow in the course of each turn, causing it to spin by a series of convulsive flicks. This I found somewhat disquieting and wondered what was going to happen when I tried the aft limit of the centre of gravity. 'So far – so good,' I said to Ernie Mansbridge, who was waiting for me on the ground – I suspect rather anxiously. And so good it remained. I completed the spinning on K5054 throughout the centre of gravity range and there was never the slightest trouble in recovery although K5054 always seemed to make a great fuss about it all while the spin was actually in progress. Thereafter I carried out the initial spinning trials on every Mark of Spitfire (or Seafire) which went into production and some which did not; there was never a case of any production Mark of either failing to recover from a spin, although I once had problems with an experimental rudder on a Seafire which resulted in a broken ankle.

When I had been flying the Spitfire for a short while I received a letter from the Air Ministry offering me a permanent commission but with loss of seniority equivalent to the time I had spent at Vickers. This was a frightful dilemma. If only they had

offered it before I had left the Service; now I was getting stuck
into the Spitfire and into Vickers and Supermarine. After much
heart-searching I turned it down.

Philip Teed, a close associate of Wallis, said in answer to my
request for advice, 'Whichever decision you make there will be
times when you bitterly regret it.' He was absolutely right.

Between 3 December 1936 (when the Spitfire first emerged
from the Works with its armament installation and other modifications) and 9 February 1937 I made a total of 37 flights on
K5054 amounting to 21 hours 55 minutes flying. The first time I
dived the aeroplane to maximum speed with the new armament
installation all the gun bay doors flew off the upper surface of the
wing.

One set of trials carried out at this time was unusual and
original. K5054 was flush riveted throughout in order to achieve
the smoothest possible surface finish which the aerodynamicists
regarded as vital for drag reduction at high speed. But since flush
riveting was difficult, expensive and time-consuming in production, a practical trial was decided upon. Several bags of dried
split peas were purchased from a local grocer. To each of the
many thousands of flush-headed rivets all over the outer surface
of the aircraft a split pea was attached by a dab of Seccotine,
thereby virtually converting each into a round-headed rivet.

I then took the aircraft up and carried out a very careful series
of level-speed runs. When Ernie Mansbridge had corrected the
figures the effect on the aircraft's performance was certainly
significant; something in the order of 22 mph. That the bulk of
the additional drag was due to the roughening of the surface in
various critical areas such as the leading edges of the wings, back
to about 30 per cent of the chord, and to certain areas of the
fuselage. So we embarked upon a programme of progressively
scraping off the split peas from selected areas in order to identify
the critical areas. (If you look closely at a Spitfire today you will
see certain areas of flush riveting and other areas where round-
headed rivets are visible.) Many flights were devoted to this
exercise and very accurate level-speed measurement and instrument calibration was needed for it. Thus was much unnecessary
flush riveting eliminated.

Towards the end of February I went down with a mild bout of
pneumonia, so that George Pickering flew K5054 to Martlesham

on 23 February for its armament trials which, in fact, went very much less satisfactorily than everyone had hoped. The A & AEE report on the early armament trials still exists (it was dated March 1937). The guns fired perfectly on the butts on the ground and also at low altitudes in the air with only a minor stoppage due to a drop in pneumatic pressure (the remote firing mechanism by Dunlop was operated by pneumatic pressure activated by a thumb button on the control column). But at high altitude they virtually refused to fire at all. This was entirely due to the very low ambient air temperature (about −53°C at 32,000 ft) which caused the oil on the breech mechanisms to freeze up. Flight Lieutenant Johnnie Dewar of the Martlesham Armament flight, on his first attempt to fire the guns at high altitude, had five guns which wouldn't fire at all, two which fired only four and eight rounds respectively and one which managed to get off 171 rounds before it stopped. The effects of the low air temperature were aggravated by the fact that, being mounted remotely in the wings, the guns had to be cocked before take-off. Thus their breeches were open in flight. As Dewar returned to the aerodrome the oil in the guns progressively un-froze itself and when he touched down on landing the slight jolt immediately resulted in three of his guns firing one round each across the aerodrome and into the peace of the Suffolk countryside. Clearly, urgent steps were now needed to provide a system for heating the gun bays and ammunition tanks. Martlesham also strongly criticised the GD5 reflector sight as being entirely unsuitable and recommended the adoption of the GM2 sight which was thereafter embodied.

The next move was for the aircraft to be returned to the Works for the installation of an effective gun-heating system but on 22 March Sam McKenna* of the A & AEE was doing some tests to try to identify some minor elevator vibration which had been observed during the period approaching a g stall when he suffered a loss of oil pressure followed by the ejection of a few con-rods through the crankcase. He put the aircraft down in some open country near Ipswich, with the wheels up, and slid to a standstill with absolute minimal damage to the structure. He did not even break the propeller because it happened to stop with its

---

* Later Group Captain and Commandant of the Empire Test Pilots School.

two blades exactly horizontal. He himself, firmly held by his Sutton harness, was also undamaged and thus the Spitfire's first emergency belly landing was most neatly accomplished. And so, not for the last time, it returned home by road.

8

Taking Silk

Towards the end of 1936, R.J. Mitchell's health deteriorated considerably and necessitated periodic absences from his office. In 1933 he had been operated on for cancer of the intestine and was told then that, provided he had no recurrence of the trouble within four years, his chances would be good. But the trouble did recur just over three years after his operation; and after consultation with specialists it was decided in February 1937 that his only hope was to visit the clinic of Dr Anton Loew, then the world's leading expert on Mitchell's form of cancer.

R.J. was flown out there in a chartered De Havilland Rapide which took off from Eastleigh aerodrome on a spring day in 1937. A large number of the Design staff from Woolston somehow found it necessary to visit Eastleigh that morning and I well remember the scene as R.J.'s aeroplane taxied out in front of a crowd of his devoted staff who had assembled on the tarmac to wave him good luck and God speed. Alas, in spite of this tide of goodwill and high hopes, R.J. returned to England late in May with any last hope of recovery finally gone. There was nothing for it but to await the end, which he did with the utmost fortitude. I drove from Brooklands to Southampton shortly after his return to see him. He was lying on a day-bed in the sitting-room of his house in Russell Place and he talked animatedly and cheerfully, but when I left I knew I would not see him again. When he died on 11 June, at the age of only forty-two, no production Spitfire had then taken the air, but he had seen the prototype of his fighter fly many, many times and knew that it was doing what he had hoped and that it was ordered into quantity production. He had every reason to expect that it would serve the Royal Air Force and his country well. It is appropriate to recall that it was during those three years following his major operation in 1933 that R.J. designed the Spitfire, knowing that his life might be cut short at any time. He was a brave man as well as a brilliant designer.

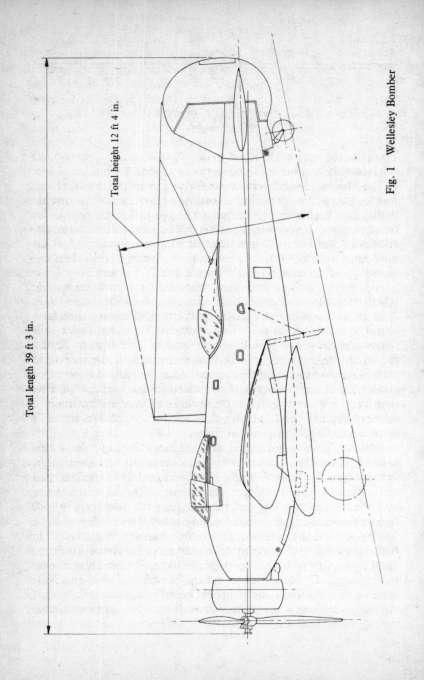

Total length 39 ft 3 in.

Total height 12 ft 4 in.

Fig. 1   Wellesley Bomber

By March 1937 the Wellesley was in production at Weybridge. My initial flight in the first production Wellesley (K7713) was on 17 March 1937 and thereafter I was testing new ones at very regular intervals. The first Squadron (76) was formed at Finningley in Yorkshire. I delivered K7714 to them on 24 March. The weather was bad with snowstorms and I had to creep along underneath it as I had no serviceable R/T and had to land at Sywell and at Grantham *en route*.

The advent of the Wellesley into production made life at Weybridge much more interesting during the intervals of flying the Venom and the Spitfire prototypes. It was an interesting and unusual aeroplane to fly, representing as it did the new generation of large single-engined monoplanes and its performance was good for its day. It was classed as a medium bomber. It was also the first all-geodetic aeroplane ever produced and its long span and narrow chord wing (aspect ratio 7) was very flexible and one could watch it, in turbulent conditions or under high g loads, almost flapping about in flight. However, its geodetic construction made the wing stiff in torsion and to achieve a dangerous condition of wing flutter it was necessary to have a combination of movement in both bending and torsion. The extreme rigidity of the Wellesley wing in torsion therefore rendered it perfectly safe, in spite of its rather lissom appearance from the cockpit. It had been Barnes Wallis's aim to achieve the aerodynamic advantages of a very high aspect ratio wing for cruising flight and to compensate for the high degree of flexure in bending by providing this great torsional stiffness.

The Wellesley was the first new aeroplane to enter production, either at Supermarine or Weybridge, since my arrival. All other production aeroplanes I had flown there such as Vildebeests, Vincents, Harts and Valentias had been rolling out of the factory before I arrived. However, I had been very surprised at what seemed a casual and haphazard approach to the testing of the production aeroplanes which was in marked contrast to the attitude towards the testing of prototypes. There was no proper schedule of tests laid down and all the test pilots seemed to be required to do was to take the aeroplane off, fly it round and ensure that it was correctly rigged, that is to say not flying right or left wing low, that the controls had freedom of movement, and that the engine was apparently functioning satisfactorily and

making the right noises. He might then do a couple of loops for
the benefit of the Flight gang on the ground, bring it in to land
and pass it as fit for delivery. He would then be required to sign
an Air Ministry Form No. 1361 and the Government represent-
atives would accept the aeroplane on behalf of the customer.
There was apparently no attempt to ensure that every production
aeroplane was checked throughout its basic flight envelope,
especially up to its maximum diving speed, nor any attempt to
ensure that the engine was providing its proper power output by
spot checks at critical heights (by now nearly all engines were
supercharged). In short, there was a lack of method about the
whole business which I thought most odd and unsatisfactory.
Mutt Summers's time and energies were wrapped up with prototypes, in future development ideas and the general politics of the
company, and he did not really interest himself much in the
production aeroplanes unless something went wrong.

As I had done the bulk of the handling and performance
testing of the prototype Wellesley K7556 I determined that,
when it came into production, each aircraft should be tested on a
much more methodical and thorough basis and that no aircraft
should ever leave our factory until both its safety and performance had been fully proven. This meant that there would have to
be a fixed and properly worked out schedule of tests which
should be mandatory before the test pilot could sign Form 1361.
With the help of Bob Handasyde I worked out what seemed a
minimum acceptable schedule for the Wellesley.

Such a proposition, however, was not likely to be adopted
without opposition. The Works had, in the nature of things, a
constant problem in keeping up to production schedules. There
was always some cause, good or bad, of delay and the flight
testing was the last significant process in production before
delivery. Rather naturally, the Works, particularly if they had
dropped behind delivery schedules, wanted the flight testing
completed in the minimum time and with the minimum of snags,
reported by the test pilot, which they would have to rectify. This
being the case, some undesirable pressures could sometimes be
brought to bear on test pilots. This was particularly the case
during periods of bad weather when pilots might be tempted to
'help out the Works' by passing aeroplanes out on the basis of
testing only at low altitude. It was also a good reason why pilots

who flew production aeroplanes should have a position in the firm which was in no way subservient to Works Management. Summers supported the idea, although perhaps he did not feel as strongly about it as I did, and together we talked to Rex Pierson, the Chief Designer, who fully agreed, as did also the Chief Inspector, Major F.C. Atkinson, who welcomed it enthusiastically. So with this amount of high-priced help, any objections to the idea were over-ruled.

So from then there was no question of a production Wellesley being passed for delivery until a proper schedule of flight tests had been completed. The schedule required that, after preliminary functional and rigging tests the aeroplane had to be climbed to a point above its full power height (12,000 ft) and a two-minute level speed done at full power to check its performance and that of the engine. This was followed by a check of its stalling speed and low-speed handling, then a full-power dive to its maximum indicated airspeed with suitable control displacements and the application of specified values of g turns to both left and right. At least three take-offs and landings with consequent operation of the retractable undercarriage and flaps were to be made as well as a list of functional tests of the multifarious items of ancillary equipment. Oil cooling and cylinder head temperatures and all indicated performance figures were to be recorded and submitted to the technical office for perusal so that any trends towards deterioration during a production run could be spotted.

Another consequence of these test requirements was that in very bad weather the aeroplanes had to sit on the ground until the weather improved. There were no wireless direction-finding facilities or 'let-down' aids at Brooklands.

However, as I knew from my time in the Met Flight, if pilots made the effort to sharpen up their cloud flying and bad weather flying in general, delays caused by the weather could be cut to a minimum. There was no point in endangering valuable aircraft unnecessarily and certainly I did not advocate taking the sort of risks we used to take in the Met Flight, but I determined to set a high standard and if other pilots did not like it they could stay on the ground and leave it to those who did – or so I said to myself rather arrogantly. In the event there were seldom any serious hold-ups as a result of the weather.

A matter for early decision was whether or not we should carry a passenger or observer in the course of production flight tests. Except in clear cases where a second crew member was needed for specific purposes, we decided against. Many things could go wrong with new production aeroplanes, which had only just been put together, and whilst the job was by no means dramatically dangerous, it obviously was accompanied by real risks. The risk of injury or death to a non-essential crew member was clearly unjustifiable.

On 5 July 1937 I taxied out Wellesley K7737 for its production test. I heard an unusual noise coming from the rear fuselage every time the tail wheel passed over a bump in the aerodrome surface so I taxied back to the tarmac and asked Charlie Boon, a Vickers inspector, to see what the problem was. He climbed aboard and after a while said he'd fixed it so I taxied out again with Charlie crouching inside the rear fuselage listening and watching, and indeed the noise had ceased. He moved up towards my cockpit and signalled that it was OK to take off. 'Have you got a parachute, Charlie?' I shouted.

'No,' said Charlie.

'Then get out and get one if you want to come with me,' I said, and taxied back to the tarmac.

A minute or two later Charlie appeared up a ladder by the cockpit and said there were no spare parachutes there – they were in the Works store – so I said, 'Hard luck Charlie – I'm off.'

I had established a routine with the Wellesley flight test schedule. When I had completed the level speed run at 12,000 ft I closed the throttle and pulled the nose up and wound the trimmer back, allowing the aircraft to climb upwards decelerating towards the stall. I took my hands off the controls and wrote the figures from the level speed run on my knee-pad. I then waited until the aeroplane stalled completely, still hands off, and wrote down the indicated stalling speed (this was primarily an instrument check). All the massive amount of testing I had done on the prototype's handling at the stall and in stalled manoeuvres had given me the utmost confidence in the Wellesley's ladylike behaviour. Perhaps I was overconfident, for while the aeroplane was wallowing about at 12,000 ft and I was scribbling on my knee-pad, waiting for the nose to drop and pick up speed, she suddenly lurched into a right-hand spin. I was taken completely by surprise for the Wellesley had never shown the slightest tendency to do this before. I immediately took recovery action but it was to no avail. In the course of the first turn and a half the nose was well down and then suddenly it reared up and the spin became very flat, slow, and stately. There was no response to normal recovery action and I tried to think of all the other things I should try. I started by trying full power and all that did was to flatten the spin still further, and speed it up, so I took the power off again. Then I tried lowering the wheels hoping that would affect the centre of gravity in some magical way, and then tried rocking the elevator throughout its full range, and finally lowering the flaps. I then remembered that in such circumstances it was quite common for pilots to try all sorts of recovery actions but never to give any of them enough time to work before trying something else so I looked over the side to see how much height I still had and started trying things all over again in an agonisingly slow and deliberate manner, ordering myself to keep calm and not to panic.

The Wellesley treated everything I did with a scornful disdain and continued solemnly spinning, down and down. Somewhere around 3,000 ft I decided I would have to go and the thought flashed through my mind, 'Thank God I haven't got Charlie Boon in the back.' I opened the canopy and crouched on the seat, grasping the windscreen. The cockpit of the Wellesley was forward of the wing and I looked at the big metal-bladed propeller windmilling round very close in front of me. In theory when I let go I should go out backwards and sideways but I was forward of the centre of gravity and had a nasty feeling that I was going to go forwards through that slicing propeller. But there was nothing I could do about it, so I cut the ignition switches and hoped for the best. I went over the port side, hit my head on some object unknown – perhaps the tail wheel assembly – delayed a little bit and pulled the rip cord. I was, as it were, falling on my back and the parachute, deploying between my legs, spun me sharply over when it opened. I immediately heard a strange swooshing noise as the Wellesley spun down past me, much too close for comfort, with its long wings slicing through the air in great sweeps.

I was then able to watch the Wellesley from above as it descended towards the ground. We were in the area of New Malden and there were built-up areas interspersed with areas of open country. It was about 7 p.m. on a fine summer's evening. I became very anxious about the Wellesley crashing in a built-up area and causing loss of life, but I could not tell when it was going to hit. Then it stopped abruptly and disintegrated. It had hit a house but, thank God, there was no explosion or fire. Then, apparently several seconds later, I heard the dull 'crump' of the impact. I could hear every sound coming from the ground as I floated silently downwards on that balmy summer's evening – dogs barking, the traffic moving along the Kingston bypass and then gradually the build-up of the municipal 'flap' caused by this large aircraft crashing into a surburban street. A maroon went off at the fire station quickly followed by the clanging of the fire engine's bell. I looked down and spotted the fire engine trying to get to the scene of the crash and taking a number of wrong turnings on the way and I considered shouting some directions to it from on high. I would have enjoyed that silent and peaceful descent but for the acute anxiety I felt about the possibility of people having been killed or maimed in the crash, and the fact that I developed a nasty swing which at one moment looked like collapsing the canopy of the parachute. Then suddenly I was getting close and could see roughly where I was likely to land; there were houses and gardens and trees and every garden seemed to have a large and uninviting glass greenhouse. I descended into the base of a small fir tree which broke my fall and so it was a comfortable landing. My head and hands were bleeding but I was unhurt. A small knot of people came running up, having invaded the large and pleasant garden in which I had landed. It was the property of a Major Petrie who turned out to be a member of the Brooklands Flying Club. He, his wife and some friends were drinking an evening cocktail when through the window they saw a strange band of people running up the drive, heads directed skywards. They came out in time to see me being helped out of the bottom of the fir tree and disentangled from the parachute. Within a surprisingly short time I had a large whisky in my hand and was on the telephone to the police and received the blessed news that no one had been injured in the crash. So I drank the whisky in the Petries' drawing-room and telephoned Vickers to put them out of their misery because by now I was, of course, well overdue. It must have been one of the most comfortable emergency parachute descents ever made. The lady who lived in the house on which the Wellesley crashed was, as it happened, pregnant, and the shock she received somewhat accelerated the birth of a baby daughter but no ill-effects were suffered by either.

The ensuing weeks were not very happy from my point of view. I put in a full report on the incident, making no attempt to disguise the fact that I had been taken completely by surprise by the behaviour of the Wellesley and I admitted that leaving it wallowing about in a totally stalled condition while I was writing figures on my knee-pad was perhaps culpable overconfidence. But I soon became aware that there was an atmosphere or under-current of suspicion which was virtually suggesting that I had put the Wellesley into the spin on purpose and then discovered that I could not get it out again. Nobody directly accused me of this but it was pretty clear what was going on and some meetings were held with the RAE at Farnborough which I was not invited to attend. Eventually I went privately to Rex Pierson, the Chief Designer, and told him that, as deliberate spinning was for-bidden on the Wellesley, I would never have contravened such a ban, that it was obvious that an aeroplane with such a huge span and a very short tail arm would probably not recover from a developed spin in any circumstances, and thirdly, had I deliber-ately exposed myself to an almost certain bale-out, I would not have chosen to do it over a partially built-up area. Rex listened carefully to this and then looked me in the eye and said he was satisfied that it had been completely unintentional on my part and that he fully accepted both my written and oral reports. This cheered me up a lot because, on reflection, I realised I did not really give a damn whatever anyone else thought as long as I retained Rex's confidence.

A few months later some trials were initiated at the RAE Farnborough and I have never been sure to what extent they were triggered off by my bale-out or what their objective was. All I know is that on 5 October 1938 Wellesley No. K7729 took off from Farnborough to do 'stalling tests' and spun into the ground near Farnham; the pilot, Flight Lieutenant Salmon, was killed. I felt greatly upset by what seemed to be an unnecessary death, and I wished I had had the opportunity to talk to him before he embarked on this test. This whole episode left a bad taste in my mouth and to some extent influenced my decision to move permanently to Supermarine. I had by then an inner certainty that my destiny lay with the Spitfire.

There is a tailpiece to this Wellesley bale-out. In about 1974, some 37 years later, one of my daughters, Virginia, born after the war, was working for the BBC in Bush House, London. There she met a girl who said to Virginia:

'Did you say your name was Quill?'

'Yes,' said Virginia.

'Was your father by any chance a test pilot?'

'Yes,' said Virginia.

'Well,' said the girl, 'he dropped a damned great aeroplane on my mother's house!'

She was the sister of the baby whose birth had been assisted by my Wellesley K7737.

9

Venom

The Vickers Type 279 Venom private-venture fighter prototype, which I flew between June 1936 and February 1938, had a short if lively flying career.

This aeroplane was designed to the Air Ministry specification F.5/34 issued in the same year (1934) as the F.37/34 specification to which the Spitfire conformed. Other aircraft built to the F.5/34 requirement were the Bristol 146 and the Gloster G.38.

The F.5/34 requirement was raised primarily to get a high performance fighter with an air-cooled engine for operation in overseas theatres.

Back in 1930 Vickers had flown a small monoplane fighter which had been designed to Air Ministry Specification F.20/27 for an 'interception single-seater fighter', capable of intercepting and destroying enemy bombers flying directly overhead at 20,000 ft at 150 mph, then estimated as the potential capability of the bomber. The Vickers aeroplane designed and built in proto-type form to meet that specification had been a small monoplane of metal construction with a Bristol Mercury IIA engine (later changed to Jupiter VIIF) with untapered wings and squared-off tips. Vickers had at that time a licence to use a method of metal construction and metal skinning developed by Wibault in France and this to a large extent determined the angular layout of the aeroplane which was named the Jockey. This little machine made its first flight in April 1930 in the hands of 'Tiny' Scholefield, then Vickers' Chief Test Pilot, and appeared at the RAF display at Hendon in 1932. It had a high wing loading for its day and a good performance but it came out at a time when official preju-dice against monoplanes was still very much alive. It is doubtful whether it would ever have been ordered into production any-way, but the matter was put beyond doubt when it 'went flat' in the course of spinning trials in June 1932 and the pilot had to bale out. That was the end of the Jockey. The aeroplane eventually ordered into production to fulfil the F.20/27 specification was the biplane Hawker Fury which equipped 1, 25 and 43 Fighter Squadrons.

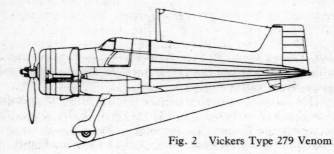

Fig. 2   Vickers Type 279 Venom

When the F.5/34 specification was issued to industry Vickers decided to update the Jockey design to meet this requirement, using the 625 hp Bristol Aquila AE 3S nine-cylinder sleeve-valve engine. Although outwardly the configuration remained very reminiscent of the Jockey, the structure was substantially re-designed, the engine completely enclosed within a long chord NACA cowling with a flush exhaust system and the pilot enclosed in a streamlined canopy. Behind this canopy a long dorsal fin stretched backward to the tail unit. This was incorporated for spin-recovery reasons and resulted from research carried out at RAE and NPL. Eight Browning .303 machine-guns were installed inside the wing, firing outside the propeller disc. The wing, of RAF 34 section, was of fully stressed skin construction with a very smooth external finish. There was a fully retractable undercarriage, large area trailing edge flaps and a three-bladed De Havilland Hamilton variable-pitch propeller of 8 ft 6 in. diameter. The Venom had its eight guns and ammunition tanks installed from the day of its first flight. Its all-up weight was 4,150 lb carried on a wing area of 146 sq. ft (as against the prototype Spitfire's 5,332 lb and 242 sq. ft.

So the Venom was more than 1,000 lb lighter than the Spitfire but had a much smaller wing, giving it a wing loading of nearly 30 lb/sq. ft – very high in those days. This Vickers design was, however, not ordered in prototype form by the Air Ministry, so

Vickers went ahead and built it as a private venture with company money.

Mutt Summers made the first flight at Brooklands on 17 June 1936. Due to some error with the fine pitch settings of the propeller he did not get the correct engine revolutions for take-off. This extended his take-off run with the result that he was very close to the Byfleet banking of the race track before the aeroplane became airborne. However the propeller settings were adjusted accordingly and I flew the aeroplane on 23 and 24 June on general handling and familiarisation flights and then found myself appointed to demonstrate it during the SBAC show at Hatfield due to take place on 29 June. As in all brand-new prototype aeroplanes the inspection departments liked to go through everything most meticulously between flights, which tended to limit its availability very severely, so I had one flight on 28 June to practise my demonstration and then the next day flew it to Hatfield early in the morning. I carried out the demonstration in the afternoon and flew straight back to Brooklands.

The machine went back into the shops to have its tailplane setting adjusted and I tested this on 5 July at Brooklands. When I chopped the throttle just before touch-down a mass of flame streamed past each side of the cockpit which singed my eyebrows and seemed to come from the lower part of the engine cowling. The main petrol tank of the Venom was immediately beneath the pilot's seat and therefore a fire on board was an unattractive proposition. The flush exhaust manifold was not readily visible from the cockpit due to the curvature of the cowling, so although I thought the fire was probably in the exhaust I could not be sure. As soon as I could stop the aeroplane I released the straps and hopped out of the cockpit to see what was going on. Sure enough the fire was in the exhaust and it fairly quickly subsided.

I had experienced this in a much lesser form on previous flights and the Bristol engineer had tried to eliminate it by reducing the fuel pressure to the carburettor. After this flight he reduced it still more.

The next day, 6 July, I flew the aeroplane to Martlesham so that it could be present at an inspection due to be carried out by King Edward VIII on 8 July. While at Martlesham it was flown by Edwardes-Jones and previously it had been flown by Flight

Lieutenant Pat Fraser* of the RAE. At Martlesham further
adjustments were made to lower the fuel pressure and I collected
the aeroplane and flew it back to Brooklands on 10 July, carrying
out some level speed runs on the way and suffering a series of
engine failures at full power. The engine ran quite satisfactory at
cruising power, however, and I landed at Brooklands without
further incident.

The Venom was a sporting little aeroplane. It could not match
up to the Spitfire's performance but it was doing around 325 mph
at about 15,000 ft. It was extremely manoeuvrable and delightful
as an aerobatic aeroplane. Its big trailing edge flaps which came
down to 90° produced a great deal of drag which killed any float
during the flare-out for landing; one could put it down very
accurately therefore on the exact spot required for landing
(which was not so easy with the Spitfire). All this time I felt that it
could use much more power with great advantage if only it was
available.

Its behaviour in a stall at high g values was good and for some
reason or another it seemed that in very tight turns the tendency
for the pilot to black-out was much reduced. I thought this must
be something to do with the seating position which was almost on
the centre of gravity whereas on the Spitfire it was further aft.
The Venom was fitted with an anti-spin tail parachute from the
day of its first flight, no doubt due to the disreputable behaviour
of its parent, the Jockey, in getting into a flat spin and shedding
its pilot at Martlesham.

The Venom had some interesting technical features: for
instance the undercarriage retraction, flap operation, engine
starting, engine cooling gills, gun heating and gun firing were all
electrically operated as well as the normal electrical services such
as reflector gunsight, navigation lights, cockpit illumination and
so on. I somewhat distrusted this arrangement but it gave very
little trouble. At the sides of the cockpit were large perspex
panels, an excellent feature which let a lot of daylight into 'the
office'. Another point of interest was that the whole engine
hinged through 90° on the ground allowing very ready access to
the back of it for maintenance purposes, all connections being
flexible. From the early performance trials which I carried out it

---

* Now Air Marshal The Reverend Sir Patterson Fraser.

was clear that the Venom was breathing down the Hurricane's neck as far as maximum speed was concerned; I was very much fretting for more power from the engine but there seemed no chance of that in the immediate future.

In January 1937 Bristol wanted some accurate fuel consumption tests and a rather strange fuel flowmeter was rigged up in the cockpit. This included a fuel supply pipe to the cockpit-mounted indicator, with a section of glass tubing, through which I could see the fuel passing. I took off from Eastleigh on 7 January with this strange contraption and proceeded to do a series of level runs between 10,000 and 18,000 ft at varying engine power settings and recording the rate of fuel flow in each stabilised condition as shown by the flowmeter. I was heading alternately east and west with Portsmouth as an approximate mid-point and I was taking a mildly academic interest in some aeration, or bubbles, passing through the glass tube when the engine abruptly stopped, throwing me forward against the straps. The propeller went on windmilling silently round. There was something very decisive in the way that Aquila engine had cut out and at once I assumed that there was an airlock in the fuel system caused by the aeration. I was too far away to glide back to Eastleigh but Lee-on-Solent and Gosport seemed to be within easy reach and I looked at them both and began to wonder which to choose. I had no R/T and saw there was a fair amount of activity in the Lee-on-Solent circuit but none at Gosport. As I would be quite unable to warn Lee-on-Solent of my impending silent and powerless arrival I thought someone was bound to get in my way at the critical moment so I decided upon Gosport although it was much smaller than Lee and the wind was blowing across the short run of the aerodrome. I was depending upon the excellent short landing characteristics of the Venom to help me get away with it. I lowered the undercarriage in plenty of time and approached the leeward side of the aerodrome, turned in left-handed and lowered the flaps at what I prayed was the exact moment. It was – and I comfortably cleared the aerodrome boundary, touched down and rolled silently to a standstill. To pull off a successful 'dead stick' landing, wheels down, and totally without damage either to the aircraft or oneself was always a matter of considerable relief and a little self-congratulation; in this instance the Venom had an extremely high landing speed for those days, Gosport aerodrome was very short in the direction I had to land, and the powerful trailing-edge flaps gave ample scope for a dangerous under-shoot.

The aircraft was rolled into a hangar by a party of airmen and I telephoned the Works to report the matter. The engine failure was, I said, certainly due to an airlock or something equivalent somewhere in the fuel system – but I thought nothing was fundamentally wrong with the engine. With that I returned to the aeroplane in the hangar which by now had attracted a small crowd of interested pilots and airmen who started plying me with questions. I was standing at the nose of the aeroplane and one of the three big blades of the metal propeller was pointing vertically downwards. I put my right hand on the blade, leant nonchalantly upon it while I was talking and promptly fell flat on my face – the propeller having spun completely freely. I picked myself up and found I could turn the prop almost with one finger. Obviously the shaft had sheared inside the gear case and the propeller was totally disconnected from the engine. I telephoned the Works, cancelled my last message and said the trouble was evidently a good deal more expensive than I had thought. In fact trouble with the sleeve-valve mechanism had caused the engine to seize solid in flight whereupon the energy stored in the heavy metal propeller had strippped the epicyclic reduction gear between the engine and the propeller, leaving the latter, as it were, all on its own. The nature of this engine failure was therefore much more serious and fundamental than had seemed at first. I went back to Southampton and then Weybridge by car and the Venom was dismantled and returned by lorry.

There was then a long delay while the reasons for the seizure of the engine and the failure of the reduction gear were being investigated. The aircraft re-emerged from the Works with a new engine on 23 June and I gave it a test flight. I was pleased to be back in the air with this lively little aeroplane although I kept a somewhat wary eye on the engine instruments and listened very carefully to the engine's note. It is no reflection upon Bristol to say that I did not have the same happy confidence in the Aquila as I had in the Spitfire's Merlin. The former was a very new and experimental engine whereas the Merlin had, even by then, accumulated many hours in the air.

Flying continued, again at a sadly low rate, during July, August and September. On 4 October I took it to Martlesham where it remained until 14 December when I flew it back again to the Works at Brooklands. Then on 3 February 1938 I took off with the object of moving the aeroplane down to Eastleigh again to continue with some full load trials. It was no doubt due to my mistrust of the engine during take-off which decided me to do the bulk of the flying from then on at Eastleigh which was a much larger aerodrome than Brooklands, had a better surface and enjoyed the inestimable benefit, in my view, of not being situated within a large concrete bowl.

I took the full run at Brooklands, heading directly towards the Byfleet banking. At about 150 ft or so, when the undercarriage was still retracting, the engine stopped dead. I could see that I was just going to clear the concrete banking of the motor race-track but beyond were trees and houses and a disastrous crash was inevitable. I closed the throttle instinctively and slowly re-opened it and the engine picked up just enough to preserve safe flying speed and climb gently away. When the engine cut it had seemed to me that even if I cleared the top of the banking I was going to certain death beyond but, strangely, I felt no fear, as I said to myself 'So this is it' and concentrated on finding the best place to point the aircraft. However, when the engine had picked up again, very much in the nick of time, I realised that my heart was in my mouth and I found my left hand, resting lightly on the throttle, was shaking vigorously. Keeping the power well down I headed off for Eastleigh saying to myself that this would be the last time I would fly this aeroplane out of Brooklands – and it was.

In fact, to my great disappointment the aeroplane never flew again anywhere. As I have said it was a private venture, built and operated with company money with the Aquila engine loaned, I believe, by Bristol. The Spitfire, for which the company already had the largest production order in its post-war history, was going very well and was substantially faster. Its powerful Merlin engine had its production future assured by big Air Ministry orders for the Fairey Battle and the Hawker Hurricane as well as the Spitfire itself. Weybridge Works was full with production orders for the Wellesley and the Wellington so if the Venom went into production it would have to be built somewhere else. Furthermore there was more power growth potential in the Merlin engine but the Aquila had no other application except some vague possibilities as a civil engine. It was not therefore an attractive proposition for production. In these circumstances there was obviously no justification for continuing to pour company money into the Venom and possibly killing a test pilot as well. Sir Robert McLean therefore decided to halt any further development.

It had occurred to me that the Venom would make an excellent ship-borne naval fighter and I believe Sir Robert McLean took up that possibility. However, Naval Staff policy favoured only two-seat fighters which would carry an observer in the rear cockpit. A small single-seat fighter such as the Venom did not respect this philosophy and the two-seat Fairey Fulmar was to be the new naval fighter. A great deal of later trouble might have been saved if the Navy had equipped themselves with a few squadrons of Venoms before the outbreak of war. As it was they went into the war without any single-seat fighter more modern than the Sea Gladiator, and had to obtain Wildcats from the USA and then ask us to turn the Spitfire into a Naval fighter, something which had never been remotely considered in its initial design. (See Chapter 23.)

Late in 1937 David Hollis-Williams, the Chief Designer of General Aircraft Ltd at Hanworth, was experimenting with a tricycle undercarriage, a concept that was then entirely new in Britain. He had modified a twin-engined Monospar aircraft and he invited me over to Hanworth to fly it. I went on 6 December 1937 and there was the Monospar standing on a fixed tricycle undercarriage with a rather spindly nosewheel leg. I did several take-offs and landings with Hollis-Williams and was at once converted to this whole idea. Taxiing was easy and foolproof, the tricycle arrangement was inherently stable directionally on the ground and eliminated any risk of 'ground looping' after landing. All one had to do after touch-down was to let the aeroplane pitch onto its nose wheel and it would run straight even in quite a stiff cross-wind. It also permitted the use of much more powerful wheelbrakes, and it rendered the difficult 'three-point' landing a thing of the past. It seemed to me a fundamental forward step of immense importance. Hollis-Williams said he was looking for a high-performance aeroplane on which to experiment – what about the Vickers Venom? I said I had to admit there did not seem to be much future for it as a fighter but would it not be a huge engineering problem to move the main gear aft and fit a nose wheel? He said it could be done at least for experimental purposes. I reported all this to Mutt Summers and to Sir Robert McLean who did not seem at all interested, still less were they interested in my enthusiastic advocacy of the tricycle undercarriage principle. Ten years, in fact, were to elapse before the first Vickers aircraft was to fly with a tricycle undercarriage – the Viscount in 1948 – which was odd for a company that had a thriving business designing and manufacturing undercarriage legs.

10

Delays and Recriminations

When the Spitfire re-emerged from the Works, on 9 September 1937, it presented a much more warlike and sinister appearance, for it had been painted in the new brown and green camouflage. Nearly all squadron aircraft in the RAF were then still in their silver dope finish with brightly coloured squadron markings, so K5054 looked purposeful and grim in camouflage paint but it had lost nothing of its elegance. It was now fitted with a Merlin II and between 10 and 23 September I made 18 flights amounting to 11 hours all on performance measurement. Then, there was a gap until 11 October when I started a further series of performance tests in addition to a demonstration for Sir Charles Craven and his friends. On 25 October K5054 departed for Martlesham to undergo more official performance trials.

I next flew the Spitfire on 14 December when I collected it from Martlesham to have its gun heating system installed in the wings. Then, on 21 December I flew the first of a series of gun-heating trials which continued throughout February into early March interspersed from 19 January with a number of night flights. On 4 March 1938 I delivered K5054 to Martlesham.

The gun-heating problem took a long time to solve. The method used was to duct hot air taken from the rear of the oil cooler into the gun bays. A great deal of modification and flying for 'trial and error' took place during which time the aeroplane was constantly shuttling between Martlesham and the Works at Eastleigh. It was not until October 1938 that the problem was satisfactorily solved and all guns could be relied upon to fire at high altitude under the coldest conditions. Before this happened, however, I flew the first production aeroplane, K9787. It was ready for flight on 15 May 1938. It differed surprisingly little from the prototype even in the details of the cockpit. The upper skinning of the wing was different, comprising large and smooth 'Alclad' panels, the 'clinker'-built appearance of the prototype wing having disappeared. The fixed-pitch wooden propeller was retained, the De Havilland three-bladed variable-pitch propeller based on the Hamilton-Standard patents being not yet available in production. Otherwise the basic configuration of the aeroplane was in essentials unchanged, although closer examination showed some detail changes arising from production methods. The tail was built as a complete unit and attached to the rear fuselage just forward of the fin. There was a joint at the wing tip outboard of the ailerons, the tip itself being another separate production unit. Operationally, the most significant difference was an increase in the maximum permissible diving speed from 380 to 470 mph IAS. As soon as I climbed into the cockpit I felt entirely at home in this apparently twin sister of K5054. The first flight of only 35 minutes was devoted to checking that everything was working as it should and produced no surprises nor anxieties for me. Thereafter we got down to a full flight-testing programme.

Two years and two months had elapsed since the first flight of the prototype and one year 11 months since the signing in June 1936 of the contract for 310 aeroplanes. The contract, No. 527113/36 called for delivery to begin on 12 October 1937 and for the completion of 310 aircraft by March 1939.

Supermarine's earliest forecast, before this contract was signed, had been for the first production aeroplane to be delivered in May 1937, but a later forecast suggested the first production delivery by December of that year, and 150 aeroplanes by October 1938. Whichever date is taken, the inescapable fact is that the Spitfire was very late in starting production. Furthermore, the planned rate of monthly production following the first delivery was also badly adrift. The 150th Spitfire was delivered in the third week of April 1939 as against the forecast date of October 1938 – six months late. Whatever the reasons for this it led to considerable acrimony between the Air Council and Sir Robert McLean, and this was not helped by production of the Wellington at Weybridge also being behind schedule. The Minutes of the Secretary of State's weekly meetings indicate that the Air Council felt a sense of outrage about the whole affair and were highly critical of McLean. They suspected he had been manipulating matters in the early stages in order to keep production work inside the company instead of subcontracting to the extent they thought he should have done. This was not a justifiable suspicion, but at one point the Air Council felt so strongly about it that they considered arraigning the whole Board of Vickers in front of them in formal session. This was averted by the tactful intervention of Sir Charles Craven, the Managing Director of Vickers-Armstrongs Ltd.

Scheme F, under which the Spitfire had been ordered, was adopted because advice had been received from Foreign Office Intelligence sources that the German Air Force might be capable of going to war by January 1939, whereas previous estimates had suggested the Luftwaffe would not be fully ready before 1942. Scheme F was announced in Parliament on 17 March 1936 and its main purpose was to enable aircraft of the very latest design to be ordered in time to be well established in service by 1939 which had now become the critical date. This accounts for the almost indecent haste with which the Air Ministry placed the contracts for the Hurricane and Spitfire in June 1936 before they had been thoroughly tested at Martlesham. It accounts equally for the strong sense of annoyance which the Air Council felt when the industry, in their view, then let them down over production deliveries. But it was not only the Spitfire which fell behind programme. The Hurricane had been designed with suitability for production very much in mind – a shrewd decision made by Sydney Camm. It was sometimes said that structurally and technologically the Hurricane was simply a monoplane Hart, and thus something which the Hawker factories were already experienced in producing. Although an over-simplification, this was true to some extent and no doubt accounted for 600 Hurricanes having been ordered as against only 310 Spitfires. Yet the Hurricane also was months late on first delivery although the production rate built up to programmed output fairly quickly thereafter.

The truth was that, in 1936, no firm in the industry was in a position to respond effectively to the sudden demand for great expansion of its production capacity simultaneously with great forward strides in the technological field. The industry had existed since 1919 on the basis of keeping a number of design-capable firms in business by spreading the small amount of peacetime design and production contracts thinly but evenly across a fairly large number of firms. The policy was sound in that it provided a sort of industrial cadre which could form the basis for expansion in time of national emergency, but it also meant that no firm had experience of really large-scale production and therefore expansion could not be switched on at short notice like an electric light. This was a factor which the Air Council, in their anger, appear to have taken insufficiently into account.

For example, between 1925 and the start of the expansion programme the largest series runs of aircraft ordered from Supermarine had been 79 Southampton flying-boats, ordered in batches over an eight-year period, 15 Scapa flying-boats and 17 Stranraers, and 24 Seagull V amphibians ordered for Australia, all at a low rate of production. These orders were marginally augmented by some small export orders. And the Stranraer was really ordered within the expansion programme as was the initial order for 12 Walrus in 1935 (746 were eventually built).

In June 1936 the total labour force of Supermarine was only 1,370 and there were acute problems in the Southampton area in recruiting skilled labour. Although an extension of the factory was in hand, floor space was limited. Therefore problems were bound to be encountered in any sudden switch to large-scale production. It was always recognised that a substantial amount of subcontracting would be necessary, indeed all the wings and the tail units were subcontracted to outside firms. The building of the fuselages and final assembly and flight testing were retained at Supermarine as well as the building of many components and sub-assemblies for supply to the subcontractors.

The initial hold-up in production was caused by the late delivery of wings from the subcontractors, who blamed the poor standard of the drawings supplied by Supermarine. There was some substance in this charge but inexperience of modern methods of structural manufacture on the part of the subcontractors was also an important factor. At any rate there were completed fuselages accumulating at Supermarine with no wings available for fitment. Additional wing jigs were installed at Woolston to speed up the supply and eventually a balanced production situation was restored. Nevertheless the early history of Spitfire production was traumatic. With hindsight, the initial shortcomings of the subcontracting scheme can really be attributable to the same original basic cause, namely that for years the industry had been starved of orders and could barely keep its factories in business on the orders it did receive. So where were the experienced and capable subcontractors to be found on the fringe of a half-starved industry? They simply did not exist.

It was all an object-lesson in the folly of allowing things to run down too much in the days of peace. It should also not be forgotten that much of the cause of this problem lay in the initial unwillingness of the Government to respond adequately to the threat from Germany. Had they taken proper steps at the proper time to expand the industry at a more reasonable rate this type of problem might not have arisen. For too long the Government had been paralysed by its fear of the vociferous pacifist and disarmament lobbies of the early 1930s.

Sir Robert McLean, always insistent upon his personal authority over, and responsibility for the aviation companies, and resentful of any outside interference, naturally had to carry the can when things went seriously wrong. Similar problems were assailing him at Weybridge. But the odium fell also upon the Board of Vickers Ltd, the owners of Supermarine and Weybridge, who responded by abolishing the erstwhile independence of the aviation companies and placing them under the overall control of Vickers-Armstrongs Ltd.

Inevitably Sir Robert McLean resigned in due course (he became Chairman of EMI), and we became Vickers-Armstrongs (Aircraft) Ltd, Supermarine Works, and our friends at Brooklands became Vickers-Armstrongs (Aircraft) Ltd, Weybridge Works.

It is also relevant that the Board of Vickers Ltd were at this time especially sensitive to any charges of inefficiency or failures of delivery on Government contracts. They had only recently emerged from a lengthy period during which they had been the prime target for a virulent and widespread public campaign conducted against the 'Private Manufacture of and Trading in Arms'. During the 1930s this campaign had grown up as part of the general 'peace at any price' and disarmament movements which had swept across Britain, fastening itself onto the League of Nations in search of international authority. Vickers, a large proportion of whose business was accounted for by Government and overseas contracts for armaments, became the principal whipping-boy, and were much pilloried in the press. The attacks came from two distinct directions. The first was from reasonably experienced professional people who argued on allegedly practical grounds that the Government did not get good value for money from private contractors who often, it was said, fell down on delivery promises (cases from the First World War were cited). The second line of attack came from a group of organisations who concentrated upon the immorality of profits being made from 'dealing in death'. These attacks tended to be emotional and ill informed, but nonetheless politically effective at the time.

The Board of Vickers were very sensitive to these attacks but had little opportunity to defend themselves publicly. Eventually the clamour became so great that the Government appointed a Royal Commission to inquire into the Private Manufacture of and Trading in Arms. The Commission sat in 1935 and 1936 (when I first joined Vickers) and took evidence from the abolitionists (those who wished to abolish the armament firms), but it also heard evidence from the other side, and this gave Vickers and others at long last the chance to have their say and respond both by written statements and evidence given in court. The 120-page report of the Royal Commission* issued in October 1936 commented that much of the abolitionist propaganda had been irresponsible and furthermore stated that if private industry were not used in peacetime, thus making it necessary for all Government defence requirements to be fulfilled by Government establishments alone, there would be no capacity for rapid expansion in wartime. This was a vital strategic consideration and Sir Maurice Hankey, Secretary to the Cabinet, made it abundantly clear that the Government did not favour abolition of the private firms.

Thereafter the clamour abated because the menace from Hitler's Germany was by now becoming patent. The tide of pacifist emotion which had swept the country died down almost as suddenly and unpredictably as it had arisen. However, the Vickers Board in 1938 were determined that delays in deliveries on Government contracts must be avoided at all costs, and this was undoubtedly the underlying reason for the reorganisation of the aircraft companies. The robust independence of the aircraft companies of Vickers, which had greatly flourished under Sir Robert McLean's energetic leadership and which had so often

* Cmd 5292.

been a source of irritation to the Air Council or the Government, was now much reduced. But it should never be forgotten that it was during this period of independence that the Spitfire and the Wellington were born and Sir Robert McLean must receive his share of credit for this.

At the time of the Royal Commission those who had so virulently attacked the private armament firms were unaware of two emergent aircraft projects called Hurricane and Spitfire – both products of the private manufacture of armaments – which were destined within four years to save the country in its hour of desperate need.

By March 1939 Spitfire deliveries were back on programme and although they briefly dropped behind again later a total of 308 Spitfires had been built and tested by 3 September 1939 and over 1,000 by August 1940 when the Battle of Britain began.

11

Last Days of Peace

After the first flight of the first production model of the Spitfire, the Mk 1 K9787, George Pickering and I had been looking forward to a build-up of the production rate giving us plenty of aeroplanes to fly. We were disappointed, for the production problems were very far from over.

The extent to which production was still in disarray and how seriously this was regarded by the Air Council is clear from item 5(c) of the Secretary of State's meeting of 5 July 1938, only two months after the emergence of the first aeroplane:

SPITFIRES

AMDP* said that the General Manager of Supermarine had promised some time ago that four Spitfires would be delivered during June. In fact none was delivered. Three might be delivered by the end of July. He had visited Supermarine with DGP† and found that production was seriously out of balance. There were 78 fuselages but only three sets of wings. He had ordered Supermarines to make additional jigs with all possible speed and General Aircraft had also been ordered to duplicate their jigs.

This is somewhat at variance with the Supermarine quarterly report to the Vickers Board of more than three months earlier (31 March 1938) which stated quite clearly that duplicate wing jigs were already being laid down at Woolston to supplement the output of subcontractors. The same Supermarine report stated that there were 35 fuselages completed but only four sets of wings. The quarterly report of 30 June stated that there were 80 fuselages at Eastleigh but only 12 sets of wings. So the problem of the subcontracted wing production was still acute in mid-1938.

Nevertheless at the Secretary of State's meeting of 3 May 1938 it was decided to increase the Spitfire order from 310 aircraft to

* Air Marshal Sir Wilfrid Freeman, Air Member for Development and Production.
† Director-General of Production.

510 for delivery by 31 March 1940 and the firm expressed confidence in their ability to do this.

It was not until 12 July 1938 that I flew the second production machine, K9788. In the meantime I made another 35 flights in K9787 devoted to handling and stability trials, cooling suitability tests, determination of acceptable centre of gravity limits, a full set of performance trials, spinning clearance and many dives to the new maximum indicated speeds of 470 mph. In the course of these the gun doors on the upper surface of the wings began to buckle, and in one or two cases to break adrift altogether. Also the radio aerial mast behind the cockpit failed altogether. The additional 90 mph on the diving speed brought the aeroplane into a speed region at which the aileron control became excessively heavy, so much so that above 400 mph the aircraft could be manoeuvred laterally only by applying both hands to the stick. George Pickering and I both reported this as being very unsatisfactory. I had the impression that even at the lower end of the speed range the aileron control of the production aeroplane was heavier than that of the prototype. Throughout the month of June K9787 kept me very busy and then at long last the second, K9788 emerged in July. I made six sorties in this aircraft on 13 July, one more on 16 July and then on the next day I flew it to Hucknall to show it to the Rolls-Royce flight development unit there before taking it on to Martlesham.

On 29 July I delivered K9792 to the Central Flying School at Upavon and handed it over to Flight Lieutenant George Stainforth, AFC, the officer commanding the handling flight (whose duty it was to prepare the 'pilots' notes' for use in the squadrons) and this was the first delivery to the RAF. Stainforth had been the pilot of the S.6B which took the world's speed record in 1931 at Calshot, and was therefore greatly intrigued with the Spitfire. The following day I gave K9789 (in serial number sequence the third production aeroplane) its first flight test and this became the first Spitfire to join a squadron. Four flights were needed to clear it and on 4 August 1938, the twenty-fourth anniversary of the outbreak of the First World War, I flew it to Duxford and handed it over to Squadron Leader H.I. Cozens, CO of 19 (Fighter) Squadron. The two Duxford squadrons, 19 and 66 then equipped with Gauntlets, were to become the first two Spitfire squadrons. I felt a particular pleasure in delivering

K9789 to the station where I had spent two such happy years.

Almost the whole station turned out to watch the arrival of the RAF's first squadron Spitfire. 'Pingo' Lester, my old Grantham instructor and by now a Wing Commander, was the Station Commander and with Cozens and Squadron Leader J.L.F. Fuller-Good of 66 Squadron we walked over to the Mess for lunch. But the old single-storey whitewashed Mess of Royal Flying Corps vintage had disappeared and in its place had sprung up a large modern building, somewhat redolent of a prosperous country club. I felt a twinge of sadness for the passing of the old Mess.

David Kay, designer of a tiny and ingenious little single-seat autogiro which I often flew, came up in our Moth G-ACIK to collect me. So I returned to Eastleigh to get on with testing the remaining Spitfires on the contract, little dreaming that there would in fact be more than 22,000 to be tested before we were finished.

Whatever may have been the practice in the past, whether at Weybridge or at Supermarine, I was determined that no Spitfire would leave our Works until it had been thoroughly and methodically test flown to a fixed and mandatory schedule. In this aim I received the full support of Joe Smith, Charlie Johns the Chief Inspector, and the Chief Inspector AID whose name, coincidentally, was Mitchell. So George Pickering and I together produced a schedule which, with suitable expansion and modification as the Spitfire developed, lasted for the next ten years. It was based on the principle that, in addition to the essential functional tests of the whole aeroplane (which were listed), the basic performance and handling should also be checked at selected points throughout the flight envelope. This meant that each aeroplane was to be climbed at maximum continuous climbing power and best climbing speed to its full throttle height of at least 18,000 ft and all instrument readings checked. This was to be followed by a two-minute level run at maximum combat power settings to check the indicated top speed and the performance of engine and supercharger. The aeroplane was then to be put into a full-power dive to its limiting indicated airspeed of 470 mph and its trim and control behaviour checked in this extreme condition. In general, and allowing for two or three short initial flights for trimming the ailerons and adjusting engine boost and propeller settings, this schedule took about 40 minutes' flying time and gave the aeroplane a thorough shake-down. A minimum of three take-offs and landings was also required before the aeroplane could be passed for delivery. There would be no concessions on any aspect of the schedule.

The question arose as to what was to happen when the weather was too bad to permit the schedule to be carried out. My answer to this was that the aeroplane would stay on the ground until the weather was fit since no aircraft would ever be delivered until the schedule was completed. I argued that in the immediate short term and with determined piloting, hold-ups due to weather would be minimal and not significant. In the longer term a R/T DF station should be built at Eastleigh and a bad-weather let-down procedure based on oral QDMs (as practised in civil aviation) would reduce weather delays to almost nothing. My position was that the Spitfire was the fastest aeroplane in the world, achieving the highest indicated airspeeds ever; to hand them over to a squadron without having thoroughly tested each one to its limits would amount to almost criminal folly. With the support of the new Air Ministry Overseer, Group Captain D.S. Brooks, the new radio station was put in hand but never com-pleted for reasons which will emerge.

Spitfire production built up agonisingly slowly throughout September and October 1938 but as far as I was concerned relief was provided by the fact that the first production Wellington L4212 came to Eastleigh because the aerodrome at Brooklands was unsuitable for high all-up weight tests. It was accompanied by the Weybridge experimental shop manager, B.A. Duncan, and a working party. So during August and September I did a great deal of flying with Wellington L4212 and L4213 accom-panied usually by Bob Handasyde and Wheatley as flight test observers. These early tests on the first Wellingtons included full-load take-offs and handling and stability tests and dives. In the course of one dive to limiting airspeed with Bob in the right-hand seat beside me a violent oscillation developed in the control column which I immediately thought was elevator flutter. I took the power off both engines as quickly as I could and hung onto the control column with both hands. Bob told me afterwards that the vibration was shaking my face into a blur. Remembering the catastrophe to the prototype Wellington with

Maurice Hare* I thought this one was about to break up also but as the speed decreased the oscillation of the control column damped out. Very gingerly I brought the aeroplane back to Eastleigh to land. The elevator trimmer tab was hanging in shreds, its fixing damaged and the elevator itself in no very good shape. Technical opinion was that it was the tab which had developed flutter. Thereafter tabs were individually mass-balanced. During this period I was glad to accumulate some 40 hours' flight testing on the first two Wellingtons as I was in danger of becoming typecast as a fighter pilot.

There were many modifications and improvements which needed trying out on the Spitfire and the fifth production aeroplane, K9791, was allocated to the firm at Eastleigh for experimental and development work. This was the small beginning of a separate flight development section which eventually grew into something large and very important.

The first priority on K9791 was to tackle the problem of the aileron control at speed and we started quantifying the problem by recording lateral stick forces in the air using an instrument developed by Henschel in Germany. We also tried to reduce the out-of-trim forces on the elevator at high speeds.

In September I did more night flying on K9791 to try out experimental exhaust manifolds to reduce glare from the exhaust flames which I had experienced on the prototype and which was obviously inhibiting in the night-fighting role. The Salon de l'Aeronautique International, an annual event which took place in the Grand Palais in the centre of Paris, was looming up. It was an indoor static display in those days at which the latest European aircraft were exhibited and most European aircraft firms of consequence and a very large number of equipment manufacturers showed off their wares. The Salon was a great meeting place for the European aviation community – especially as the Grand Palais was within easy walking distance of some of the best Parisian restaurants and hotels.

It was decided that we should exhibit a Spitfire and that I would fly it to Le Bourget where it would be dismantled and trucked to the Grand Palais and re-erected there for exhibition in

* The prototype B.9/32 (Wellington) suffered a total structural failure with Maurice Hare at the controls in 1936.

the centre of the main hall. The aircraft selected was K9814, the twenty-eighth production aeroplane, still with a fixed-pitch wooden propeller.

Here was a chance, I decided, to beat whatever was the record from Croydon to Le Bourget by a handsome margin. Ernie Mansbridge and I worked out a flight pattern designed to do the 200-odd miles in the shortest possible time, which involved a full power climb from take-off to 18,000 ft at best climbing speed followed by a fast level cruise, at full power, then a steady descent to Le Bourget at a calculated rate and somewhat reduced power so as not to risk blowing up the engine. We estimated it would take about 40 minutes depending on the wind strength. In any event it should mean flying from London to Paris very much faster than ever before and this was obviously a great opportunity to get publicity for the Spitfire. The Hurricane had already achieved a big publicity boost by flying from Edinburgh to Northolt, riding a tail wind of around 100 mph.

This was before the days of highly organised publicity or public relations staff employed by firms. Vickers, in fact, probably spent more time and money avoiding publicity than generating it. The directors' floor of Vickers House in Broadway, London, panelled with fine mahogany, carpeted in discreet and rich dark red, with oil paintings on the walls of cruisers and battleships of yesteryear interspersed with portraits of former Chairmen, including that of Sir Hiram Maxim, was inhabited by Board members to whom the very idea of deliberately generated public relations was vulgar and thoroughly undesirable. A little discreet advertising in reputable and professional periodicals was perhaps permissible otherwise the less the Company had to do with the public and vice-versa the better they were pleased. If the press were too stupid to inform themselves of what was going on, so much the better.

So I took off from Croydon on 17 November 1938 with no advance publicity of any kind nor the presence of any official Royal Aero Club or FAI* observers or timekeepers. Jimmy Jeffs, the Chief Air Traffic Control Officer at Croydon, a well-known character in aviation circles, promised to record my departure time accurately and to arrange for his French colleagues to do the

---

* Fédération Aéronautique Internationale.

same on arrival at Le Bourget. Apart from that he gave me an
avuncular pat on the shoulder and said, 'Don't bump into any of
my airliners and be sure not to frighten the horses,' and away I
went. In less than an hour I was back. I had no radio and it was
essential to my plan that I should see enough of the ground,
preferably the French coast itself, from 18,000 ft so that I could
pinpoint my position exactly and 'let down' at precisely the right
moment and then hit Le Bourget bang on the nose, going as fast
as possible. From midway across the Channel there was a solid
carpet of stratocumulus cloud obscuring all view of the ground
and when my watch told me I had crossed the French coast and it
was nearly time to let down I could still see nothing. So I eased
back the throttle and cruised gently back to Croydon determined
to try again the next day rather than lose the opportunity to put
up the fastest possible time. The advantages of having had no
advance publicity were immediately apparent. The next day the
cloud was broken and I crossed the French coast between Dieppe
and Abbeville and began my let-down by watch. I passed through
the broken cloud at about 4,000 ft to find thick haze beneath with
severely limited horizontal visibility. I could only see the ground
directly downwards and found reading the map impossible, so I
just hung on to my compass course and rate of descent and
prayed. I realised that I only had to miss Le Bourget by half a mile
and I would pass it by without seeing it and the whole attempt
would be a wash-out. Then to my intense relief I passed right
over the top of it at about 500 ft exactly $42\frac{1}{2}$ minutes after take-off
from Croydon.

I handed the aeroplane over to the Supermarine ground crew
who were to dismantle it for transport to the Grand Palais and just
managed to catch the Imperial Airways HP42 service to Croydon. This old four-engined biplane trundled from Le Bourget to
Croydon in about $2\frac{1}{2}$ hours but it was a comfortable ride and the
luncheon was excellent. When the Salon de l'Aeronautique was
over and the Spitfire had been re-erected at Le Bourget I went
over and brought it back to Croydon, this time with a marginally
better upper wind component, doing the trip in 41 minutes flat.
The initial flight out to Paris had passed almost completely
unnoticed by the press, largely because Vickers had done
nothing whatever to bring it to their attention but by the time of
the return flight some of the more alert aeronautical journalists

had begun to analyse these flight times and concluded that the Spitfire must be a very fast aeroplane indeed. This triggered off a great deal of press speculation, some of which became very exaggerated, about its performance and the Air Council evidently considered this undesirable. So on 8 March 1939 they released their first official statement to the press giving a top speed for the Spitfire of 362 mph at 18,500 ft.

I got back to Croydon from Paris in K9814 rather late in the afternoon of 16 January 1939 and by the time the aircraft was refuelled it was dark. The weather seemed fair, however, so I decided to fly back to Eastleigh and land by the Chance lights on the aerodrome; I arrived at Eastleigh in the midst of a violent rainstorm. I managed to land without too much difficulty and, as I taxied to the tarmac, I saw a light burning in the flight office. Inside was Flight Lieutenant D.S. Wilson MacDonald, of 41 Squadron, probably the tallest and largest Spitfire pilot in the RAF at the time. He looked somewhat startled to see a Spitfire taxi up in pitch darkness and torrential rain but I managed to pass it off as if it was an everyday occurrence. 'Well,' I told him, 'it's supposed to be a day and night fighter, isn't it? Although I confess that on the whole I'd prefer to do my fighting by day.'

During this time (1938 and 1939) we had a continual stream of visiting Missions. They were usually brought down by Vickers London Office staff, often accompanied by McLean, and I was asked to give flight demonstrations for them. They included the Swiss, Turks, French, Estonians, Greeks and Portuguese, almost all of whom placed orders for Spitfires. The French flight evaluation team which came to Eastleigh included Michel Detroyat, a well-known French aviator, who was some sort of adviser to the Minister, and a young and very competent officer of L'Armée de L'Air called Rozanoff to whom I took an immediate liking. He spent some days at Eastleigh flying the Spitfire and I encountered him again after the war when he was Chief Test Pilot of Dassault. He was killed soon after when demonstrating an Ouragan in Paris.

The number of requests from foreign governments to purchase Spitfires became an embarrassment to the Air Council. Sales to the Turks and the French were approved and at least one aircraft was delivered to France but the Turkish order was cancelled after the outbreak of war, although we did dispatch two of their machines. They were diverted *en route* and finished up in Cairo.

Another visitor in 1939 was Charles Lindbergh. He arrived in his own aeroplane and I showed him round the erecting shops at Eastleigh and explained the points of the Spitfire. He had recently returned from a tour of the German Aircraft Industry, made at the invitation of Hermann Goering, and they had put out the red carpet for him as the Nazis well knew how. The Spitfire erecting shops at Eastleigh, in old hangars dating from the First World War, were not immediately impressive to the eye. They were old-fashioned in appearance and totally lacked any atmosphere of chromium-plated modernity. But they were producing Spitfires at a good rate at the time and I knew, although Charles Lindbergh did not, that the Spitfire was the finest fighter in the world. I noted his eye roving upwards to the old wooden trusses of the roof and I could tell exactly what he was thinking after his visit to the ultra-modern German factories. He was perfectly polite and pleasant but showed what seemed to me only a condescending interest in the aeroplane. When I walked with him back to his aeroplane and bade him goodbye I was suddenly aware of a feeling of burning anger and resentment which I hope I managed to disguise. As he taxied out I felt like shouting after him something in the American idiom like 'OK – wise guy – just you wait.' My annoyance was unreasonable; Lindbergh was a very great aviator whom I much admired and he was not alone in his misinterpretation of the signs.

By this time Supermarine had been for several months under the overall control of Vickers-Armstrongs Ltd. McLean had resigned and Alex Dunbar took over control of the Weybridge and Supermarine Works. Trevor Westbrook had become General Manager at Weybridge. We at Supermarine had a new General Manager, H.B. Pratt, who came from Vickers at Barrow. Pratt was an old airship man and adopted a very different style of management from Westbrook. He took over at a particularly difficult time at the end of 1937, inheriting the difficulties of the Spitfire production for which he was in no way responsible. Yet he was on the receiving end of the Air Council's wrath for the firm's failure to live up to the delivery forecasts. He was a calm, methodical and unexcitable man who set about recovering the situation in a calm and methodical way and in fact production deliveries were back on schedule by March 1939.

About 6 months after the outbreak of war, however, Pratt died tragically, no doubt as a result of the strain of the task which was compounded by wartime problems. He was replaced by Jimmy Bird (Squadron Commander James Bird RNAS (ret)) who was one of the very early directors of Supermarine and who had become the Managing Director when he bought out his original partner, Hubert Scott-Paine. In 1928 he had sold out to Vickers Aviation Ltd but had remained a member of the Supermarine Board under Sir Robert McLean. Now after Pratt's death, Vickers-Armstrongs Ltd brought him back as General Manager in which capacity he served with distinction and success until 1946. The appointment of Bird to be wartime head of Supermarine was an important step in the history of the Company – and of the Spitfire. Jimmy Bird was a cheerful and convivial character, a good leader and a good manager and did much to keep the firm's spirits up in the darkest days. He was knighted after the war and in my opinion he well deserved it.

During the latter part of 1937 the idea of using a Spitfire for an attempt on the world's landplane speed record had begun to develop. This depended upon the ability of Rolls-Royce to develop a special 'sprint' or 'Schneiderised' version of the Merlin engine to give, for a strictly limited time, a power output of some 2,000 bhp running on the same special fuel as was used in the Rolls-Royce 'R'-type engine for George Stainforth's world speed record flights in 1931. Bench testing was started at Derby on two Merlin II engines, Nos. 529 and 1765, and data survive of these development tests carried out between August 1937 and May 1938. Some were done at 3,200 rpm and at boost pressures as high as plus $28\frac{1}{2}$ lb, giving power outputs of over 2,000 bhp. At such high boost pressures special fuel was obviously required. Various fuels were used during the bench testing and eventually we flew with a 20–60–20 mix of Californian or Romanian Gasoline, 'Nineties' Benzol and Methanol, with Tetra-ethyl-lead added at 4 cc per gallon. The engine in all essential respects remained unchanged from standard. The supercharger gear ratio was standard and the high boost pressures were obtained by running the engine completely unthrottled at ground level. The forty-eighth production Spitfire (K9834) was modified to take this 'Schneiderised' Merlin. The main changes made to turn it into N.17, the high-speed development Spitfire, for a possible attempt on the landplane speed record were the fitting of the 'Schneiderised' Merlin engine; wings of shortened span; a main coolant radiator of substantially increased area to satisfy the increased cooling requirement; a long streamlined perspex windscreen with no clear-view front panel; a four-bladed fixed-pitch wooden propeller of greatly increased pitch angle; a streamlined tail-skid and finally the aircraft was given 16 coats of high-gloss Regal blue paint rubbed down to a superbly smooth finish. (This paint job was done by the Rolls-Royce car company.)

The aircraft was ready for flight on 10 November 1938. Still nominally Chief Test Pilot of Supermarine as well as Weybridge, Mutt Summers exercised his right to make the first flight. Thereafter it went into the shops to have its super-gloss paint finish applied, which was a long job, so it was not until 14 December that I flew it. Engine 'life' was severely restricted so I took off and went straight into a level speed run down Southampton water at 1,000 ft to get a speed figure and check the pitch setting of the propeller, the functioning of the engine and cooling etc. It was certainly a novel experience to see plus $27\frac{1}{2}$ showing on the boost gauge. I flew it again on 4, 13 and 24 January, on 12, 16 and 25 February and 6 March. All these flights were of the shortest possible duration, seldom exceeding 15 minutes, and all were devoted to speed performance measurements. Various propellers, including a De Havilland three-blade variable pitch, were tried. At full power and full speed the aeroplane had a tendency to crab sideways no doubt due to the effect of transmitting so much power through a relatively small diameter fixed-pitch propeller, so it had to be flown rather carefully.

By the end of these trials it was clear that the maximum speed in level flight was of the order of 408 mph, but this was not fast enough to take the record. The Air Ministry, who were paying for the venture, had at the outset stipulated that any record attempt should be made by a Royal Air Force pilot and Squadron Leader 'Bruin' Purvis of the RAE had been selected. The flying that I had been doing was in the nature of contractor's trials with the prime objectives of checking the proper functioning of the airframe and powerplant and of establishing whether the aeroplane was fast enough to take the record. When we had got it going as fast as we could 'Bruin' Purvis used to come down from Farnborough and fly it to confirm our figures. On 8 March he flew the aeroplane to Farnborough where it remained for a few days, but did no flying while there.

Eventually it was agreed that the only way to get a substantial increase in speed was to get rid of the cooling drag. It was decided to remove the large external ducted radiator unit altogether and substitute a total loss coolant system. This was to be done by converting the lower fuel tank into a coolant tank-cum-condenser losing over the side in the form of steam what could not be condensed and it was calculated that the fuel endurance from the upper tank would balance the coolant endurance and provide enough flight time for the record attempt. The aircraft therefore returned to the shops for this work to be done.

When this job was completed, which took a long time, I taxied the aeroplane out at Eastleigh and before I got to the take-off point I became enveloped in dense clouds of steam. A coolant pipe had burst. I emerged from the Turkish-bath atmosphere of the cockpit feeling lucky not to have been badly scalded. By this time there were more pressing things to think about than putting up speed records. The aircraft had been modified so extensively that it could not be restored to operational status. The coolant system was reverted to standard, we fitted a production Merlin XII, put in a proper windscreen and canopy and the aeroplane was given to the PRU as a hack, presumably because it was already painted blue. It was never fitted with cameras, never flew operationally and survived the war.

I mention this Spitfire because it rendered one extremely vital and significant service. It demonstrated for all to see, and particularly to Joe Smith at Supermarine, the enormous power growth potential of the Merlin engine. The plain fact was that in January 1939, before the outbreak of war, I was actually flying at the firm's aerodrome at Eastleigh a Merlin engine which was pumping out over 2,000 bhp at 3,200 rpm and running at the then incredible boost pressure of plus $27\frac{1}{2}$ lb. Yet it was to all intents and purposes a basic Merlin II engine with a standard supercharger. To be sure it had to run on one of Rod Banks's specially devised 'cocktail' fuels, and it had to have greatly increased cooling capacity and special spark plugs and could be run at maximum power output only for a very few minutes at a time. But the flying done on N.17 with its 'Schneiderised' Merlin did more to convince Joe Smith of the power growth we could expect out of the Merlin during the ensuing years than any number of Rolls-Royce brochures of technical forecasts.

It is not possible to look back and identify a particular moment, nor any great conference or meeting of official and industrial minds, at which a conscious policy decision was taken that from thenceforward the full Supermarine design effort should be directed towards the continued development of the Spitfire rather than dabbling with new designs. Nevertheless there is no doubt that the abortive attempt of N.17 to gain the relatively unimportant prize of a world's landplane speed record had an impact upon the thinking of Joe Smith and his colleagues which was crucial to the future of the Spitfire. Certainly it pointed the way to a far greater prize than anyone could then foresee. J.D. Scott wrote in his history of Vickers that '. . . by 1940 Joe Smith, Mitchell's successor as Chief Designer, had reached the conclusion that the Spitfire design was capable of the most extensive, and indeed of almost infinite, development. This conclusion had two merits. In the first place, it was correct. In the second place, it was a conclusion which suited Joe Smith's own temperament and abilities.'

So, from some unspecified and unidentifiable date either just before or just after the outbreak of war Supermarine became committed to the proposition that the Spitfire would be kept one jump ahead of the enemy for as long as possible and as long as could be foreseen. No directive was issued, no statement of intent was ever made, nobody knew what the future would hold, but all of us in Supermarine knew what we had to do.

R.J. Mitchell's death in June 1937 had at once posed a vital problem of succession. He had a technical assistant, Major H.J. Payn AFC RAF (ret), who had come to Supermarine from Weybridge, and had been appointed by McLean to assist Mitchell when Vickers bought Supermarine in 1928. He had engineering qualifications, had been commissioned in the Royal Engineers before transferring to the RFC, and was an experienced pilot when he left the Air Force in 1923. He had served with distinction in 29 Squadron, RFC, in 1916 and had flown with Major James McCudden VC DSO MC, one of the great air fighters of the First World War. Indeed Payn's name appears in several of McCudden's accounts of engagements with German aircraft over the Western Front. He was also, by 1928, an experienced flying-boat pilot which no doubt accounted for his appointment to work with Mitchell. Thus, when Mitchell died, Payn was appointed Manager of the Design Department (not Chief Designer) and Rex Pierson was put into overall design supervisory position over Supermarine as well as being Chief Designer at Weybridge. It is not certain whether McLean intended this to be a permanent arrangement or merely temporary, pending the selection and appointment of a new Chief Designer as such. In fact it turned out to be short-lived. As events moved towards war there was not only a great scramble to revive the strength of the Armed Forces and the industries which supported them but there was also a scramble to improve the security situation. One result of this sudden revival of consciousness and sensitivity about official security was that Payn came under investigation by the security services. This was due to a divorce and re-marriage to a lady of foreign origin. The immediate and direct result was that the Air Ministry withdrew their approval for Payn to hold his position of high responsibility in an area where security was obviously of the utmost importance. McLean dismissed him from his post and he left the Company. Personally I had always liked 'Agony' Payn, as we called him, and felt that he was the victim of overzealousness on the part of the officials and of a rather ruthless response on McLean's part. He could never have replaced Mitchell because neither by training nor experience was he in the same category, but he took his position as advisory assistant to Mitchell seriously and conscientiously. As a result of this security affair Payn became unemployable in the industry and had a very hard time during the ensuing years.

With Payn's departure Joseph Smith, who was Chief of the Drawing Office under Mitchell, became Manager of the Design Department still under Rex Pierson's overall supervision, but before long he was appointed Chief Designer, thus effectively restoring full autonomy to the Supermarine Design Department as it had existed under Mitchell.

Joe Smith was a thoroughly practical engineer of great determination and tenacity, with a strong personality and an ability to impose his authority over the now large and expanding Design Department. Joe, who served his apprenticeship with the Austin Motor Company in Birmingham, had joined the Supermarine

Company as a senior draughtsman in 1921 and had become Chief Draughtsman in 1926. So he had had some eleven years of working closely with R.J. Mitchell and understood his methods and thinking as well as anyone. As head of the Drawing Office he had presided over the detail design of the Spitfire and so had a deep and exact knowledge of the whole aircraft.

Recognising the essential strengths of Mitchell's design Smith set about the task of expanding its capabilities and performance to the maximum. He recognised and exploited the whole area of advancing technologies within the industry, more especially the potential power growth of the Merlin and Griffon engines, and the advances in aircraft ancillary equipment. 'If Mitchell was born to design the Spitfire,' wrote J.D. Scott, 'Joe Smith was born to defend and develop it.' The verb 'to defend' perhaps needs some explanation. Although much liked by pilots from the outset the Spitfire never found much real favour with the Air Council until it had decisively proved its mettle in battle over Dunkirk. Originally many technical people were suspicious of it, many production advisers in the Air Ministry did not care for it, and the Air Council were outraged during the latter part of 1937 and during 1938 by the delays in production.

On 7 June 1939 a memorandum was sent to the Chief of the Air Staff by the Air Member for Development and Production (AMDP), Sir Wilfrid Freeman, in which he referred to 'orders to be placed now with certain firms whose existing orders will run out early in 1940'. On the subject of Supermarine he wrote: 'Supermarine will run out of their order for Spitfires in February or March 1940 and since it will be impossible to get a new aircraft into production at Supermarine before September 1940 there is certain to be a six-month gap which we will have to fill.

'In order to be able to bridge the gap with as few machines as possible, Supermarine will be told later on to reduce the amount of subcontracting and get their men onto single shift so that although Supermarine production is likely towards the end of the present contract to exceed 48 aircraft per month it is hoped that we can reduce the gap production to 30 aircraft a month.'

He went on: 'Vickers are pressing for a more generous release of Spitfires for foreign orders, and it seems to me that provided no releases are made until October, we could go some way to meet them this year and could release aircraft for foreign orders freely after the spring of next year, when the Castle Bromwich factory will be coming into production.' Later in the same memorandum he wrote: 'The type of aircraft that could be put into production at Supermarine after the end of their contract would be Beaufighter, Gloster Fighter, Lysander or Westland (F.37/35).'

Two things are clear from this memorandum. First, that although the Mk I Spitfire had been in squadron service for nearly a year the Air Staff had really failed to appreciate the potential of the aircraft they had in their hand. Second, by planning to allow Spitfire production to phase out at Supermarine (in favour of the Beaufighter) they obviously had no ideas whatever for developing the Spitfire beyond the Mk I stage, nor had they much appreciation of the way operations would develop when hostilities broke out. The whole tone of this memorandum suggests that the Air Council had already decided they were not much interested in going on with the Spitfire beyond their current contractual obligation to Supermarine, and that the planned shadow factory at Castle Bromwich could look after any additional production that might be required so the only outstanding question was what to do with Supermarine. Castle Bromwich had been planned to produce bombers as well as fighters so the Air Council had flexibility of choice at that time.

It is a sobering thought that this talk of phasing out the Spitfire was going on only 14 months before the start of the Battle of Britain! That was what Scott meant when he wrote of Joe Smith having to *defend* as well as develop the Spitfire.

By the beginning of 1940 the proposal to turn Supermarine over to the production of Beaufighters was entirely serious; I remember it well and Wilfred Elliott, our Works Manager, and his staff were making frequent visits to Filton in connection with it. Joe Smith knew that this would be the end of the Spitfire and that if it were phased out of production at Southampton it would never be developed properly at all. So he pressed on with the first two stages of development, the first a minor one and the second more substantial.

The Spitfire Mk II was an aeroplane of only detail differences from the Mk I and it represented the agreed standard of aeroplane to be produced at Castle Bromwich. Perhaps its most important difference, apart from a slightly more powerful Merlin, was the incorporation of the Rotol constant-speed propeller fitted with blades of processed wood, in place of the De Havilland metal-bladed variable-pitch propeller. The firm of Rotol had been created by Rolls-Royce and Bristol in order to provide a greatly increased capacity for the production of propellers.

Joe Smith's next development of the Spitfire was the Mk III N3297, which I first flew on 16 March 1940, powered by the Merlin XX engine (the first of the Merlin series to be equipped with a two-speed supercharger) of 1,240 hp. It also had a re-designed windscreen which incorporated flat glass side-panels in place of the curved perspex side panels while the section of armour-plated glass in the sight line had been moved from an external to an internal position, thereby cleaning up the lines of the screen and reducing its drag. The wings of the Mk III were clipped, lessening the span by more than 6 ft and thus somewhat reducing the span of the ailerons. In this case the main structure of the wing was shortened whereas the later so-called clipped-wing versions of the Spitfire (some Mk Vs, IXs etc) were achieved simply by removing the already detachable wing tip units and replacing them with wooden blanks. For a variety of reasons, however, the Mk III never went into production.

These two Spitfire variants can be said to mark the beginning of the process of Spitfire development which, under Joe Smith's leadership, grew and expanded to such a spectacular degree during the war.

Before the war Rolls-Royce already had plans to revive the 'R'-type racing engine used in the S.6 Schneider seaplane (itself a derivative of the old Buzzard engine) and to turn it into a pro-duction engine for military purposes. It was to be called the Griffon and was a larger and heavier engine than the Merlin, with 37 litres capacity as against the Merlin's 27. Obviously a pro-duction version of this engine, intended for general military service, would initially be drastically de-rated in horsepower from the 2,700 bhp achieved by the sprint engine in the S.6B in 1931. But just as the special engine in N.17 had demonstrated the potential of the Merlin so did Joe Smith at once recognise the still greater future potential of the larger Griffon engine. Even before the outbreak of war he had set about studying the feasibility of squeezing the Griffon into a Spitfire which some people thought would not be possible. It was an inspired decision.

12

Production Testing

During the latter half of 1938 and the early part of 1939 the tempo of Spitfire production at Supermarine had at last increased. By the end of 1938 we had produced 48 aircraft and by the end of March 1939 130 aircraft which was 14 ahead of schedule. This gave George and myself plenty of flying to do on the production aeroplanes. In mid-1939 there was a temporary drop in production rate due in part to a shortage of embodiment loan items (essential items of equipment which it was the responsibility of the Government to deliver to the Works) and in part to the effect upon Supermarine of the amount of help which had to be given to the emergent 'shadow' factory at Castle Bromwich under the control of Lord Nuffield. His organisation was finding that putting a high-performance fighter into quantity production was a very different matter from the mass-production of cars.

When it had become clear, during 1937, that the aircraft industry had insufficient capacity to deal with the increases in production which the expansion programmes demanded, the Government moved towards the concept of large new 'shadow' factories which would produce aircraft under direct contract from the Air Ministry.

The Secretary of State, Lord Swinton, discussed with Lord Nuffield, the head of Morris Motors, the establishment of a factory to produce Spitfires in large quantities. In due course the site was chosen at Castle Bromwich near Birmingham. The Nuffield Organisation was, of course, very experienced in the mass-production of automobiles on a scale unknown to the aircraft industry, which was accustomed only to the batch production of aeroplanes in very modest numbers. The aircraft firms, responsive to the demands of their customers, had on the other hand developed a system of batch production which could accommodate frequent modifications and changes of specifications, something which was completely foreign to the car industry.

During 1939, the Nuffield Organisation, applying car production methods and attitudes, got deeper and deeper into trouble and Supermarine – not fully aware of what was going on, beset by problems of its own, and bearing no contractual responsibility for production at Castle Bromwich – were not able to help much initially nor pull Nuffield's management chestnuts out of the fire. The result was that this great shadow factory, specially built for the production of Spitfires in very large quantities and superbly equipped, had not by the outbreak of war produced a single aeroplane.

Lord Beaverbrook, who became the first Minister of Aircraft Production in May 1940, by which time the situation had reached crisis point, put the Castle Bromwich factory under the direct management of Vickers-Armstrongs Ltd, who were then able to co-ordinate the production efforts of Supermarine in Southampton and Castle Bromwich in Birmingham. Thus, by co-ordinating the resources of Supermarine and Castle Bromwich the deadlock in getting the latter started was overcome. Once production really got going, Castle Bromwich became the largest single source of Spitfire production in the country and at one time reached a peak output of 320 Spitfires per month.

By the outbreak of war production at Supermarine was running at about 10 per week and Pickering and I were kept busy. During that September I flew 21 new production aircraft (apart from the experimental work) and 33 were built altogether. With the expected increases in output from Southampton and the amount of experimental development flying which was building up it was clear that we should need another test pilot. We were determined to get someone of our own choice.

While we were considering this I heard that Alex Henshaw had been taken on at Weybridge. Alex was a well-known private aviator at that time, having made a great reputation for himself as a racing pilot in his specially modified and tuned Mew Gull single-seat racing aeroplane and more particularly by reason of his record flights from Gravesend to Cape Town and back in 1939 in the course of which he collected three records: London–Cape Town, Cape Town–London, and London–Cape Town–London. The last of these records still stands, 43 years after it was set up.*

* London–Cape Town: 1 day 15 hours 25 mins;
Cape Town–London: 1 day 15 hours 36 mins;
Total time for round trip: 4 days 10 hours 20 mins.

Henshaw's air-racing achievements were impressive but to my mind they paled into insignificance by comparison with that incredible flight from London to Cape Town and back in 4½ days in that tiny aeroplane half the size of a Spitfire. I had never met Alex Henshaw but a man who can do that, I thought to myself, must have plenty of fire in his belly and this is the sort of chap we need. So, after Pickering and I had talked it over I got into a Spitfire and flew to Brooklands for the specific purpose of trying to have a word with Alex and form some impression of the man. I had met a few of the civil racing and record-breaking fraternity and whilst there were some I liked and admired, there were others I certainly would not want involved in our test flying at Supermarine. I knew that Alex was a wealthy young man who had always owned his own aeroplanes and his rather unusual brand of flying experience had been acquired by his own enterprise and effort and at his own expense and that he had not, as George Pickering and I had, been trained in the Royal Air Force. So I did not know what to expect.

I climbed out of my Spitfire at Brooklands and walked into the little flight office by the bridge at the edge of the aerodrome. As luck would have it, Alex was in there alone. After only about two weeks he was thoroughly fed up at Weybridge. Mutt's general approach to the flying there at the time was rather casual and outwardly disorganised. Mutt Summers was an excellent experimental test pilot and a shrewd judge of an aeroplane but when the expansion programme started and the flying became more complicated and urgent and much larger in volume, it required organisation, method and discipline. Mutt was temperamentally unsuited for this and so Alex had joined one of the great firms of the industry, expecting to find the flying side highly organised, efficient and challenging and had been surprised to find what seemed to him the reverse, or at least the outward appearance of the reverse.

Alex described our first meeting in his book *Sigh for a Merlin**:

I went back to the pilots' office to think things over. I would tell Mutt that morning that I was leaving, meet Barbara later and tell her what I intended and then see Dad at the weekend. I was deep in thought as the door opened quietly and a trim dark-looking boy in

* John Murray, 1979.

black flying overalls, carrying a helmet and test pad, walked in. 'Hello,' he said, 'you must be Alex Henshaw. I'm Jeffrey Quill.' I liked him at once and was soon telling him how fed up I was kicking my heels around there. He said, 'That's ridiculous. You must come to us; we've got more work than we can cope with.' He then told me of the experimental work on the Spitfire, the sea trials in the Solent and the Channel with the Walrus and the development work on the new Sea Otter, so that I regretted very much I had not seen him when I first arrived at Weybridge. We parted with Jeffrey saying, 'We'd love to have you at any time if you would like to come.'

It was not long before Alex turned up at Eastleigh.

With the accelerated drive to increase production, monthly output (with cumulative totals in brackets) of production aeroplanes at Supermarine ran as follows:

1939　Sept. 33 (341), Oct. 48 (389), Nov. 50 (439), Dec. 40 (479).

1940　Jan. 37 (516), Feb. 45 (561), March 42 (603), April 60 (663), May 77 (740), June 94 (834), July 134 (968), Aug. 128 (1096).

As far as the production flying was concerned, my chief interest lay in devising ways and means of minimising hold-ups due to bad weather and, as my hopes for a radio let-down system had come to nothing, it seemed that everything was now dependent upon the skill and determination of individual pilots. I wanted to set a new standard in this matter and my experience in the Met Flight gave me reason to believe I could do so. At the outbreak of war the flying control at Eastleigh (such as it was) passed from the civil aviation authorities to the Royal Navy because there was a Royal Naval Air Station situated on the far side of the aerodrome.

Our gleaming white-painted hangars, in which the final assembly of the entire British output of Spitfires at that time took place, were hurriedly camouflaged and blacked out and soon a balloon barrage appeared to protect the aerodrome. The balloons were moored to mobile winches and were normally kept close hauled but if there was an air raid alert up they went, and stayed up until the all clear.

Very early on George Pickering and I were summoned to a meeting presided over by Commander Gerald Saunt RN who commanded the Royal Naval Air Station. He, poor fellow, had on his desk about three pounds of bumph constituting the official instructions detailing the regulations for the control of non-operational flying in wartime. It was soon apparent that it would be impossible for us at Supermarine to be bound by these regulations if we were to keep up the tempo of test flying required to match the factory's output of Spitfires. Six or seven flights were needed to clear a single aircraft and often we had several aircraft on the go at once. We could never afford to have serviceable aircraft standing around on the ground.

After much discussion I had to state clearly that as soon as each new Spitfire aircraft emerged from the factory we proposed to fly it whatever the state of air raid alerts, whatever the time of day, balloons up or balloons down, ack-ack guns or no ack-ack guns, rain or shine, Germans or no Germans, and Sundays included. This certainly put Gerald Saunt into a difficult position as he had no real jurisdiction over us, but goodwill and common sense on both sides soon sorted it out. In short, the Navy accepted that we would operate as we deemed necessary and they would be kept informed all the time about our movements.

By studying the exact position of all the balloon winches we were able to work out a 'route' through the balloon barrage which, by keeping right down at ground-level, enabled us to take off and come into land picking our way through the barrage without hitting a cable whilst the balloons were actually flying. This procedure was, naturally, frowned upon by the authorities but we were able to keep up the tempo of our test flying. It was also arranged that, when we were operating through heavy cloud cover, we would have a specific area out to sea south of the Isle of Wight where we could climb to height to complete our test schedules. This would cause the minimum inconvenience to the Fighter Command radar stations and the understanding was that if we got picked off by a marauding Me 109 that was our hard luck. This suited us very well.

It was at about this point that Alex Henshaw came on the scene. He soon became fully familiarised with the Spitfire and the flight schedule. At that time when the weather was very bad we would take off from Eastleigh, creep along the railway line towards Fareham at 'nought feet', cross the Solent and fly to a point south of St Catherine's Point to begin our climb and then let down and return by the same route. Before long Alex was doing this in weather which was as bad as it was possible for anyone to fly in at all without 'aids'. On one occasion, when the solid base of wet and rain-laden stratus cloud was very low indeed, I had just landed back at Eastleigh and was wondering whether it was not already a bit too much of a good thing before making another sortie. Then Alex's Spitfire appeared through the murk and as he crossed the airfield he did a slow roll as close to the ground as I had ever seen it done in that category of aeroplane, with his wing tips literally brushing the base of the cloud. Because of the rain there was no horizon and there was no margin for error either way. The roll was perfectly executed yet it shook me considerably. He came into the flight office, and as we were stripping off our Mae Wests I said, 'You're asking for it, Alex, aren't you?' This developed into a sharpish row between us which died down as quickly as it flared up. It was already obvious to me that in Alex Henshaw we had a pilot of the most exceptional skill and ability and totally unorthodox in his approach to flying. Things that would be regarded as lunacy by normal standards seemed perfectly manageable to him. He seemed to be a sort of aeronautical phenomenon and there was no point in trying to impose restrictions upon him which he would not accept anyway.

For some months I watched Alex's flying with growing amazement and respect. There was a period when I thought it was only a matter of time before he 'bought it' but, thankfully, he never did. Later in 1940 he moved up to Castle Bromwich to take over the mammoth production testing task there which is described in his *Sigh for a Merlin* on the jacket of which are quoted some words of mine:

There is no doubt that the job of Chief Pilot at Castle Bromwich was one of exceptional difficulty and challenge. It was fortunate for us all that Alex was there to do it. I know of no other pilot who could have handled it as he did, nor who could have set such a standard for his subordinate pilots to follow. It was a case of leadership by example if ever there was one. I refer, of course, to the formidable task of flight testing such a huge output of aircraft in abominable weather with no 'aids'.

Although I had now been flying Spitfires for some three and a half years, with a great deal of performance testing at full power, I had never had a total engine failure. This was a remarkable tribute to the Merlin, but I knew it could not last for ever. Sure enough, on 25 September 1939, I was doing a set of level speeds on K9791, which was a sort of prototype Spitfire Mk II destined for production at Castle Bromwich, when the engine stopped dead. I was at about 15,000 ft heading west and it was a day of broken cloud. It seemed to me that I might just perhaps reach Yeovil on the glide but it was the sort of aerodrome where a minor error or misjudgement in a 'dead stick' landing could have disastrous results and in any case from where I was I could not see it because of the cloud cover. I could, however, see the flat and relatively treeless area of ground round Weston Zoyland and here, I thought, I would put the Spitfire down in open country, wheels up if necessary. So I made my approach accordingly. By the time I was down to a few hundred feet my propeller had stopped rotating completely and it was then that I saw that the field I had selected had some dykes crossing it. I touched down, wheels up, where I had intended, skidded along merrily and jumped the first dyke with a resounding bang, then slid along until the Spitfire buried its nose in the second dyke. I was unhurt but the Spitfire was somewhat the worse for wear. I knew that this sort of thing could be expected to happen more often in the future, and sure enough it did, but when I look back on the intensity of the flying in those years, and the tremendous bashing one gave various Merlins in the course of rigorous performance testing, I marvel at the relatively few times it let me down and I look back with gratitude.

During 1939 there were the beginnings of some development flying and the testing of early modifications mostly aimed at reaching a standard for the Mk II aeroplane with the modified Merlin XII in the course of which we tested, among other things, various designs of propeller blades and different radiators. The Mk II could be described as a refined version of the Mk I with some alterations introduced for production as well as technical reasons. Also, of course, I began to fly the Mk III early in 1940.

After the outbreak of war the pressures upon the production organisation were intense and the small number of aeroplanes which had been allocated to Supermarine by the Director of Technical Development for experimental and development work (known as DTD aircraft) were handled and maintained by the production shops. The Works were quite properly trying to squeeze every possible production aircraft out of the shops and into the air by each Friday night (when the official week's production was counted and signalled to the Air Ministry) and so they had difficulty in devoting labour and man-hours to work on the experimental or DTD aircraft. As a result these experimental aircraft were being pushed aside in the flight shed during the week and it was noticeable that often they only made their appearance on the flight line on Saturdays and Sundays when the pressure was slightly eased on the production shops. At that time the experimental flight test department of Supermarine, although it had no such grand name, in effect consisted of Ernie Mansbridge and myself. The situation was highly frustrating and Joe Smith was fuming in the background due to the time it was taking to get the DTD flying done. I realised then that sooner or later we should have to organise a separate experimental flight unit, such as Rolls-Royce had at Hucknall.

Temperamentally I was much more interested in development test flying as it seemed to me to be essential to get on with improving the breed. I studied the techniques of accurate performance measurement and thought a great deal about the testing of handling qualities. I enjoyed testing the production aeroplanes and was determined to see they were properly tested and that nothing was skimped, but my prime interest was with the development testing. George Pickering, on the other hand, seemed more interested in the production testing so perhaps we made a good complementary pair.

Had it not been for the experimental flying and the urgent need to increase the performance and capability of the Spitfire, and Joe Smith's evident determination to do so, I should have left the firm at that time to return to the Royal Air Force. Indeed I went through agonies of doubt as to where my proper course lay but felt that to abandon the Spitfire at this crucial time would be a sort of betrayal.

13

Eastleigh and Sea-Spitfires

The Royal Naval Air Station at Eastleigh, which had been established on the west side of the aerodrome in hutted accommodation and with Bessoneau hangars of First World War vintage, became, at the beginning of the war, a pilot refresher training school. As late as 1938 the Fleet Air Arm had come under the sole and direct control of the Admiralty who virtually had to form a new Naval Air Service from scratch. A number of ex-short-service officers from the RAF were given commissions and one shrewd move by the Admiralty was to write, during the pre-war period, to every male holder of a civil private pilot's licence and offer an immediate RNVR commission in the event of the outbreak of hostilities provided they were of a certain age and medical standard. The result was that, in September 1939, a most unusual and motley band of aviators turned up at Eastleigh to be trained as Fleet Air Arm pilots – jockeys, motor racing drivers, actors, solicitors, bankers, stockbrokers, farmers and those of no particular occupation apart from doing what seemed to them interesting and amusing at the time. They arrived in an impressive assortment of mechanical transport with a good smattering of Bentleys. Ralph Richardson, for example, turned up on a 1000-cc four-cylinder Ariel motorbike.

They had varying amounts of flying experience, mostly in light types, and the naval instructors did their best to sort them all out and grade them accordingly. They flew in a variety of obsolescent and superannuated service types. Aerodrome control was virtually non-existent and when the weather was fine the circuit and surrounding air became crowded with these heterogeneous aircraft with their still more heterogeneous pilots going about their somewhat unpredictable business. On one occasion, as I was 'holding off' prior to touch-down, a Percival Vega Gull, which I had not seen, passed about 2 ft over my cockpit canopy on a course about 90° to mine.

In the thick, hazy, autumnal conditions, of which there was

much that year, the hazards associated with bringing Spitfires in to land were great, but this invasion of 'mature students' clad in brand-new sub-lieutenants' uniform did much to liven up our daily activities.

Later on, when the initial course of newly joined RNVR officers had passed through 'Narkover Nautical College', as it became known, a rather more serious unit in the shape of a Fighter School under the command of Lieutenant-Commander Brian Kendall was established at Eastleigh. Some preliminary deck-landing training in the form of ADDLs (aerodrome dummy deck landings) took place which necessitated marking out on the aerodrome surface the rough shape and size of an aircraft carrier's flight deck upon which, stationed on the port side aft, was a deck-landing control officer (DLCO) with his bats controlling the landing approach of aircraft to this dummy deck. Each time I came back to land at Eastleigh, if the dummy deck and DLCO were in place, I would 'pick up the bats' and land on the 'deck'. So did George Pickering and Alex Henshaw. We found that in spite of the blind forward view of a Spitfire it was possible, by making a carefully judged curved approach at minimum speed, to keep the bats in view and touch down neatly at the stern end of the 'deck'. The Spitfire had excellent lateral stability and aileron control right down to the stall and thus had what was needed for very slow approaches. I had, at that time, never been aboard an aircraft carrier but on the basis of these ADDLs with Spitfires it did not seem that there would be any great problem in landing a Spitfire on the deck providing it had a hook.

At the outbreak of war the Royal Navy's fighter situation was very far from being rosy.

The only single-seat fighter in the Fleet Air Arm suitable for front-line operation from aircraft carriers in September 1939 was the Sea Gladiator, a Naval version of the RAF's last biplane fighter. On order, but not due to fly even in prototype form until January 1940, was a new two-seat Merlin-engined monoplane fighter called the Fulmar which had been developed to Naval specification 0.8/38. Actually in front-line service with the Fleet in September 1939 were the Blackburn Skua, an aircraft designed as a dive bomber with secondary role as a fighter, and the redoubtable Fairey Swordfish Torpedo Spotter Reconnaissance (TSR) aircraft which was destined to play an historic role in

Naval air warfare. So, on the outbreak of war with Germany there were no high-performance single-seat monoplane fighters available for operation from aircraft carriers. In view of the then current building programme of armoured Fleet carriers, the first of which, HMS *Illustrious*, was in the final stages of completion, this was an ironic situation.

It is easy to be critical of the Navy's attitude towards the air during the period between the wars, but in fact the Naval Staff's inter-war logic was not so much flawed as overtaken by the forward march of aeronautical development during the years immediately before the Second World War, the pace of which they had tended to under-estimate. In the days when the Battle Fleet was the principal and dominant instrument of Naval power and when the aircraft first teetered uncertainly onto the world stage in the early part of the century, the first impact of the aeroplane upon Naval tactics lay in its potential for reconnaissance. It could become the eyes of the Fleet at sea. It could locate an enemy fleet at sea sooner and at a greater distance than could any scouting force of cruisers or destroyers. Seaplanes carried in special ships and lowered over the side by crane (the earliest form of aircraft carrier) could thus have a vital impact upon a fleet engagement. Nowhere was this more clearly recognised than in the Royal Navy.

Only three weeks after the Battle of Jutland in 1916 (a battle much bedevilled by confused information about the enemy's whereabouts) Admiral Jellicoe, then Commander-in-Chief of the Grand Fleet, wrote: 'The first requirement [is] for the Fleet to be provided with sufficient carriers and efficient seaplanes for scouting and spotting, manned by trained personnel.'* Obviously it was equally important to prevent the enemy fleet from playing the same game and therefore the need to intercept and destroy the enemy's shadowing reconnaissance aircraft, which made a point of keeping out of range of the fleet's guns, at once produced a role at sea for the fighter aircraft since it took an aeroplane to destroy an aeroplane at a distance. Then as aeroplanes developed in performance and load-carrying capacity, the Admiralty became faced with the problem of providing the fleet at sea with a defence not just against reconnaissance aircraft but

---

* G. Till, *Air Power and the Royal Navy* (Jane's, 1979).

also against a potentially devastating form of air attack – the air-launched torpedo. At this stage the doctrine that it takes an aeroplane to destroy an aeroplane still held sway, but later, in the inter-war period the Navy's attitude towards the air defence of the Fleet changed. It was considered the best defence against high-level bombers and torpedo-launching aircraft would be the intense and concentrated anti-aircraft fire which could be mounted in capital ships, rather than by dependence upon the then uncertain and unreliable operations of single-seat fighters. Gunnery was the Navy's stock-in-trade and they placed great faith in certain technical developments in anti-aircraft gunnery which were being studied in the early 1930s. Therefore they reasoned that carrier-borne fighters should be confined to the minimum required to destroy enemy shadowing aircraft.

But common sense and the restricted space available on air-craft carriers demanded that the fighters which were embarked should have at least a dual role. Since enemy carrier-borne reconnaissance aircraft were unlikely to be of very high performance it was argued that the fighters to intercept them need not be of very high performance either. These views, taken with the concept that Naval fighters should be capable of attacking enemy aircraft carriers and putting their flight decks out of action with machine-gun fire and by dive bombing attacks with light bombs so as to immobilise their aircraft very early on in a fleet action, led to the Skua, a dive bomber with a fixed gun armament and just sufficient performance to fulfil the now secondary task of defending the fleet against enemy shadowing aircraft. Thus by the late 1930s the single-seat fighter had all but disappeared from the Navy except for the small force of Sea Gladiators which was retained to protect the older carriers, *Furious*, *Glorious*, *Courageous* and *Eagle*, whose flight decks were not armoured and whose anti-aircraft fire was not yet up to the latest standards.

It should be remembered that until the late 1930s the single-seat fighter suffered from severe limitations, especially at sea. It had no bad-weather capability, no navigation capability when out of sight of land or the Fleet, very little night capability, very restricted range and firepower and no radio communication air-to-air or air-to-ship. Their Lordships could hardly be expected to commit the safety of the Fleet to such a dubious mode of defence.

The gunnery philosophy, however, failed to take fully into

account the advances made in the late thirties in the land-based bomber in terms of speed, range and bomb-load or the extent to which the Fleet in war would find itself operating within the range of such shore-based bombers. This was to be brought home forcibly to the Admiralty very early in the war when on 25 September 1939 the Home Fleet put to sea from Scapa Flow to cover the rescue by the cruisers and destroyers of 'Humber Force' of a British submarine in trouble near the Horns Reef off the coast of Denmark. The Home Fleet included the aircraft carrier *Ark Royal* with the Skuas of 800 and 803 Squadrons on board and the battle cruiser *Hood*. Early next day this Fleet was detected by three German reconnaissance flying boats (Do 18s) and in accordance with their design function the Skuas were launched to intercept. One of the flying boats was destroyed by a Skua of 803 Squadron (the first German aircraft to be destroyed by the Fleet Air Arm in the war) but the other two managed to escape to radio a sighting report back to base. The result was an attack on the Fleet by four Ju 88s from the Island of Sylt operating as dive-bombers in the course of which one of the Ju 88s planted a 1000-lb bomb just off *Ark Royal*'s bow throwing a huge wall of water over the forward end of her flight deck and another scored a hit on HMS *Hood*, fortunately without the bomb exploding. This was a let-off for both ships and significantly no German aircraft were destroyed by anti-aircraft fire. Weather conditions were overcast which no doubt influenced both the effectiveness of the German attack and the ship's anti-aircraft fire but obviously the incident called into question the wisdom of having no high-performance interceptor fighters at sea.

So far as Supermarine were concerned the upshot was that in October 1939 inquiries were received from the Air Ministry about the possibility of producing a 'hooked' Spitfire for the Navy followed by a request early in December for details to be worked out for a folding-wing 'hooked' Spitfire with a folded width of no more than 18 ft to suit the lifts of the new armoured carriers. So we had to turn the Spitfire into a Sea-Spitfire (later to be called the Seafire), capable of operating at sea from an aircraft carrier, a thing which had not been even remotely considered in the initial design of the Spitfire in 1934–5. Certainly the undercarriage had not been designed with this arduous mode of usage in view. If the Spitfire never made a wholly satisfactory Naval fighter until it had been much further developed, it is not necessary to look beyond this for the reason. However, drawings and data for a Sea-Spitfire were produced and submitted to the Air Ministry on 2 January 1940 and on 5 January the Director of Air Materiel at the Admiralty, Captain Mathew Slattery RN, inquired of the Ministry the possibility of having 50 Spitfires (or Hurricanes) supplied with folding wings and arrester hooks as soon as possible.

In the meantime the prototype Fairey Fulmar two-seat fleet fighter with the Merlin engine had made its first flight at Ringway near Manchester on 4 January 1940 and predictions for its performance and hopes for its success were soon running high. The Air Ministry obviously hoped that the success of this aircraft, designed specifically to Naval requirements, might mean they would hear no more of the Admiralty's request for Sea-Spitfires or Hurricanes, which they feared would seriously interfere with their own production plans, but in February the Admiralty renewed their request for 50 folding-wing Spitfires, adding that they would like some available by July 1940!

Supermarine estimated that an order for 50 hooked and folding Sea-Spitfires could be completed within 16 months from order, but at a cost of 75 Spitfire deliveries to the Royal Air Force. Sir Wilfrid Freeman, however, took a different view and argued that the Admiralty's Sea-Spitfires would take as long to produce as the Fulmar and would cost the RAF 200 Spitfires in lost production. On 30 March he received a note from the Admiralty to say that the then Fifth Sea Lord, Vice-Admiral Royle, had given instructions to drop the folding-wing Spitfire proposals. Thus was production of the Spitfire enabled to continue uninterruptedly for the battles that lay ahead for the Royal Air Force, but the decision also meant there would be no Sea-Spitfires – or Seafires – for the Royal Navy until mid 1942.

In 1935 a new aircraft firm, which was not a Government shadow factory, had been formed by Sir Hugo Cunliffe-Owen and established in a hangar at Eastleigh, not far from ours. They procured the manufacturing rights, from Burnelli in the USA, of a so-called 'flying wing' design. Cunliffe-Owen considered, evidently, that there was a civil market for this aeroplane in 1938, but when the expansion programme got under way in 1936–7

Cunliffe-Owen, obviously with a view to getting lucrative Government contracts, built himself a large factory on the edge of the aerodrome and was filling it up at that time with subcontract work. Later he built Seafires to Government contract.

Meanwhile the main Spitfire assembly remained in our old First World War hangars on the edge of the tarmac apron at Eastleigh.

Late in July 1940 I was standing on the tarmac outside our hangars talking to Commander 'Shorty' Ermen RN who was visiting from the Admiralty. It was a cloudless day but with upwards visibility into the blue sky much restricted by haze. The sound of a large formation of aircraft approaching at altitude could be heard but there was no alert and we paid little attention to it. Eventually I picked them out at about 12,000 ft. 'I don't know how it strikes you, Shorty,' I said, 'but those look very much like Heinkel 111s to me.' No sooner had I said it than we heard bombs whistling down.

I forget which of us first made the air raid shelters – only about a hundred yards away – but by the time that short raid was over the Cunliffe-Owen factory had been severely blitzed. On the other hand our flight shed and the Spitfire assembly sheds were wholly untouched. They evidently did not appear important or grand enough to the German bombers. We had had a very lucky escape. Our flight shed was full of completed Spitfires and the DTD aircraft and, had the assembly shops been hit, it would have brought Spitfire production to a standstill.

We had therefore to find a more secure location for the DTD aircraft and then somewhere to put the production aircraft between flight test and delivery. The Naval Air Station at Worthy Down was the nearest, most convenient and inconspicuous place and we acquired a hangar by arrangement with the Navy. We moved the DTD aeroplanes up there, established a flight gang under a very competent and hard-working foreman, Edgar Woolridge, and at last we had the makings of a separate experimental flight test department coming under the control of the design department rather than under the production department.

From that point onwards we built it up. I had some hutted office accommodation erected and we established a small flight test branch of the technical office under the supervision of Murry

P. White.* From then on the development flying ceased to be the poor relation, and we were able to work directly and more closely with the design department.

* Later President of British Aerospace USA (Inc).

14

The Battle of Britain

As a brief summing-up and a neat placing of the Battle of Britain in a global context the following passage from J.M. Roberts's *The Pelican History of the World** is admirable:

> It was soon clear that only defeat after direct assault was going to get the British out of the war. This was even more certain after a great air battle over southern England in August and September had been won by British science and the Royal Air Force . . . This victory made a German seaborne invasion impossible (though a successful one was always unlikely). It also established that Great Britain could not be defeated by air bombardment alone. The Islands had a bleak outlook ahead, but this victory changed the direction of the war, for it was the beginning of a period in which a variety of influences turned German attention in another direction. In December 1940 planning began for a German invasion of Russia.

In scale the Battle of Britain was small by comparison with air operations which took place in the course of later campaigns of the war, but its effects were enormous. The morale of the British people was uplifted to an extent which enabled them to respond to the positive leadership of Winston Churchill and his coalition government; the effect on opinion in the USA was substantial and greatly strengthened Roosevelt's political hand in providing aid to Britain on a scale which stretched neutrality to the limit. As Dr Roberts pointed out, it convinced Hitler that he could not eliminate Britain by invasion. It also had a powerful effect in the Commonwealth countries who had instantly committed themselves to the support of Britain on the outbreak of war in 1939 only to witness a series of military reverses and disasters until suddenly the RAF achieved this decisive victory. From 10 July to 31 October, which is deemed officially to be the period of the Battle, a total of 2,945 aircrew fought, out of which 507 were

* Penguin Books, 1980.

killed and approximately 500 wounded.

This compares with 15,000 British and Allied troops lost in one day at Waterloo. Perhaps aerial warfare is economical in lives, provided it achieves really important strategic objectives.

At the beginning of the Battle there were 19 squadrons of Spitfires operational in Fighter Command and 38 squadrons of Hurricanes. In No. 11 Group the ratio of Spitfires to Hurricanes was more even. During the months of July to October (inclusive) the combined output of Spitfire and Hurricane was 1,653 of which 1,025 were Hurricanes and 628 Spitfires. In June the ratio of Hurricanes to Spitfire deliveries had been exactly 3 to 1, but for the four months July to October (inclusive) Spitfire production increased considerably so that the ratio ran at around 1.6 to 1. This figure gives a fair assessment of the relative numerical participation of those two aircraft in the battle. Surprisingly British fighter output in this period exceeded that of Germany by a considerable margin. Sir Maurice Dean, in *The Royal Air Force and Two World Wars**, writes:

> The number of fighters available for operations in Fighter Command rose steadily throughout June, July, August and September. Of course, Fighter Command was too small; not surprisingly surely after years of financial stringency and the collapse of France but, given this qualification, aircraft were not the most severe problem. This arose partly from a shortage of pilots and partly from the vulnerability of fighter and radar stations to attack.

Apart from the broad strategic issues, what were the special circumstances which affected the Battle? First, the fact that German forces had overrun The Netherlands, Belgium and northern France meant that the Luftwaffe, which was primarily a tactical Air Force having no heavy long-range bomber force to speak of, now had airfields within easy reach of south-eastern England and London which could then be attacked by its medium bombers. Furthermore these bombers could be escorted by high-performance fighters, thereby greatly compounding the problem of Fighter Command in mounting an effective defence.

The second vital circumstance was the availability to the

* Cassell, 1979.

British of a fighter control system based on a chain of radar (with the cover name RDF – radio direction finding) stations. The practical effect of these was that incoming raids could be spotted at a considerable distance from our shores, thus providing essential early warning; the strength of the enemy formations could be assessed with reasonable accuracy, and their position, height and track plotted. Not only did this enable the British fighters to be controlled or vectored towards their targets by the controllers on the ground but it contributed greatly towards economy of force in that fighters could generally be kept at readiness on the ground until an attack was positively observed. The development of radar stations was a breakthrough of incalculable value but almost as important was the fact that the Luftwaffe High Command had failed to appreciate its significance and was taken largely by surprise. Even if, as has often been claimed, their Intelligence may have been aware of it, the Luftwaffe High Command appears to have failed to benefit from the information. Perhaps this was because German Intelligence was somewhat in disarray due to the rivalry between the Abwehr and the SS, which meant that available information was not always presented in a coordinated manner.

Third, there were the British fighters. The Hurricane and the Spitfire ideally complemented each other. The Hurricane had been designed with ease of production very much in mind; it was rugged and more easily maintained than the Spitfire, and was thus available in greater numbers, but some performance had been sacrificed for these qualities. The Spitfire had a significant edge over the Hurricane in performance which made it more suitable for tackling the German fighters which escorted the bombers. Neither the Spitfire nor the Hurricane could have won the Battle on their own because, apart from anything else, there would not have been enough of them. It took both of these great aeroplanes to win the Battle. Both should always be honoured for the great fighters they were.

Fourthly, there was the aggressiveness and determination of the air crew in Fighter Command. By and large the pilots had the advantage of fighting over their own country in defence of their own homeland. In the case of the pilots from the Dominions the 'old country' still had a very real meaning and significance for them and they were determined to fight for it. In the case of the foreign pilots – Free Frenchmen, Belgians, Dutch, Poles, Czechoslovaks and Norwegians – they had the stimulus of extreme anger arising from how their own countries had been overrun. A strong element of anger influenced the British pilots as well. Although it is not fashionable to talk about it today, those of us who fought believed we were fighting a just war against unprovoked aggression with Right entirely on our side. We had seen enough of the pre-war Nazi regime to believe it was evil and dangerous and although we were by no means sure it could be beaten, not to fight against it was unthinkable.

The RAF had yet a fifth advantage over the Luftwaffe; it was far better commanded. In 1918 the RAF had been the largest air force in the world in numbers of aircraft, in squadrons and in manpower and it was backed up by the largest and most powerful aircraft industry in the world. At the conclusion of that war the RAF had been run down to a shadow of its former self and had existed on very short rations financially until around 1935. But it was never destroyed, it never went out of business, and indeed the best of it was preserved throughout the lean years; it also had a world-wide role between the wars. Formed as it was from the old Royal Naval Air Service and the Royal Flying Corps it had absorbed many of the best traditions and habits of command of the older Services. In 1939, therefore, the RAF was a mature service with the priceless asset of having senior officers with the experience and maturity gained from long and uninterrupted service to the Crown.

The German Air Force had had no such luck. Completely dismantled after the war in 1918, its officer corps was disbanded and scattered at random over the chaos and despair of post-war Germany. But in fact the German Air Force was never quite out of business – General Hans von Seeckt, Commander of the Reichswehr from 1920 to 1926, had seen to that. Using every possible device and subterfuge to thwart the Versailles Treaty, he kept a tiny cadre of officers and the basis of a planning staff alive and training took place secretly in Russia. The basis of an aircraft industry was created, under the guise of developing civil aircraft within the very limiting terms of the Treaty. The German Air Force in short, beaten, destroyed and dismantled in 1918, refused to lie down although it may have feigned dead. In the 1920s enormous encouragement and support was given to gliding clubs and thousands of young Germans were able to take this first step towards flying. But it needed a major political upheaval and a direct defiance of the Versailles Treaty before anything like a new Air Force could be created. Hitler provided these conditions and the Luftwaffe was the result. It was in fact an amazing achievement to create a new Air Force, with the industry to back it, on such a scale and in such a short time. But its fundamental weakness was that it was the child of an aggressive political dream and of the appalling corruption of the Nazi party. In such circumstances the command structure of the Luftwaffe was bound to lack mature experience and training in spite of the often valiant and courageous efforts of officers of an older school. This was how the Luftwaffe had to fight the Battle of Britain. It is not surprising that it failed in its first confrontation with a large and really professional air force fighting in defence of its own country.

The personal memories and accounts of individual participants in any great battle are bound to vary enormously according to the form of their participation. One of the Duke of Wellington's private soldiers, after he had returned from Waterloo to his West Country village to a hero's welcome, was asked for his account of the battle. He replied, 'I'll be damned if I know aught of the affair for all day long I was rolled in the mud and galloped over by every rascal who had a horse.' On that note I start an account of my own modest participation in the Battle.

The fall of France in June 1940 had created a most desperate situation, and I felt I simply must get back into a fighter squadron. My best chance to overcome the opposition that I knew would come from the firm was to put forward the case that, in order to do my job properly, I must gain first-hand experience of fighting in a Spitfire. Group Captain D.S. Brooks, an old friend of Upavon days, helped me and the Air Officer Commanding (AOC) No. 11 Group, Air Vice-Marshal Keith Park, agreed to post me to 65 Squadron at Hornchurch. I reported there on 5 August 1940, privately hoping that it might turn out to be a permanent arrangement. The Hornchurch wing at that time comprised 74 Squadron, commanded by 'Sailor' Malan; 65 Squadron, whose CO, Squadron Leader Sawyer, had just been killed; and 56 Squadron, commanded by Squadron Leader

Leathhart, who had recently distinguished himself by landing near Calais in a Miles Master, picking up his then Squadron Commander, who had been shot down, and lifting him safely back to Hornchurch more or less under the noses of the Germans.

I took over my room in the Mess and in the evening met many people I already knew. There was Piers Kelly who had recently distinguished himself by getting a hole blown in his top fuel tank large enough to get your head and shoulders into, but miraculously without catching fire. 'Sailor' Malan and H.M. Stephen and Mungo Park of 74 Squadron were there and Al Deere of 54 Squadron and Webster and Norman Ryder of 41 Squadron, all of whom had been amongst the early RAF pilots to collect their Spitfires from Eastleigh. There were many others too, including quite a few who were not to live very long.

Number 65 Squadron was at Rochford so none of them was in the Mess at Hornchurch that evening. I drank a few beers with various people in the Mess. They had all fought in the operations around Dunkirk and so had some lively experiences to recount; but they had also begun to develop definite ideas about air fighting and tactics as the result of hard experience. Al Deere, a New Zealander later to become one of our greatest fighter pilots, talked at length about the recent air fighting at which he was now very experienced. I learned much which I have no doubt contributed towards my own subsequent survival. From this and other sources I acquired that evening many nuggets of sound advice such as 'Get in as close as you can, you're usually further away than you think'; 'You get shot down yourself by the man you don't see'; 'If you hit a 109 don't follow him down to see him crash – another will get you while you're doing it'; 'You need eyes in the back of your head'; 'Scan the sky constantly – it's essential you see them before they see you'; 'Never get separated if you can help it – and don't hang about on your own.'

The next morning I reported to Group Captain Bouchier, the Station Commander, known variously as 'Boy' or 'Daddy' Bouchier, who gave me a very friendly welcome, told me how the CO of 65 Squadron (Sawyer) had been killed the previous night and hinted that he thought I might be better off in 74 Squadron on account of its more experienced leadership, by which he obviously meant 'Sailor' Malan; however, I said to Bouchier that I was due to fly to Rochford in the afternoon and thought that at least I should join the squadron to which I was posted, even if a transfer were arranged later. He agreed and so, having drawn some essential kit and spent an hour talking to the station intelligence officer, I flew one of 65 Squadron's Spitfires (which had just emerged from workshops) down to Rochford.

Sam Saunders, 'B' Flight Commander, had taken over command of the Squadron after the death of Sawyer. He was a tall, fair-haired and quietly authoritative man, and I instinctively felt no qualms about being led by him in the air. I was also glad to meet the Flight Commander of 'A' Flight, Gordon Olive, wearing the dark blue uniform of the RAAF. Not long before he had taken off at night in his Spitfire and, at a very low height, had baled out because his oxygen system had apparently caught fire. This was a unique case and puzzled us very much at Supermarine. An inquiry had concluded that a form of spontaneous combustion had been caused by some particles of oil penetrating the system.

I was then lifted back to Hornchurch in the 'Maggie' as I was to fly a Spitfire to Sutton Bridge the following morning for practice air firing. But flying was cancelled at Hornchurch the following day due to bad weather, which irritated me partly because I wanted to get my practice air firing over and done with and start real air-firing at the Luftwaffe, and partly because I did not consider the weather to be all that bad. However the day after I got away early to Sutton Bridge in YT-J, the squadron aircraft allotted to me, and did some firing against a sleeve target towed behind a Henley cruising at about 150 mph. I had only 200 rounds per gun but made several passes at the sleeve and finished up with a score of 54 hits which I was told was good, which cheered me up a bit as I feared I was still a poor shot. I flew back to Hornchurch by lunchtime and found that 65 had lost two sergeant pilots, Kirton and Phillips, that morning. A big force of about 250 German aircraft in the neighbourhood of Manston had been engaged by 65 and 41 Squadrons and the two sergeants had been shot down and killed. Five Me 109s had been claimed – mostly by 41 Squadron – and an E-boat had been shot up off Calais.

The news that two of 65 Squadron's pilots had been killed made me realise I must get to Rochford without further delay. I had, after all, done more flying in Spitfires than anyone else in the

Air Force at that time and I had done my air firing to satisfy the Book; so as far as I was concerned I was operational. But as soon as I got there I was asked to lead three recently joined pilots up to Sutton Bridge for more air firing which seemed to me to be wasting another day. These new pilots comprised a nineteen-year-old fresh-faced young Pilot Officer straight from OTU called Derek Glaser whom I had known as a boy, and two Polish pilots, Szulkowski and Gruszka. According to my diary notes at the time, they did their air-to-ground firing and we had some tea in the Mess and flew back to Rochford. It was a beautiful evening and I much enjoyed the trip over Cambridgeshire and the old familiar Met Flight country. When we got back to Rochford I had a talk with Saunders and it was decided then that I should start off operationally in the morning.

While we were having tea in the Mess at Sutton Bridge I had the chance to ask the two Poles about their escapes from their country, but their English was limited and they were obviously confused by the trauma of their recent lives, culminating in being trained to fly Spitfires in a foreign land and in a foreign tongue and then pitched into the strange environment of a Royal Air Force fighter squadron. I wondered how they would ever understand anything over the R/T, for in those days we still had old TR9D H/F sets whose sound quality was so poor that I had difficulty enough myself in hearing distinctly. Young Glaser was extremely good with them, and they seemed to feel at ease with him, as they had joined the squadron together. Until the day that Gruszka was shot down and Szulkowski became inconsolable and silent, they spent hours poring over an English dictionary. (This was before separate Polish squadrons and wings were formed.) The other pilots in the squadron at the time were Gordon Olive, Nicholas, Wigg, Lee Pyman, Hart, Smart, Paddy Finucane and Gregory, with Sergeant pilots McPherson, Orchard, Franklin and Kilner; and our Intelligence officer was Flying Officer Hardy.

Rochford, in peacetime, had been a small civil aerodrome; it was entirely grass, just to the north of Southend and what had been the old flying club building served as our Mess. There was a small lawn outside the Mess with some garden furniture where one could relax in good weather when not over at dispersal. There were two dispersals on opposite sides of the field, one for each flight and the Flight Office, and rough sleeping accommodation for those on night readiness was in wooden huts. 'B' Flight's dispersal was quite close to the Mess, ours a good deal further away.

In the morning we were at 30 minutes' readiness but nothing happened, which gave me time to look around. At 1300 hrs we took off for Manston aerodrome (code-named 'Charlie Three'). We flew in four sections of three, sections in line astern, Sam Saunders leading. I was in the fourth section led by Nicholas with me as his number two and Pyman number three. As we headed off across the estuary, passing over the mile-length of Southend Pier, I realised that I had not flown in a squadron formation of fighters since the Bulldog days in 17 Squadron. When our section closed up behind the rest of the squadron and became an integral part of 12 Spitfires, alive and animated and glistening in the summer sunlight, I suddenly felt enormously elated and excited. I had been flying this aeroplane for over four years; four years of wondering how it was really going to work and acquit itself when the real test came, four years of reports and meetings and discussions and continuous flying, day in and day out. But, looking back, it all seemed to have been one stage removed from reality, as if I had in a sense been a spectator or a planner rather than a participant; a coach rather than a player. Now, as we headed south-east across the estuary for Manston at a brisk clip and in quite tight formation, I felt a participant at last, and experienced a great sense of fulfilment.

The formation which we were flying, comprising four Vics of three in line astern, amounted in effect to three parallel lines astern of four aircraft each, with the leaders' line staggered slightly ahead. It could be rapidly opened out sideways, required a minimum of concentration on the actual flying, thereby enabling everyone to scan the sky methodically; and it lent itself to a sudden 'break', if necessary, with the minimum of confusion or collision risk. We broke into sections and landed individually on the large grass field at Manston and taxied to our dispersal, which was on the west side of the aerodrome, adjacent to some small hangars. There were a few wooden huts including one for the pilots to use while at readiness, and of course the inevitable direct telephone line from the Ops room at Hornchurch. During the ensuing weeks we were to spend about half of each day at readiness at Manston and that hut became very familiar.

When at readiness we would sit in the hut and play cards, usually gin rummy or sevens, and talk about nothing in particular. I had a paperback copy of Izaak Walton's *Compleat Angler* which fitted into my tunic pocket and this I found absorbing when we were not playing cards.

When the telephone rang, which it very frequently did, a silence would descend upon the assembled company while Sam Saunders answered it. It was usually one of the controllers at Hornchurch as, whenever possible, they passed us advance warning if the RDF stations were picking up signs of a build-up of German formations on the other side of the Channel; but often enough the call was an executive order to 'scramble', and 'scramble' it really was.

Our aircraft stood outside the dispersal hut within easy running distance. Our parachutes were already in the cockpit seats, the harnesses disposed carefully so that we could nip into the seat, fasten the harness very quickly, then fasten the Sutton harness on top of it. The airmen were mostly very skilled in giving essential help in this process as they stood on the wing beside the cockpit; then we plugged in the R/T lead and connected the oxygen tube and started the engine all at once. The airmen snapped shut the little shoulder-height cockpit door and, with an encouraging pat on the shoulder, would jump to the ground while other airmen unplugged the ground accumulators and pulled away the wheel chocks. It was all done in very quick time, and we were away. I was always puzzled by the publicity photographs so frequently seen of pilots running awkwardly towards their aircraft, trailing their parachutes over their shoulders. It always struck me as a completely daft way of going about the job because to start off with you could not run easily when toting a parachute and it took much longer to get into the cockpit. No doubt all those pictures had been taken in the piping days of peace.

'Charlie Three' (Manston) aerodrome was geographically the closest to France (with the possible exception of Hawkinge) and it really was not the ideal place from which to take off to intercept and attack enemy raids which were already formed up and heading across the Channel with their top cover of fighters in position. If we climbed directly out to sea from Manston we had no chance of gaining enough height from which to attack, so we had first to climb inland and then turn southwards to deal with whatever was coming. Logic suggested that we might just as well operate from Rochford, and this logic seemed to have even more to commend it when, on 12 August, we were comprehensively dive-bombed while taking off from Manston, not to mention being beaten up by a force of Me 109s. However, there was one over-riding reason why there should be Spitfire squadrons operating from Manston, which was that if they were withdrawn the local inhabitants might get the impression that this heralded a general withdrawal from the area. Indeed, as we usually arrived at 'Charlie Three' from Rochford at dawn (we never spent the night there) we were briefed to fly low over Margate and Ramsgate and Deal before landing.

The first time I sighted Me 109s in the air we had been vectored out over the Channel towards a formation of 'bandits' which was alleged to be coming in in roughly the opposite direction. I was flying in the fourth section, to the rear of the squadron, when I was aware of black smoke coming from the exhausts of our leading aircraft as Sam Saunders had started climbing furiously and turning left-handed. Then I saw them, about 1,000 ft higher than we were, over to our left, and in a fairly tight formation heading in exactly the opposite direction; about 20, I estimated. They looked like silvery minnows with their down-swept noses and I could see the black crosses on their fuselages. Then they started to swing round in a diving turn towards us. They had the advantage of speed and height, so we continued climbing and turning furiously. To my astonishment the 109s, having turned left-handed through 180°, dived away towards the French coast without making the slightest attempt to attack us. We immediately gave chase but only our leading few aircraft were close enough to open fire. I could see the tracer trails and was mightily impressed by the bullet drop thus displayed, at once realising why one needed to get close to get a hit. Nevertheless we all blazed away at them but Sam Saunders called off the chase – very properly, because the 109s, losing height rapidly as they were, could well have been leading us into a trap. We reformed and went on with our patrol but encountered nothing else. It seemed to me the 109s had missed a great opportunity because we had been in a very disadvantageous position. However, at least I had seen them and knew what they looked like and had fired my guns.

Most days we would take off from Rochford at first light and proceed directly to 'Charlie Three'. Sometimes we would be sent to patrol over a convoy proceeding along the east coast either to or from the Thames estuary, in order to use up our fuel usefully before landing at 'Charlie Three'. This involved milling about over the sea at low level within sight of the convoy and keeping a sharp look-out for Dorniers or Ju 88s which might make a quick attack, particularly if there was any cloud about to cover their approach. It was impressive and startling to see the masts and superstructures of so many sunken and wrecked merchant ships sticking out of the shallow sea around the estuary and the Goodwins. On one occasion we were covering a convoy at first light when we spotted some other aircraft which we first assumed to be 109s but they turned out to be Hurricanes. In my diary notes I wrote:

> The clouds were low and we were going along at about 1,500 ft in the usual squadron formation. . . . There were some Hurricanes knocking about but they were in twos and threes and seemed to be messing about in the most extraordinary manner. Three of them actually did a 'peel off' on us from behind and it looked rather ugly for a moment; it was evidently a very undisciplined squadron . . .

At that very early hour in the morning, and after all the commotion of getting the squadron airborne and formed up and on station, without having had anything but a lukewarm cup of tea, I was not brimming over with the spirit of peace on earth and goodwill towards men. I remember saying to myself: 'If one of those buggers so much as makes a mild pass at me I'm going to break away and let him have it.'

There were also days when we remained at readiness at Rochford during the morning and went to 'Charlie Three' for the latter half of the day, flying back to Rochford at dusk. But Manston was where the main action was. When a big enemy raid was seen to be forming up over on the other side, we were usually alerted by the Hornchurch controller and sometimes climbed into our cockpits awaiting instructions to move. When it came we would take off and be climbing up and often there would be a big formation of Dorniers coming in over the Channel at about

12,000 ft. We would be told to ignore them and go on up to where we would be vectored on to their top cover of Me 109s. The main objective was to engage these formations of Me 109s, so that when the fighters were thus milling around between 20,000 and 30,000 ft the bombers would still be bumbling along towards their targets. If their escorts were by then out of position the bombers were easier to attack for the other squadrons which were vectored on to them later. My recollections are therefore almost exclusively of combats with Me 109s, although I claimed a Heinkel 111 destroyed when leading a section. My diary notes describe one particular such occasion:

> To 'Charlie Three' after breakfast. Today there was a lot of cloud about, white broken stuff low down and more wishy-washy alto-stratus at 20,000 ft and around. We were sent off early and went straight out towards Dunkerque. Control kept telling us we were 'right in the middle of them' but we had a tremendous scout around in and out of cloud in line astern, snaking about from right to left without seeing anything for a long time; that 'snake' was effective and we felt very secure from surprise. At last we saw some 109s above and in front going at right angles to us; they turned left to get round behind us and when I looked behind I saw Pyman was very far behind and below and one German was streaking after him. I turned and went to head him off and Nicholas followed me and the 109 saw us and changed his mind and all was well before we had got too much separated. Why won't these people keep up?
>
> There were other 109s knocking about but they didn't seem keen for a fight. We were going back towards Margate now and when we reached there we were told there were bandits at Dover and at that moment we could see balloons going down in flames. We turned and dived down towards them and on coming through the broken cloud we saw a lot of what were presumably 109s ahead. We went straight for them, still in line astern, and as we were nearly there I saw a single 109 passing across underneath them. I had a quick look round and all seemed fairly clear so I broke away and went after him, Nick following; I opened fire from fairly short range and saw my tracers going right into his fuselage; I expected him to swerve or half-roll or something, so was all keyed-up to follow but he just went straight on down so I gave him another burst and another and still he went on downwards and not very fast and then I thought I had been spending too long on him and turned quickly to see if anyone was behind me and found all clear but a lot of aircraft swirling around some way away. Thinking about it on the way back I came to the conclusion

that I must have hit the pilot in the head or the back with the first burst because of his complete indifference to my fire. . . . Anyway I put in a combat report to that effect and feel very confident in my mind that he was in fact dead or unconscious. We landed back at 'Charlie Three' and I was anxious because Pyman did not return. We were not long there before we had instructions to return to 'Don One' (Rochford). . . . Then we got the news that Pyman was at Manston, his aircraft too badly shot up to fly back to Rochford. This was good news for we should be sorry to see Pyman go.

Early in August we were dive-bombed while taking off from 'Charlie Three'. Manston was an entirely grass aerodrome and we would form up on the ground and take off in squadron formation in four sections of three in Vic formations. Sam Saunders, of course, led the first section of three with a second and third section on his right and left and on this occasion I was leading the fourth section on the extreme right of the whole formation. When Sam began to roll we would all take off together and once airborne we would, section by section, drop into line astern, our section bringing up the rear. It was a somewhat stately or even ponderous method of getting the squadron airborne, but it minimised the problems of forming-up in the air. It also cut down on the R/T chatter inseparable from forming up in the air after individual take-offs. Anyway, rightly or wrongly, in 65 Squadron we took off as a complete squadron whenever we had room to do so. On this occasion (12 August) we were just formed up on the ground and awaiting Sam's signal to start rolling. I was therefore looking out to my left towards the leading section when I became aware of, rather than actually hearing, a sort of reverberating 'crump' behind and to my right. I looked quickly over my right shoulder in time to see one of the hangar roofs close behind us ascending heavenwards followed by showers of earth and black smoke, and then more and louder 'crumps'. I caught a glimpse through smoke of what looked like a Me 110 pulling sharply out of a dive and immediately concluded it was high time for Quill to be airborne. We were being dive-bombed. I put my head down and slammed the throttle open and went without further cere-mony, wondering what chance I had of getting airborne before a bomb dropped immediately ahead of me, or even on me. We had, in 65 Squadron, a local modification consisting of wide-angle convex rear mirrors mounted inside our canopies at the top of the windscreen, which gave a good wide rear-vision coverage although somewhat restricted due to the convexity. As I became airborne I glanced in the mirror and saw nothing but bomb-bursts and showers of earth and smoke immediately behind me. I thought I must be the only member of the squadron to have got away. Then I saw a Spitfire, and another and another, emerge through the smoke and at that point a Me 109 went shooting past me – very fast. 'Hell,' I thought, 'Me 109s! That's all we need now,' and I flew right down on the deck just beyond the aero-drome and started weaving and trying to look behind. My diary notes written immediately afterwards say:

. . . those seconds when I was cold meat for any swooping Messer-schmitt were interminable but at last I could pull the nose up into a steep spiral turn and look behind. There were no Germans on my tail and more amazing still there was a cluster of Spitfires; I never expected to see so many. There was one immediately on my left now – I could see his fuselage markings YT-W, in fact we almost collided. It was Paddy Finucane, and he turned very suddenly to the left and at that moment a 109 shot straight up in front of my sights. Finucane must have seen him at the same moment for he turned in again and we both opened fire together. Our tracer was plainly visible and my immediate reaction was how badly we were both shooting. We were out of range and the Me 109 was going fast (which we weren't). I pressed my boost control cut-out and felt the surge of power as the boost went suddenly up and black smoke poured from my exhausts. We were amongst the broken low cloud now and as we began to close range we could see the German making for a white cumulus. I opened fire again, aimed high, but still my fire was going low and as I released the trigger button and tried to curb my excitement, he was gone. We followed him into the cloud and were out of it in a second but no Messerschmitt. The fight, such as it was, was over.

During that attack the Germans had planted 148 bombs on the airfield. Miraculously the whole squadron got airborne except one, Hart, who had been marginally slow in getting started. A bomb dropped immediately behind him, the blast from which blew his propeller round backwards and stopped his engine. He was left sitting, as it were, in the middle of the target area but suffered no ill-effects except to his peace of mind. The rest of us considered we had beaten the world record for getting 11 Spit-fires airborne. We had, of course, been extremely lucky, but our best bit of good fortune was that the Me 109s, who came boring down at us just as we were getting airborne, hopelessly overshot us as they were going much too fast. They should have slaughtered us.

To our astonishment we were instructed to land at 'Charlie Three' the following morning, all the bomb-holes having been filled in and made good by the Pioneer Corps. When we arrived at Manston there was the remains of a Me 110 which had been hit by a Bofors shell and had dived straight into the middle of the aerodrome. So, there was at least one confirmed German and no British aircraft lost in that little disturbance.

Nearly all our many engagements with Me 109s took place at around 20,000–25,000 ft. We had the edge over them in speed and climb and particularly in turning circle, but there were one or two glaring defects with the Spitfire which needed urgent action. I used to talk with Joe Smith on the telephone or write short notes with promises of a full report later. One point was the immense tactical advantage accruing to the side which saw an enemy formation first and in good time, and conversely the rapidity with which one was in trouble if one failed to see them first. One of the most remarkable pilots in 65 Squadron was Sergeant Franklin. He had eyes like a hawk and it was noticeable that he was often the first to see and identify distant specks in the sky and draw the leader's attention to them. I found my own ability to do this improved rapidly with practice, but I never achieved anything like the skill that Franklin and some others possessed. The Spitfire was fitted with a thick, armoured-glass panel in the centre of its windscreen but the side panels were of curved perspex and the optical distortion from these made long-distance visual scanning extremely difficult. I was determined to have the design altered and indeed I succeeded in getting optically true glass into the side panels by 1941.

When milling around in an engagement at around 25,000 ft or more at full power and usually at very low airspeeds it was not long before the ethylene glycol, which comprised the coolant for the engine, began to boil at around 130°C, when it would eject a jet of steam from a small overflow pipe on the starboard side of the cowling and this would freeze all over the windscreen. Also if one had been flying at high altitude for some while and then suddenly dived down into the low, warm and moist air the inside of the screen and canopy promptly became covered with an opaque layer of frozen condensation. This blinded one for several seconds or even minutes. However, this had already been reported during test flying and steps were in hand to cure it.

One engagement with several Me 109s at about 25,000 ft over the Channel sticks in my memory. It all happened very suddenly, in fact we were mildly 'bounced' and soon I found myself behind two 109s in a steep left-hand turn. I was able to turn inside the second one and fired at him from close range. He went on pulling round as sharply as he could and I followed him without any difficulty and went on firing bursts at him and saw puffs of black smoke and then a trail of white vapour streaming from him. By this time I could no longer see the first 109 and then realised he was on my tail. As I was by now just shuddering on the g stall, I quickly turned inwards and dived. I pulled up again when I was sure I had shaken him off and, as usual on these occasions, found myself apparently completely alone in the sky and thoroughly disoriented with wildly spinning compass and gyro instruments. Eventually I found one or two other aircraft and joined up with them to return to base. I was pleased with that little episode, partly because I was damn sure that the first 109 was not going to get home and, secondly, because I was now absolutely sure the Spitfire Mk I could readily out-turn the 109, certainly in the 20,000 ft area, and probably at all heights. It was at about this time that Lee Pyman was shot down. He was a quiet and thoughtful fellow but extremely aggressive as far as attacking the Luftwaffe was concerned. He was very prone, however, to trail off on his own and expose himself to getting picked off (I had already scooped him out of one such incident), but once on to a target he would pursue it regardless of his own vulnerability. He had been peppered full of holes on 14 August, so it seemed just a matter of time before the inevitable happened.

At about this time also (18 August) Gruszka the Pole failed to return from a sortie. It had been a very active day and those two Poles of ours, both very aggressive, were also much inclined to go off on their own once anything began to happen and we assumed that Gruszka must have been shot down into the sea as there were no reports of crashed Spitfires inland which could have been his. Needless to say the unfortunate Szulkowski was terribly upset but could shed no light on the matter.*

Laurie Holland, with whom I had served at Grantham and in 'C' Flight of 17 Squadron and who was by now a Squadron Leader, now arrived to command the squadron. Very sensibly, and in view of the intensity of the operations at that time, he left Sam Saunders to lead the squadron in the air while he himself flew in Sam's section. Not long after his arrival we were again shot up on the ground at Manston by some Me 109s. This time our aircraft were being refuelled and re-armed, so were sitting ducks; but we lost only two aircraft, set on fire. Here again the Germans missed their opportunity.

Although the continuous fine weather was a feature of the Battle during August and September, there were occasional days of heavy cloud and on one such I was sent off leading a section comprising Dave Glaser and Wigg in pursuit of a lone German aircraft. This involved much vectoring around in and out of heavy cloud and at times, according to the controller, we were close to him but we never made contact. In the end it turned out to be an abortive sortie and we were all fairly tired by the end of it. The Spitfire was neither an easy nor comfortable aircraft to fly in cloud or at night and I began to reflect about possible improvements; but other than greatly increasing its stability margins about all three axes, which would probably destroy some of its good points as a fighter, there seemed to be little that could be done about it. Whatever the original specification may have said, the Spitfire was essentially a day fighter, not a night fighter.

At about this time a somewhat bizarre incident took place. Sir Charles Craven, Managing Director of Vickers-Armstrongs Ltd, had been made Chief Controller under Lord Beaverbrook in the Ministry of Aircraft Production; I received a message from him one day through Vickers House in London that on the next available opportunity I should call at Millbank for an interview with Beaverbrook. Very soon after that the squadron was 're-leased' for 24 hours so I went to London, telephoned Craven's office and was given an immediate appointment to see him and Beaverbrook. Full of curiosity and some misgiving I was ushered into Craven's outer office where I was startled to find Air Marshal

---

* In 1975 Gruszka's Spitfire was discovered in Kent with his body still in the cockpit. He was buried with full military honours at Northwood cemetery in the presence of many members of the Polish community in London. Dave Glaser and I also attended.

Sir Edgar Ludlow-Hewitt also waiting. I greeted him with due deference but it was soon clear that his visit was in no way connected with mine, and as he would be sure to be ushered into the presence ahead of a mere Flying Officer I resigned myself to a long wait.

At that point, Craven walked briskly into the room, shook me by the hand and said, 'My dear Quill, how nice of you to come'; and then, tapping my AFC ribbon with his finger he said, 'Surely you haven't got that already.'

'No, Sir', I said, 'I had it before the war.'

'Well,' he said, 'come in. The Beaver will see you now,' and whisked me into his office.

I had no chance to ask what it was all about. As I caught a glimpse of a decidedly displeased Air Marshal as we passed through the inner door, I idly wondered what would be my chances of slipping out through some other exit when my interview with Beaverbrook was over.

'The Beaver' was sitting at his desk conducting a telephone conversation in anything but a soft or mellifluous voice. To whom he was speaking I had no idea but this strange gnome-like little man was certainly making his wishes abundantly clear to whoever was on the other end of the line. He put the receiver down and Craven introduced me, and Beaverbrook said, 'Ah. Yes. Quill – good! I know all about you, young man, and I want to talk to you but right now I'm too much engaged. Come to dinner at my house tonight at eight. Stornaway House – don't be late' – and with that the little man sprang to his feet and shot out of his office by another door.

Sir Charles Craven looked at me and laughed and I said, 'Have you any idea what all this is about, Sir Charles?'

'Not much' said Craven. 'I think it may be something to do with cannons in Spitfires.'

'But I don't know anything about cannons, except that at the moment they don't work very well.'

'Ah well,' said Craven, 'I expect you'll get quite a good dinner.'

I arrived at Stornaway House in good time by taxi. There were several other people assembled and drinking pre-dinner cocktails, amongst whom were Brendan Bracken, who was Minister of Information, and Lord Hardwicke who I knew was in some way connected with Hispano-Suiza cannons. It was soon clear that they had even less idea than I as to the reason for my presence. The Beaver was nowhere to be seen and from the general drift of the conversation I gathered that the precise time of dinner was largely a matter of speculation as far as the guests were concerned. Eventually the Beaver arrived in the house with one or two acolytes and soon we were shepherded into dinner but as Beaverbrook kept going in and out of an adjoining room to speak on the telephone or deal with secretaries we were left very much to our own devices. There were some seven or eight of us at table and I sat next to Hardwicke and opposite to Bracken. The conversation was lively, amusing and sophisticated and I listened with interest, hoping for some light to be shed on the reason for my presence. Dinner wore on, with the Beaver's absences becoming longer. Eventually, and by the time the brandy and cigars were circulating, I had begun to give up all hope of finding out what it was all about and the rest of the guests were clearly beginning to wonder when our host would return. A door into an adjoining room was standing open and from the other side of that door there suddenly emerged a loud and unmistakable snore. Brendan Bracken tiptoed in to investigate and we all peered in. Beaverbrook was in an armchair, a telephone on a table beside him, sleeping soundly. After a long day at his level of furious activity this was hardly surprising. We finished our brandies and quietly and discreetly left the house.

I returned to duty at Rochford the next morning at the end of the 24-hour release period with a sense of a return to reality, rather like emerging from a darkened cinema into the sunlight of a summer's afternoon. I chatted to the Flight Sergeant and to the airmen and thought to myself, cannons or no cannons today's problem is simple: it just amounts to what the Luftwaffe will do this afternoon when we come to readiness.

In the operations rooms of fighter stations sat the Fighter Controllers. These were the men and, later, women, who, surveying the plotting-table on which was indicated the position, height and course of all incoming enemy aircraft and also the position of our own squadrons (from a locating device known as the radio contactor or 'pipsqueak'), controlled and directed us in the air by voice transmission over the R/T. When in the air everyone in the squadron could hear the controller passing information and directions to the leader. He was our prime contact with the ground and one could picture him sitting on his raised platform and looking down at the whole scene displayed in front of him. The manner in which he spoke, the clarity and authority with which he passed his information and directions and the atmosphere of calm efficiency which a good controller could impart were vital factors in the success or otherwise of the operations.

In the air everyone, quite naturally, became tense and excited. Often it was difficult enough to know what was going on anyway and this was when a really good controller was a fighter pilot's best friend – he could calm everything down and make everyone feel relaxed and well informed. At Hornchurch we had some splendid controllers but one in particular stands out in my memory: his name was Ronald Adam and in civilian life he was an actor of some distinction. Apart from being highly competent at the actual job, his voice had a quality of calm and unhesitating certainty which would have done credit to an archbishop in his pulpit. Often after an engagement one found oneself alone and disoriented in a hazy sky and calling for a homing course to steer. Adam's voice then almost shamed one into feeling 'What the hell am I getting all steamed up about?' The contribution of such men to the outcome of the Battle of Britain was incalculable.

Towards 20 August, word seeped through the grapevine that the squadron was shortly to be moved up north (to Kirton-in-Lindsey) for a rest. No doubt the squadron needed a break as they had been fighting hard since before Dunkirk, but I was a comparatively new boy. So I resolved to take the next opportunity to fly into Hornchurch, see 'Daddy' Bouchier and ask if I could be transferred to 74 Squadron when the time came for 65 Squadron to move up north. As it happened the next few days were very active and my log-book records several affrays with Me 109s, one with Dorniers and some convoy patrols. No date was yet fixed for the squadron to move and I was still awaiting an opportunity to get up to Hornchurch to see Bouchier when the blow fell.

On 24 August a signal arrived from Group instructing me to return to Supermarine because, it said, my services were required for test flying the Spitfire Mk III. I was very put out by this because I was just getting into the swing of things, still had a great deal to learn and the fighting was undoubtedly hotting up.

Furthermore I was sure that the Mk III was still in the Works being modified, and I suspected it was just a manoeuvre by Supermarine to get me back. I felt like rushing off to 'Daddy' Bouchier to try and get the order reversed, but I was advised there was little chance of this. So I spent a few hours that evening sorting out in my mind what I felt I had learned from my spell of operations and what recommendations I could make for improvements to the Spitfire. Broadly they amounted to the following: the first priority was a 'crash' programme for a huge improvement to the aileron control at high speed. The present state of affairs was a severe tactical handicap. My mind went back to the many occasions of struggling with both hands on the stick at well over 400 mph on the clock and swearing and sweating profusely as one always did, and feeling totally restricted in manoeuvre. I felt this situation had to be treated as an emergency and began to feel that the sooner I got back to Supermarine and to Joe Smith to get something moving the better. Perhaps then I could arrange to return and continue my attachment to Fighter Command.

Next, I was determined to obtain a major improvement to the optical qualities of the windscreen side panels. Also necessary was an improvement in direct rearwards vision. I did not quite see how this could be achieved in the short term although probably something could be done in the way of further bulging of the canopy (it was). In the longer term I believed a big change must be made to the lines of the rear fuselage and the shape of the canopy. This would take time but in the immediate future I felt I could try to draw attention to the urgency of the need.* I knew that most pilots were shot down by a Hun they could not see, and having had them on my own tail from time to time I felt very strongly about it. The problem of engine cutting under negative g had also been a great disadvantage in combat. The excellent Miss Schilling at the RAE, Farnborough, had already achieved a substantial amelioration of this problem but by no means a full solution. I had no idea what the final answer would be but was sure I should press very hard for it to be found. (It was, with the Bendix Stromberg carburettor, but it took a long time.)

I also wanted round-counters. You became involved in a fight and blasted off in a few bursts of fire. Then it was over for the

* In fact this came in with the Mk XVIs, XVIIIs and FR XIVs in 1944/5.

moment and you reformed with some, if not all, of the squadron. Everybody's fuel state was immediately available because both tanks of the Spitfire were accurately gauged. But how much ammunition was left? Nobody knew, except those who had not fired at all. This meant that pilots tended to assume the worst and return to base to re-arm when in fact further action was probably quite feasible. I felt, therefore, that a round-counter would be of great value and not beyond the wit of man. (This was never done.) There were many other details which needed immediate attention, such as something to stop the inside of the bullet-proof screen and interior of the canopy icing-up during a rapid descent from altitude, and a fuel spray to wash oil deposits off the outside of the screen (a fine oil deposit on the screen used sometimes to come from the De Havilland propellers which impaired vision, especially up sun).

And, finally, we all needed more performance, more fuel, and heavier fire-power. I put all these points into a report to Joe Smith and I made a strong plea for pressing on with the cannon armament. We needed better hitting power and the sooner cannons could be made to work and be introduced into regular service the better.

I also emphasised that, despite anything that pre-war doctrines may have postulated, the Spitfire was primarily an air combat fighter and also, again contrary to a widely held pre-war belief, the day of the dogfight was *not* over – it would continue to remain with us for the foreseeable future. Therefore the Spitfire should always be considered with this fact very firmly in mind.

I said goodbye to my friends in 65 Squadron with considerable sadness. I had a feeling of great unease and indeed almost shame that they would be going on fighting and I would not. I went away determined to do my best to help make the Spitfire into a better fighting machine for them and also I made up my mind that somehow I would return to that squadron. But I under-estimated the problems and the pressure of events.

The experiences of fighting against Me 109s had, however, made an indelible impression on my mind. The Spitfire's ability to out-perform, outfly and preferably outgun enemy fighters in all circumstances was now, in my view, paramount. Some sacrifice of other qualities in the aeroplane would be acceptable if it were necessary in order to achieve these aims.

15

Aileron Problems

Back at the Works the first priority was to solve the aileron problem. I have often been asked how it was that we found ourselves in the thick of the Battle of Britain with such a lamentable standard of aileron control on the Spitfire at high speeds. Indeed I asked myself the question often enough, especially when a Me 109 was on my tail.

The answer was that the problem developed by stages, was therefore not fully appreciated soon enough and, when it was appreciated, it could not be dealt with effectively in the midst of all the other development and production problems. Then the war was upon us.

The prototype aeroplane was, due to considerations of wing stiffness, limited to a maximum diving speed of 380 mph (indicated), so the quality of the aileron control could only be explored in flight up to that speed, and it was by no means too bad. It was light and effective at low and cruising speed, and at 350 mph it was firm but still responsive. Although it had become a bit heavy at 380 mph the aeroplane was still fully manoeuvrable in roll. The A & AEE at Martlesham Heath had reported on K5054 in September 1936: 'The aeroplane was dived to 380 mph ASI and up to that speed the ailerons were not unduly heavy, and gave adequate response.'* This lined up precisely with my feelings at the time and those of Mutt Summers and George Pickering. Indeed our general assessment of the aileron control of K5054 was 'very good' and no one seemed to disagree.

Then, in May 1938, out came the first production aeroplane (K9787) with a much stiffer wing and its maximum diving speed increased by nearly 100 mph to 470 mph IAS. This was much higher indicated airspeed than had been achieved by any of the Schneider Trophy seaplanes or indeed by any other aeroplane anywhere at that time and I well remember, after I first dived

* A & AEE Report No. M/692/Int 2.

K9787 up to 470 mph on the clock at a height which produced a true airspeed of well over 500 mph, Ernie Mansbridge gave me a jocular slap on the back afterwards and said, 'How does it feel to be the fastest man in the world?' So, unsatisfactory as the ailerons on K9787 were, it is all too easy to forget today that at the time we were probing well into previously unexplored speed regions. On K9787 I did a number of these high-speed dives and found the ailerons almost solid at 470 mph IAS. It was a two-handed job to manoeuvre the aeroplane even a small amount laterally at that speed. Even at 400 mph it was very heavy, though manageable, and at 380 mph it was, in my judgement, heavier than the proto-type at the same speed. All this was reported, and the A & AEE reported it too. Indeed their comment on K9787 (issued in October 1938) stated quite categorically that the ailerons were excessively heavy at high speeds and that 'this characteristic may make it difficult to obtain accurate gun aiming at high speeds'.

By the time that report was written, however, we at Super-marine were already trying to find a remedy. In August 1938 I made several flights in K9791 (the aircraft we had at Supermarine for development work) using the Henschel stick force recorder to measure aileron loads in flight so as at least to quantify the problem. Then, using the same aircraft, we tested a modified pair of ailerons with an improved surface finish achieved by flush stringing. This produced some improvement at medium speeds, bringing the production aeroplane more into line with the proto-type, but the ailerons were still much too heavy above 400 mph. We then tried a set of ailerons with double the number of ribs, which it was hoped would eliminate ballooning of the fabric covering or distortion of the aileron structure at speed. Again there was no noticeable improvement above 380 mph.

Therefore it is fair to say that from the initial flights on the first production Spitfire (K9787) it was observed and reported by test pilots – not only George Pickering and myself at Supermarine but also by the RAF test pilots at Martlesham and Farnborough – that the aileron control of the Spitfire, though excellent at low and medium speeds, was much too heavy at speeds above 400 mph. The design department at Supermarine, the aerodynamics and flight handling research people at RAE, and the technical branches at Air Ministry all took note of the matter. Initially, however, it tended to be registered in everyone's mind as one of those problems (and there were plenty of others) which would have to be solved when we could get around to it. Moreover, the heaviness of the ailerons at high speed did not represent any safety hazard. On the contrary, I have always taken the view that technical and design people concerned with structural strength, wing stiffness and flutter aspects were privately somewhat relieved that at these very high diving speeds pilots could not apply large aileron displacements nor manoeuvre the aeroplane too briskly.

It may seem strange that no one at that time suggested that severe tactical limitations would be imposed by the heavy ailerons. This can probably be accounted for by the fact that the Air Staff regarded the Spitfire (and the Hurricane) as being primarily for home defence and hence bomber destroyers rather than as being designed for dog-fighting against other fighters. The air threat to this country was seen to comprise massed raids by enemy bombers and it was not thought that German single-seat single-engined fighters could ever appear over Great Britain because they had no bases within range. Moreover those surviving officers with operational fighter experience from the First World War had fought in Sopwith Pups, Camels and SE5As in fighter-to-fighter dog-fights over the static Western front and their aeroplanes had been capable of not much more than 100–120 mph. Now here was a fighter flying more than four times as fast and the concept of a dog-fight at such speeds seemed to them grotesque. Contemporary wisdom, certainly amongst senior officers, therefore simply assumed that the day of the dog-fight was long past. Thus the sort of operational scenario with which we were in fact confronted after the fall of France in 1940 had not been foreseen before the war, nor had that of the offensive sweeps in 1941 and 1942 which led to daily fighter-to-fighter combats over northern France and the Low Countries. So in 1938–9 the aileron problem was not regarded as critical nor so desperately urgent as the need to catch up the shortfall in the delivery programme, to form and train the squadrons, to develop the aircraft to full operational standard and get spares delivered and to establish how the squadron pilots were taking to the aeroplane and how the maintenance crews were coping with it. These were the things then uppermost in most people's minds. This is not to say that nobody did anything about the problem, but it was not until the beginning of 1940 that Supermarine and the RAE initiated a formal aileron improvement programme to try to improve the situation.

Towards the end of 1939 Sam McKenna of the A & AEE flew a French Air Force Curtiss Hawk and reported favourably on its aileron control, saying it was more manoeuvrable at high speed than either the Hurricane or the Spitfire. I got my hands on this aeroplane at Farnborough on 2 January 1940 and the aileron control was indeed excellent, but the limiting diving speed of the Curtiss was less than that of the Spitfire so the comparison was not entirely valid. Moreover the gearing between stick and aileron was lower on the Curtiss giving greater mechanical advantage to the pilot, so although one could move the stick about more easily at high speed the response in terms of rate of roll was not all that much better; however, the Curtiss was certainly more manoeuvrable. This was really the beginning of a general acceptance that the lateral manoeuvrability of the Hurricane and Spitfire was simply not good enough. Meetings were held at the RAE and at Supermarine towards the end of 1939 and at the beginning of 1940, and possible solutions were discussed. A programme was agreed for the testing of various modifications and a certain number of Spitfires on charge of the Air Member for Development and Production (AMDP) were allocated to Supermarine and the RAE for use in the programme; but when in May 1940 the Germans overran the Low Countries and penetrated deeply into France, the war entered a stage of extreme crisis and the decision was made on 20 May that all these AMDP aircraft were to be returned at once to front-line squadron service. Thus the first aileron improvement programme came to an abrupt halt.

By this time I was bitterly blaming myself for not having thumped the table much harder about the aileron problem from the moment I first flew K9787 in May 1938. If we had tackled it a bit earlier and with more urgency we might perhaps have cured the trouble before the outbreak of war. However production problems at the time made any design changes almost impossible to embody.

The aileron problem was further compounded by what could be described as 'non-repeatability' or variations in manufacturing accuracy. On first take-off a new production Spitfire would usually be found to be flying severely one wing low, sometimes to the extent that it was almost a two-handed job to hold it. The aircraft would immediately be brought in to land again and a trimming strip, comprising a piece of cord sewn inside a length of fabric, would be attached to the upper trailing edge of the aileron on the 'wing low' side. It usually took several flights to achieve the right length of trimming strip to make the aircraft fly level in cruising flight. Then the flight test schedule would be continued, culminating in a dive to the limiting speed of 470 mph. Usually, but not always, if the aircraft had been successfully trimmed at cruising speed it remained in trim at this very high diving speed. But sometimes it would develop a strong bias one way or the other. In these circumstances an aileron had to be changed and discarded or tried again on another aeroplane. Thus very small production variations in the hinges, the slotted shrouds in the wing, the profile of the aileron nose balances and the aileron profile aft of the hinge could have a spectacular effect on the lateral handling of each production aeroplane.

So the ailerons virtually had to be individually 'tuned' by the test pilot (who had to know what he was about) and it usually took several flights to achieve this. Sometimes if an aileron had been discarded as untrimmable on one aeroplane it could be refitted to another and found to be quite all right, so it was a question of matching the variations on both aileron and wing. If, however, after delivery to the Service, an aileron was changed the whole matching process was destroyed and the aeroplane might fly very badly indeed. There were frequent reports from squadrons of so-called 'rogue' aeroplanes and it usually transpired that an aileron had been changed or that someone had monkeyed about with the trimming arrangements.

The reports which floated in to the A & AEE and RAE through HQ Fighter Command on these so-called 'rogue' aeroplanes did much to confuse the issue during our early efforts to deal with the problem. Provided the ailerons were correctly 'tuned' and the aeroplane correctly flown, there was really only one central problem – the ailerons were much too heavy at speed.

When I got back to the firm after my service in 65 Squadron a new aileron improvement programme had been set up but on a strictly ad hoc basis, in that only such changes as could be quickly tested and quickly and easily applied retrospectively to existing aeroplanes should be allowed. This had been agreed between Joe Smith and John Serby, AD/RDL* at the Ministry of Aircraft Production and Irving of the RAE at a meeting in August. The various items to be tested were variations to the area of the entries and exits to the slot (or shroud) between the wing and the nose of the aileron; variations to the shape of the nose of the aileron forward of the hinge; the incorporation of geared tab balances at the trailing edge of the ailerons; and lastly metal skinning of the whole aileron and particularly thinning of the trailing edges. (Some tests at the National Physical Laboratory had suggested that very thin trailing edges would do much to lighten aileron control at high speed.)

I started on this programme on Spitfire X4268 within two days of returning from Hornchurch, and we worked our way through a whole series of variations including geared tab balances and blunt noses, but nothing showed much result, while some, indeed, made matters worse. George Pickering and Alex Henshaw flew on this programme too. Then, just as we were beginning to feel thoroughly depressed about the situation I tested, on 7 November, a pair of metal-skinned ailerons with thin trailing edges on Spitfire R6718. I remember doubting, as I taxied out, whether they would make much difference. In fact they changed the situation in the most spectacular way, being much lighter at the top end of the speed range without any loss of effectiveness at low or medium speeds. The aeroplane was transformed. I flew it four times more that day and threw it about violently to try to find some snag or some undesirable feature, but I could not. George and Alex flew it and agreed it was a huge improvement. I called Joe Smith and reported to him. I flew again twice more on 8 November and then in some excitement I flew R6718 to Farnborough where it was flown by Willy Wilson (OC Aerodynamics Flight) and Roly Falk and they reported a 'vast improvement on anything so far tested'; 'excellent control'; 'control gently stiffens up in the correct ratio'; 'consider all Spitfires should be modified as soon as possible'.

These ailerons were transferred to X4268 for check tests and on 19 November I took this aircraft to Westhampnett where it

---

* Assistant Director, Research & Development (Landplanes).

was flown by the OC 602 Squadron, Squadron Leader 'Sandy' Johnstone, on orders from HQ Fighter Command. On the same day the A & AEE at Boscombe Down reported that 'all pilots agreed a vast improvement in aileron control' the only criticism being that the control was now perhaps 'a little too light'.

It was quickly agreed that an urgent programme to metal-skin all ailerons should be initiated at once and all Spitfires should be fitted with them as soon as possible. Supermarine and Castle Bromwich put them into production at once and Air Service Training (AST) at Hamble started a programme of modification of existing ailerons.

After 'Sandy' Johnstone's flight at Westhampnett the word swept round Fighter Command like wildfire and in no time the air around Hamble was thick with the Spitfires of Wing Leaders and Squadron Commanders all trying to jump the queue to get their aircraft fitted with the new metal ailerons – Douglas Bader leading the hunt!

It certainly was a blessed relief to me. Although the 'non-repeatability' problem remained and there was too much variation between individual aircraft and ailerons still had to be individually tuned there was nevertheless an enormous overall improvement and the Spitfire became a vastly better fighter almost overnight.

I have mentioned how badly I felt about the ailerons of the Spitfire at the time of the Battle of Britain. In October 1940 I flew a captured Me 109E; to my surprise and relief I found the aileron control of the German fighter every bit as bad, if not worse than, at high speed as the Spitfire I and II with fabric-covered ailerons. It was good at low and medium speed but at 400 mph and above it was almost immovable. I thought the Me 109E performed well, particularly on the climb at altitude, and it had good stalling characteristics under g except that the leading-edge slats kept snapping in and out; but it had no rudder trimmer, which gave it a heavy footload at high speed; while the cockpit, the canopy and the rearward vision were much worse than in the Spitfire. Had I flown the Me 109 earlier I would have treated the aeroplane with less respect in combat.

The A & AEE reported on the Me 109E in October 1941: 'The flying controls have excellent response and feel at low speeds but are far too heavy for manoeuvring at high speeds. The extreme heaviness of the ailerons makes rolling almost impossible at speeds above 400 mph.'

So we were not the only ones in trouble in 1940. The metal ailerons solved the immediate problem but the non-repeatability difficulty persisted and I always felt that the aileron characteristics fell far short of perfect at high indicated airspeeds. Joe Smith believed this too. He began to plan a fundamental change in the aileron design, but it was not possible to introduce this until the arrival of the stronger and stiffer wing in the Mk 21 series.

On 24 September 1940 at about 1330 hours a daylight raid by the Luftwaffe severely damaged the Itchen Works, Southampton. An air raid shelter received a direct hit and 90 Supermarine employees were killed with some 40 other casualties.

Two days later (26 September) a further raid finished off the Itchen Works and completely destroyed the Woolston Works killing a further 37 of the work force and killing another 52 people in the surrounding areas. Spitfire production at Southampton was brought to a standstill.

Such a possibility had obviously been foreseen and during 1939 L.G. Gooch had been appointed Works Engineer, which meant that he was responsible for the proper maintenance and functioning of all the plant and machinery. In particular he had been given the task of planning a dispersal scheme for the Southampton production area, should enemy action make it necessary. As a start he had requisitioned a bus station in Southampton and three sizeable garages.

Some vital jigs and tools had already been moved out of Woolston into these premises at the time of the bombing so the works were not caught completely unprepared. Nevertheless the situation was critical and when Lord Beaverbrook, the recently appointed Minister of Aircraft Production, saw the damage to the factory and to the work people's homes surrounding it he ordered the immediate dispersal of the whole of the Supermarine Works over southern England.

The design department and drawing office were transferred immediately to University College in Southampton, the Management into a floor of the Polygon Hotel and the accounts and commercial departments moved into a requisitioned house.

Planning and implementation of the complete dispersal of the works started at once from the temporary headquarters in the Polygon Hotel and a number of Beaverbrook's personal staff moved down from London to assist in the whole complex operation which spread over Hampshire, Dorset, Wiltshire and Berkshire. Some time later both Design and Works administration moved into Hursley Park, near Winchester.

The dispersed manufacture, assembly and flight testing of Spitfires by Supermarine in the Southern Region – as distinct from the Castle Bromwich factory outside Birmingham – was split up into the Trowbridge, Newbury, Southampton, Salisbury and Reading areas. Each area was put in the charge of a single area manager answerable to Len Gooch as overall Works Manager who in turn was responsible to the Works Superintendent, W.T. Elliot, and ultimately to Jimmy Bird as General Manager. Thus Len Gooch became the man responsible for the efficient working of the dispersal scheme he had planned and set up. He was thirty years old.

Each area had its own airfield to which fully equipped wings and fuselages were trucked and rapidly assembled where they were flown and tested by our test pilots and then collected by the Air Transport Auxiliary. There was a total of 35 dispersal sites where details, sub-assemblies and main assemblies were manufactured and these sites were requisitioned garages, bus stations, laundries, a rolling mill and a traction engine factory! The total productive work force grew to about 10,000, of which at one time 45 per cent were female, and altogether some 8,000 Spitfire aircraft were produced in the Southern Region after the bombing of the main works in 1940. The whole of this extraordinary effort was administered from the company headquarters at Hursley Park but the management structure was starkly simple and is shown in Appendix 1.

One of the great merits of the Southern Region dispersal scheme* was its flexibility. It was the very antithesis of a monolithic structure and the area managers had great scope for the exercise of their initiative and powers of improvisation. Therefore as new Marks of Spitfire had to be brought into production, often involving the most complicated modifications, such as, for

* See Appendices 2 and 3.

instance, turning the wing leading edge structure into an integral fuel tank for the PRU aircraft, and the early conversion of the Mk V into the Mk IX, the Southern Region had the flexibility to get production going in the minimum time. Often there were several different Marks of Spitfire in production simultaneously.

The men and women who performed this remarkable feat of improvisation and production have gone largely unsung and unhonoured but in my opinion no words of praise for them can be adequate. Len Gooch, who was really the driving force behind it, was awarded a well-deserved OBE. He really did rescue, resurrect and expand Spitfire production at a most critical time after the disastrous bombing of the works in September 1940.

16

The Tide of Development

Some idea of the scope of the development which actually took place between 1939 and 1945 can be gathered by the list of operational variants of the Spitfire which were produced for front-line service*, a total of 52. Some of these, admittedly, were very minor variants confined to small differences in armament or the supercharger characteristics of their engines. Other variants were fundamental and the outward configuration and appearance of the Spitfire changed a great deal over the years.

In the course of the development process the all-up weight of the aircraft, the horsepower and other characteristics of its engines and the punch of its armament all increased dramatically. A favourite statistic, as a rough illustration of the extent of the development achieved, is to quote the maximum all-up weight of the last of the operational variants of the Spitfire to enter service, the Seafire F. Mk 47, and to point out that it was equivalent to the first service version, the Mk I of 1938, taking off with 32 airline passengers plus baggage on board (see Appendix 10).

The extent of the development of the Spitfire achieved by Supermarine would not have been possible without the parallel development of its engines, the Merlins and the Griffons, achieved by Rolls-Royce. In fact, to a large extent it was engine development and power growth that led the way, in parallel with the need to enhance the military effectiveness of the aircraft. The power of the Merlin engine increased from 1000 bhp in 1936 to over 1700 bhp in 1944 and the band of heights at which this power was available widened greatly, which was of vital tactical significance. The power of the larger and basically more powerful Griffon engine increased from 1735 bhp in 1941 to 2350 bhp in 1945. In both cases this was achieved primarily by improvements in supercharger technology.

* See Appendix 4.

Before the arrival of jet propulsion the horsepower developed at the shaft of an aero-engine had to be converted into forward thrust by means of a propeller rotating in the air. The early Spitfires had been fitted with simple two-bladed fixed-pitch wooden propellers, but these were soon replaced by three-bladed variable-pitch propellers and, later, constant-speed propellers; and, as the amount of horsepower to be converted into thrust progressively increased, the number of propeller blades had to be increased and we moved from two blades to three, then four, then five, and finally to six-bladed contra-rotating propellers. Propellers were therefore a crucial factor in the development process and credit for this must go to De Havilland and Rotol.

It was not only in performance as a fighter aircraft that the Spitfire greatly improved. It expanded and extended its capabilities to embrace other military roles. For instance, as the Seafire, it became a Naval carrier-borne fighter, something which had never been even remotely considered at the time of its original design. Also, fitted with automatic cameras pointing vertically downwards and special long-range fuel tankage, the Spitfire became an unarmed high-speed high-altitude long-range Photographic Reconnaissance aeroplane, relying on its speed and height for survival.

However, the main thrust of its progress was concentrated upon the fighter roles, whether operating ashore or afloat, so that the main development effort went into achieving continuous improvement in the basic characteristics required for better fighting in the air – more speed, higher rate of climb, better manoeuvrability, more firepower, more range and endurance. These central objectives determined the main march of events and the other role variants benefited from them. The Photographic Reconnaissance Mk XIX, for example, an aircraft of spectacular performance, derived directly from the Mk XIV fighter. The fact that the operational effectiveness of the Photographic Reconnaissance Mks X and XIX was greatly enhanced by the provision of a pressure cabin for their pilots resulted directly from the initial development of pressure cabins for the Mks VI and VII fighters which were produced in response to the urgent need for a high-altitude fighter to meet a high-altitude bomber threat foreseen early in the war. So the fighters constituted the central lines of development and led the way. The Photographic

Reconnaissance and Naval variants followed in their wake.

The main lines of development of the fighter variants from which sprang all the many sub-variants can be shown diagrammatically, but covering only those aircraft which went into production and front-line service:

Merlin-Engined Spitfires   *Griffon-Engined Spitfires*

Mks I & II
|
Mks VA VB
|
Mk VC_____
| |
Mks VI & VII
(pressure cabins)   Mk XII
|
Mks IX & VIII_____
| Mks XIV & XVIII
Mk XVI |
                      Mk 21
                          |
                      Mks 22 & 24

All other variants, whether Photographic Reconnaissance or Naval, sprang from this basic line of combat types.

The availability in production of an improved version of one of the Rolls-Royce engines, offering more power, or the same power at a greater height, or both, was the principal factor leading to the design of a new mark of Spitfire which would then incorporate heavier armaments, longer range, more speed and height or an expansion of role capability. The Mk III, for example, which flew only in prototype form, was really designed to exploit the first Merlin engine to be fitted with a two-speed supercharger providing increased power over a wider height band. So the opportunity was taken to redesign the windscreen, develop a retractable tail-wheel and experiment with a wing of considerably reduced span and greater armament potential. Although the Mk III did not go into production these other refinements found their way into other production marks.

By 1941 an improved Merlin, the 45, had been developed. It retained a single-stage supercharger, but provided more power

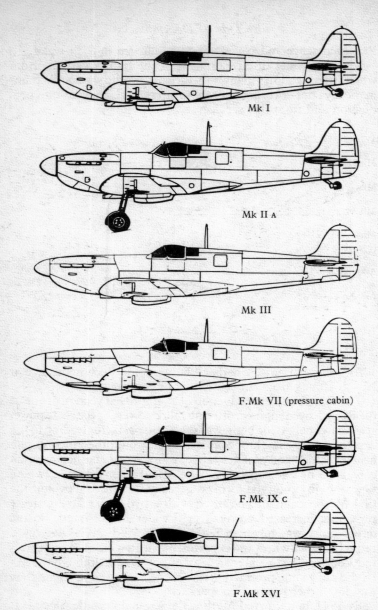

Mk I

Mk II A

Mk III

F.Mk VII (pressure cabin)

F.Mk IX c

F.Mk XVI

Fig. 3   Merlin-Engined Spitfires

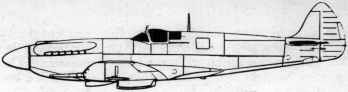

Mk XII

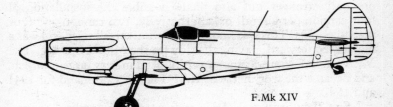

F.Mk XIV

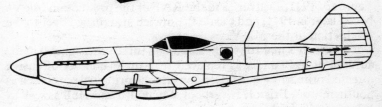

F.R.Mk XIV E

Mk F.21

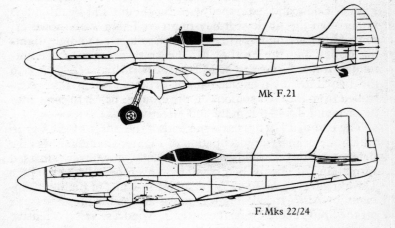

F.Mks 22/24

Fig. 4 Griffon-Engined Spitfires

and ran at higher manifold pressure. This produced the Mk V Spitfire, which came out in three basic versions: the VA, VB and VC, the principal difference being in their armament. The VA retained the eight .303 machine-guns of the Mk I, the VB was fitted with two 20-mm Hispano-Suiza cannon and four .303 machine-guns and the VC had a more advanced wing which was not only stronger but also made possible the installation of four cannon per aircraft or, alternatively, two cannon and four machine-guns. This was known as the 'universal' wing and was a major step forward, paving the way for the Mk IX Spitfire. The Mk V, in its various forms, was produced in very large numbers and became the workhorse of RAF Fighter Command for 1941 and 1942.

I first flew Spitfire X4922, converted to a Merlin 45, on 1 February 1941. Deliveries to the RAF of the production Mk VA began later in 1941, and Castle Bromwich also turned over to the production of the Mk V.

The enemy's main daylight assault on this country ended in the autumn of 1940 and was replaced by a night-bomber offensive directed primarily against London and the principal ports such as Southampton, Bristol, Liverpool, Plymouth and Hull as well as various industrial centres, such as Clydebank. This period, 'the blitz', obviously concerned the night-fighter squadrons of Fighter Command, equipped with Blenheims and Beaufighters rather than the single-seat day-fighters. There were, however, some Hurricane and Spitfire squadrons allocated to night-fighting duties, but the Spitfire was never a very practical night-fighter. It was during this period that airborne radar (AI) fitted to the two-seater twin-engined night-fighters, which were controlled from the GCI stations on the ground, began to come into its own and develop rapidly and effectively.

The end of 1940 thus saw the end of the phase of the war in which the primary preoccupation of Fighter Command was the defence of these islands against daylight assaults by massed formations of enemy bombers. In November 1940 Sir Hugh Dowding was replaced as Commander-in-Chief of Fighter Command by Air Marshal Sholto Douglas and as the pressure came off the Spitfire squadrons the latter initiated a series of offensive operations designed to carry the air battle into the skies over enemy-occupied territory. These operations took, broadly, three forms. First, when the weather was suitable, large-scale fighter sweeps or offensive patrols across the Channel and over enemy territory; secondly, day-bomber raids against some specific target or targets escorted by very large numbers of fighters disposed as close escorts and top cover, and perhaps some diversionary activities as well; and thirdly, 'rhubarbs'. These were low-level marauding sorties by pairs of fighters, operating below cloud against ground targets of opportunity, in poor weather. All this, started at the end of 1940, can be said to have general rather than specific objectives. The intention was to move Fighter Command into an offensive posture – 'leaning towards the enemy', Sholto called it – and this would be healthy for the morale not only of Fighter Command but of the country as a whole. Secondly it would bring the enemy into the air to fight and so force him to maintain substantial fighter strength in France and the Low Countries, thereby drawing them away from other theatres of operation. Thirdly these were the only offensive daylight operations, on a reasonably large scale, which were available to us within Europe at that time. These operations increased in scale and scope during 1941 and 1942 and the Mk V development proceeded primarily in response to their requirements – greater range by the incorporation of external and jettisonable fuel tanks; increased firepower by the continued refinement of the two-cannon wing (VB) and the development of a redesigned wing accommodating either four cannon or two cannon with four machine-guns (VC), the substitution of VHF radio for the old TR9D HF sets, and many other refinements to improve fighting efficiency. Mark Vs were later sent to the Middle East and other overseas Commands and a total of 6,479 was produced altogether by Supermarine and Castle Bromwich.

During the latter half of 1941 a new German fighter began to appear over the Channel and northern France. This was the FW 190 and it was soon apparent that it could outfight the Spitfire V. It appeared to be more heavily armed and to have a higher rate of roll. As more FW 190s appeared the tactical initiative swung away from Fighter Command and in favour of the Luftwaffe. The nature of the operations placed the prime emphasis upon fighter-to-fighter combat and so upon relative fighter performance. When engagements took place the Fighter Command squadrons tended to be at the limit of their range, a long way from their bases, and so were fighting at a severe tactical disadvantage. When the enemy also had the additional advantage of having an aircraft of apparently superior performance the situation was becoming extremely serious, and Fighter Command losses began to mount.

An aircraft of much better fighting performance than the Mk V was urgently required to redress the balance of tactical advantage. Fortunately, in the nick of time, it was developed in the form of the Spitfire Mk IX (see Chapter 17).

17

Quantum Jump:

Spitfire Mks IX and VIII

In October 1939 the firm of General Aircraft Limited (GAL) had submitted to the Air Ministry a design for a high-altitude fighter embodying a pressure cabin. Amongst much else, this design proposal contained a statement of considerable significance. It said that a study of German patent specifications had revealed that Germany was well advanced in her thinking about aircraft operations at very high altitude. This served to concentrate the Air Staff minds upon the threats of attack by high-flying German bombers against which the only defence would be very high-altitude fighters which, at the time, did not exist. The GAL design proposals were considered on 1 November 1939 and again on 18 April 1940 when a meeting took place at the Air Ministry presided over by Air Vice-Marshal Roderick Hill, Director of Technical Development. At this meeting reference was made to the strongly expressed wish of the Air Staff to 'develop high-altitude fighters' and the meeting decided that a Specification should be issued for a fighter suitable for use up to 45,000 ft (the General Aircraft design had envisaged only 37,500 ft). Certain firms were to be invited to tender designs, including General Aircraft Ltd.

Clearly such a requirement implied two essential needs: the development of pressure cabins to enable the crew to function efficiently, and special engines able to take an aircraft up to such a great height.

At the meeting of 18 April it was also decided to ask the Deputy Director of Research and Development (Engines) to advise on how engine development could lead to an engine capable of such performance within two years.

There was also discussion of the development, as an interim measure, of variants of existing fighters (which really meant the

Spitfire) for use up to 40,000 ft using pressure suits instead of pressure cabins. All this implied developments to the Merlin engine toward significant improvement in its high-altitude performance. Rolls-Royce's work on the development of two-stage supercharging for the Merlin really dated from this period.

Moreover, an equal stimulus to the work on very high altitude engines lay in the Air Staff's desire to develop pressure cabin bombers and a high-altitude version of the Wellington was already under development at Weybridge.

Two-*speed* supercharging had been largely a mechanical problem involving a gear change mechanism to speed up the rotation of the supercharger impeller at the higher altitudes. This had already been incorporated in the Merlin XX engine, which had been fitted to the Mk III Spitfire. Two-*stage* supercharging was another matter altogether. It involved the provision of a second stage of compression – the fitting of a second supercharger in series with the first – but this would cause heating of the fuel/air mixture to an unacceptable extent thus causing detonation in the cylinders. Therefore the fuel/air mixture needed to be cooled, and for this it was passed through an inter-cooler, or heat exchanger, situated between the supercharger and the engine. This produced a larger more complex and longer and heavier supercharger unit at the rear of the engine and increased the overall length of the engine by 9 in. This engine, designated the Merlin 60, produced great increases in power throughout the height range and in particular at the higher altitudes.

Once the crisis of the Battle of Britain was over urgent thought was again given by the Air Staff, and the Ministry of Aircraft Production, to the development of a defence against high-altitude bombing. Intelligence reports indicated that Germany had developed a high-altitude version of the Ju 86, and that at least one such aircraft had already been operating over the UK.

In January 1941 the concern of Air Chief Marshal Sir Charles Portal, the Chief of the Air Staff, himself was indicated by a question he addressed to the Assistant Chief of Air Staff (Tactics): 'What is being done to develop high-altitude fighters to deal with enemy bombers with pressure cabins enabling flight at, say, 45,000 feet?'

As a result on 29 January 1941 Air Vice-Marshal Hill, then Director-General of Research and Development at the Ministry of Aircraft Production, visited E.W. Hives at Rolls-Royce at Derby, to discuss modifications to increase the ceiling of the Merlin, which might be applied to a small number of engines for special high-altitude duties. He afterwards reported that Rolls-Royce were experimenting with the use of Methanol to cool the charge temperature, with a higher 'S' gear in their two-speed supercharger, and also with a supercharger with a second stage of compression. Under Ernest Hives, the man at Rolls-Royce responsible for design aspects of the Merlin was Arthur Rubbra and under him were two senior development engineers, Cyril Lovesey and Stanley Hooker. The latter was charged with the task of extracting ever-increasing power outputs from the Merlin, which he did primarily by developing increased levels of supercharging, whereas Cyril Lovesey's task was the preservation of the mechanical integrity and reliability of the engine as the power outputs were increased.

Meanwhile, by late 1940 the Air Staff had accepted the idea of two classes of day-fighter: one with a pressurised cabin for high-altitude operations, the other unpressurised for operations at more normal heights. This concept, which they had previously resisted, was formally accepted by them in a minute dated 29 April 1941 in which future fighter requirements policy was stated as follows:

(1) A pressure cabin aircraft with a ceiling of 41,000 ft at first, later increasing to 45,000 ft;

(2) An unpressurised fighter able to fight up to 35,000 ft with a maximum speed of over 400 mph at 20,000/25,000 ft and a service ceiling of 38,000 to 40,000 ft.

Not only did this add further impetus to the development of two-stage supercharging for the Merlin engine at Rolls-Royce, it also confirmed the requirement for Supermarine to develop a pressure cabin version of the Spitfire which eventually led to the Mk VI and Mk VII Spitfires.

By April 1941 Rolls-Royce were running, on the test-bed, an engine with a two-stage supercharger, with a view at that stage to its applicability to a high-altitude pressurised Wellington and to a pressure cabin Spitfire, and by June they were ready to proceed with a trial installation. The old Spitfire Mk III prototype N3297 happened to be at the Rolls-Royce experimental flight unit at Hucknall at the time and it was decided that this (non-pressurised) aeroplane should be used for flight tests of the new engine. Spitfire N3297 first flew with the experimental two-stage engine, designated the Merlin 61, on 20 September 1941 at Hucknall and on 8 October it was decided that a duplicate installation should be built by Rolls-Royce in a Mk I aeroplane, R6700, to enable more flying to be accumulated on the engine. I started flying this aeroplane at Worthy Down on 7 January 1942.

Meanwhile N3297, fitted with the prototype Merlin 61 engine, had gone to Boscombe Down for official performance checks on 20 October 1941. There were a number of features about the aeroplane which would tend to give over-optimistic performance figures (such as radiator areas insufficient for service use, non-representative weight and no cannon fitted in the wings). Nevertheless, the results showed a spectacular improvement over the Mk V Spitfire – a maximum speed of 422 mph at 27,000 ft and an operational ceiling of 38,000 ft with an absolute ceiling of nearly 43,000 ft.

In August 1941 the AOC-in-C of Fighter Command, Air Marshal Sholto Douglas, had submitted a 'Most Secret' memorandum to the Chief of the Air Staff expressing grave concern about the ability of Fighter Command, equipped with Spitfire Vs, to maintain its present relative position against the Luftwaffe by the spring of 1942. He drew urgent attention to the need for improvements to the performance of the Spitfire which, above 31,000 ft, was already inferior to the Me 109F both in speed and climb. As a result a very high-level meeting was held at the Air Ministry in London on 10 September 1941 with the Chief of the Air Staff in the chair to discuss this problem and the performance of fighter aircraft which would be available by April 1942.

The technical branches of the M.A.P. were not optimistic about the future, but the Controller of Research and Development (CRD, Linnell) reported that 300 pressure-cabin Spitfires, with Merlin 61 engines, had been ordered and it was thought that the engine could, if necessary, be fitted to 'an unpressurised version of the Spitfire Mk VI' (which in effect meant the Spitfire V). This was only a suggestion at that stage, but within a couple of months figures for the performance of the Spitfire with the two-stage Merlin (N3297) became available.

These at once indicated the answer to Fighter Command's worries. However, the appearance of increasing numbers of the FW 190, which was showing itself more highly manoeuvrable and heavily armed than any other Luftwaffe aircraft, in the early spring of 1942 intensified the need for a greatly improved Spitfire, and the result was a 'crash' programme to convert the Spitfire Vc to Merlin 61 engines and to put them into squadron service as quickly as possible. The conversion required a substantial modification to the cooling system, involving the fitting of an additional external radiator under the starboard wing in place of the old oil cooler unit, and so considerable modification to the pipe runs was needed and a good deal of engineering adjustment. New engine cowlings and a four-bladed Rotol propeller were required. The first conversions for service use were made, some at Hucknall and some at Supermarine, and were not entirely interchangeable. The aircraft was designated the Spitfire Mk IX and was soon in proper production at Supermarine and later at Castle Bromwich. A total of 5,665 were eventually built, the bulk of them at Castle Bromwich.

When I started flying R6700, I was so impressed by its performance that I decided one day, without any official sanction, to fly it to Hornchurch and get Harry Broadhurst, who was by then a Group Captain and commanding the station there, to fly it. He was a very experienced operational pilot in Spitfires. I also knew that if he was as much impressed with it as I was the word would very quickly be passed to his AOC in 11 Group, Leigh-Mallory, and thence to the C-in-C, Sholto Douglas.

So I rang Broady, arranged to have lunch with him at Hornchurch, and flew there in R6700. I told him I had a Spitfire with a new engine and thought he might like to fly it and I kept things as casual as possible because I did not want to enthuse over the aeroplane before he had flown it. We arranged that he would fly it after lunch. The Hornchurch Wing, which was led by Pete Powell, was due to take off on a sweep that afternoon and Broady and I saw them off, sitting in his staff car. I then saw him into R6700 and as he climbed aboard he said, 'I've told my driver to take you to the Ops Room. You can sit with the Controller and watch the Wing in action.' The underground Operations Room at Hornchurch was a little way from the airfield and by the time I arrived and sat beside the Controller, Ronald Adam, whom I remembered from 65 Squadron days, I could see from the plots on the table that the Wing was over the Channel heading for the French coast. Adam told me they were going to sweep round behind Lille at about 25,000 ft and return. As the Wing was approaching the coast at Boulogne I noticed that behind them, there was a single aircraft plot. I watched this for a bit, without thinking much about it, and then at a suitable opportunity I said to Adam: 'What's that plot there?'

'Oh,' he said, 'that's the Station Commander.'

'Goddammit,' I said, 'he's in my aeroplane! Do you realise that's the most important prototype fighter in the country right now – and what's more the guns aren't loaded!'

'Well – there's nothing I can do about it,' Adam replied, 'but right now he seems to be well over 35,000 feet.'

'Thank God for that,' I said and resigned myself to a very anxious wait, for there was a great deal of reaction from the Luftwaffe that day and the Wing was quite heavily engaged. I began to consider how I would explain away the circumstance that I took off from Worthy Down in the morning in the trial installation Merlin 61 aircraft belonging to CRD and before the day was out it had been shot down in France.

Fortunately Broady returned safely, duly impressed with the aeroplane, and, as I had expected, it was not long before the word spread into the upper reaches of Group and Command Headquarters. The first Squadron to be equipped with Mk IX aircraft was No. 64, at Hornchurch, which was commanded by another old friend, Group Captain Duncan Smith*, who had also flown R6700 on the day that Broadhurst did. They began to receive their new aircraft in June 1942 and very sensibly decided that they would not go into action against the enemy until they had a complete Squadron, for they did not want to lose the element of surprise.

The great thing about the appearance of the Mk IX at that juncture was that it was extremely difficult for the German pilots to distinguish a Mk IX from a Mk V in the air. Therefore every Spitfire in the sky soon became potentially a Mk IX to the German pilots. This had a marked effect upon their confidence and thus upon the level of their aggressive tactics.

---

* Duncan Smith has described their first engagement with FW 190s in *Spitfire into Battle* (John Murray, 1981).

However, the almost euphoric atmosphere which accompanied the introduction of the Mk IX into RAF operational service was destined to be somewhat short-lived. On 23 June 1942 Oberleutnant Arnim Faber, having become disoriented in the course of an air combat over the Channel with Spitfires operating from Exeter, landed his FW 190 at Pembrey in south Wales. The aeroplane, completely undamaged, was immediately sent to the RAE at Farnborough. This enabled Farnborough to carry out some proper performance measurements on it (flown by Willy Wilson) and also enabled the Air Fighting Development Unit of Fighter Command to conduct a tactical trial of the FW 190 (flown by Ian Campbell-Orde) in the air against a Spitfire IX. The results of these trials indicated that the edge of the performance of the Spitfire IX over that of the FW 190 was much narrower than supposed, and that between about 15,000 and 23,000 ft the rate of climb of the FW 190 was actually superior. Also the FW 190's excellent lateral manoeuvrability, already noted by our fighter pilots in combat, was confirmed and measured.

On 14 July the new Minister of Aircraft Production, Colonel Llewellyn, made a somewhat injudicious statement to the House of Commons in which he virtually said that British fighters were superior to their German counterparts in all respects. This triggered the Chief of the Air Staff into writing a long 'Most Secret' memorandum on 17 July in 21 numbered paragraphs to the Secretary of State for Air (Sir Archibald Sinclair), which said that the Minister's Statement to Parliament had been inaccurate and misleading. He emphasised that, whilst the Mk IX was superior to the FW 190 in speed at most altitudes, it was inferior in rate of climb in one very important height band (approximately 15,000–25,000 ft). He also added that since the bulk of the Spitfires in Fighter Command were Mk Vs, which were much inferior to the FW 190, and since the latter was in service in the Luftwaffe in large numbers and could be expected to improve in performance as time went on, the situation was extremely serious. In short, there were no grounds for complacency and urgent improvements in our fighters' performance were required if we were to maintain control of the daylight air over northern France and the Channel. On 21 July Sir Archibald Sinclair wrote to the Minister of Aircraft Production: 'We are being left behind

. . . A turning point in the war has been reached. Our mastery of
the daylight air is threatened . . . The Mk IX is dangerously
inferior to the FW 190 in climb up to 25,000 ft.' Sinclair was
over-stating the case, but these brisk reactions to the general
fighter situation galvanised the Air Staff and the technical
branches of the Ministry of Aircraft Production into demanding
even greater performance of the Mk IX as quickly as possible and
also into studying critically the future of our fighter position.

There were immediate consultations with Rolls-Royce on ways
and means of extracting even more power from the Merlin 61.
This resulted in an early up-rating of the engine involving an
increase in the allowable manifold pressure for combat from plus
12 lb to plus 15 lb, with investigation into increasing this further
to plus 18 lb. In the slightly longer term it resulted in a scheme to
re-schedule both the low and high blower gear ratios in such a
way as to provide an increase of performance for the aeroplane at
the low and medium altitudes at the expense of the higher
altitudes. This had the effect of filling in the gap between the
climb performance of the Spitfire and the FW 190 between
15,000 and 25,000 ft.

The engine with the re-scheduled blower gear ratios, the
Merlin 66, came into production and general use in early 1943.
The higher-altitude engines, Merlin 61 and 63, were retained in
production for use in the high-altitude Photographic Recon-
naissance Spitfires, and with modification, in the pressurised Mk
VII fighters.

The Mk IX aircraft fitted with the Merlin 66 engine came to be
known in the Service as the Mk IXB but its proper nomenclature
was LF. Mk IX. Some weight-saving exercises were carried out
on the aeroplane and some changes to propeller reduction gear
ratio were studied in order to improve the climb.

There was also a political reaction to the FW 190 situation. On
24 July 1942 the Minister of Aircraft Production sent a memorandum (through Lord Cherwell) to the Prime Minister outlining
the performance situation between the Spitfire and the FW 190
and not disguising that the bulk of the Spitfires in Fighter
Command were Mk Vs, which were at a severe disadvantage.
The fact that this issue reached the Prime Minister shows how
seriously it was taken in Whitehall. The Americans had now been
in the war for seven months and major issues of Grand Strategy

were in discussion between the two Allies, such as the relative priorities between the European and Pacific theatres and the issue of when and how to plan for an assault on the European mainland, and whether an assault on Europe should be preceded by a landing in North Africa. Such discussions were by no means easy between the Allies and this was no time to have to admit that we were in danger of losing control of the daylight air situation in Europe.

However, any performance gap between the FW 190 and the Spitfire IX was soon closed and I was confident that, on balance, the Spitfire IX was the better of the two aeroplanes for I eventually had the chance to fly the FW 190 myself. However, it was a most formidable opponent. The fighter-to-fighter combats in the Battle of Britain and subsequently the offensive sweeps across the Channel had set the opposing fighters clawing for more and more height, and the development of both the Spitfire and the Me 109 had responded to this increasing search for altitude.

Then, at some indefinite time in 1942, there seemed to be a change of tactical philosophy on both sides. It was rather as if, by some sort of tacit mutual consent between enemies, it was realised that the band between 30,000 and 40,000 ft was a silly place in which to have an air battle, and the fighting tended to drop down into the more practical regions roughly between 15,000 ft and 25,000 ft. I remember how, at the time, this trend interested me very much indeed. It was clearly reflected in the LF. Mk IX (Merlin 66) with the engine performance adjusted to the reduced height band. It was also reflected in the fact that, by removing the wing tips of the Spitfire, an improvement in lateral control could be achieved, but because it thereby increased the wing loading and the span loading of the wing, an aerodynamic penalty was incurred at high altitude. Such a proposition would have been unthinkable in 1940/1 but in 1942/3 the idea was enthusiastically adopted by some squadrons in No. 11 Group, and the 'clipped-wing' Spitfire became a common sight in the sky.

When the decision was taken to go ahead with the two-speed two-stage supercharged engine in an unpressurised Spitfire there were other improvements requiring to be made in the fighter apart from simply increased altitude performance. Foremost amongst these were increased range and endurance, implying more internal fuel capacity as well as external jettisonable tanks (the latter had just been developed) and also increased fire power, which clearly meant at least four cannon. Although the Mk Vc (with the 'universal' wing) had provision for four cannon it was normally possible to fit only two, because heating for the outboard cannon was inadequate. Only some Squadrons operating overseas in low-level roles ever operated the Mk Vc with four cannon fitted, so a fully operational four-cannon installation was now required. The increasing importance of the Middle East and, later, other overseas theatres also demanded the modification of future fighters to suit them for tropical conditions.

So the aeroplane which Supermarine designed to take the two-stage engine, the Mk VIII, embodied extra internal fuel tanks in the wing roots, bringing the internal fuel capacity up to 124 gallons, a four-cannon wing, full tropicalisation and a retractable tail wheel. It also embodied ailerons on which the long overhang outboard of the outer hinge was shortened in order to increase the stiffness of the aileron structure. Because the emphasis was, at the time the aircraft was ordered, still firmly on improved performance at altitude, the Mk VIII was originally designed with extended wing tips similar to those designed for the Mk VI and Mk VII pressure cabin aeroplanes. These changes to the Mk VIII obviously took time to get into production, and the Merlin 61 engines were available ahead of the aeroplanes so the Mk IX, essentially conceived as an interim type, came into service well ahead of the Mk VIII. Paradoxically the 'interim' Mk IX was produced in greater quantities than any other mark of Spitfire.

The Mk VIII, however, was by far the better aeroplane and because of its tropicalisation, improved range and other refinements it was allocated to the overseas commands while Fighter Command soldiered on with the Mk IX in the temperate conditions at home.

I flew the first Mk VIII (JF274) in November 1942 and after some delay, due to the need to re-position the oil tank, the first three aeroplanes were delivered to Gibraltar on 12 April 1943. By mid-June they were being delivered overseas in quantity.

I considered the extended wing tips on the early Mk VIIIs entirely unnecessary. The aeroplane was not, in my view, a specialised high-altitude machine – it was an air combat fighter of excellent all-round performance and destined for theatres of war where it would have to operate in a wide variety of circumstances. The extended wing tips did nothing for it except increase the lateral damping and spoil the aileron control. I complained incessantly to Joe Smith about them and did my best to get rid of them. Eventually, God be praised, when the Merlin 66 engine was brought in on the Mk VIII, we reverted to the standard wing tip configuration. We then had an excellent aeroplane, very pleasant to handle and of performance as good as the Mk IX with many other advantages added on.

18

Pinckney's Plan

During 1942 No. 12 Commando was stationed for a time near Bursledon where I had my house. It was commanded by Lieutenant-Colonel Robert Henriques and later by Lieutenant-Colonel S.S. Harrison; 'E' Troop was commanded by Captain Philip Pinckney.

Philip was a man of rare and timeless character. One might have encountered him accompanying Drake's raid on the Spanish treasure trains in Panama, or steering a fireship amongst the Armada anchored off Calais, or with Shackleton on his epic open-boat journey from Antarctica to South Georgia. Equally he was in no way out of place in the Ritz bar; he was a man for all seasons.

Much dedicated to the outdoors, a keen shot and a naturalist, he had, after Eton and Cambridge, travelled on foot in the Himalayas and in Iceland until the war swept him into the Army. He was a complete individualist, basically somewhat of an ascetic, and it was only necessary for an organisation such as the Commandos to be formed for Philip to join it; indeed if the Commandos had not existed it would have been necessary to invent them for Philip. When I first knew him he had already taken part in a number of operations and had trained 'E' troop of 12 Commando according to his own highly individual and unorthodox methods. 'E' Troop was tough, competent, splendidly fit and highly belligerent. When Mountbatten, as Head of Combined Operations, paid a visit to 12 Commando he wrote afterwards to Colonel Henriques, 'I was particularly impressed with Pinckney's Troop.'

Cheerful and ebullient as Philip was I became aware of a sort of bottled-up intensity within him and a great force of character and determination. Knowing a little of the sort of things the Commandos used to do, and the sort of man that Philip was, it occurred to me that he was very unlikely to survive the war.

In the spring of 1942 the FW 190 was forming the prinicpal opposition to our fighter squadrons in their almost daily offensive sweeps over northern Europe, and it could outfight the Spitfire V. The losses of No. 11 Group were mounting. Equally serious was that very little was known about the 190 or its capabilities, and in the absence of such knowledge there was a tendency to paint the enemy ten feet tall. However, it was abundantly clear that the Spitfire V was being outclassed and I personally felt, as did many others at Supermarine, that we had failed to keep up and had let the Air Force down.

The Spitfire Mk IX with the Merlin 61 engine was, we hoped, going to produce the answer but it was only just coming into production. In short, we badly needed a FW 190, preferably undamaged, for evaluation.

One evening I casually mentioned the FW 190 problem to Philip. He made no comment but the next evening he turned up at my house, steered me out into the garden and said: 'I've been thinking about what you said last night. Why don't we go and grab a 190 from a French aerodrome?'

'You are, I presume, joking,' I said, 'or are we about to open the second front?'

'No,' he said, 'I'm quite serious – we'd do it as a Commando operation but we'd need someone who could fly it back.'

His meaning was all too clear and I went into the house to get us each a beer and give myself a moment to think it over. I was familiar with Fighter Command aerodromes and began to consider what would be the chances of pinching a Spitfire if one really set about it in the right way. I concluded that the chances were not all that bad, and that logically they should not be too bad the other way round. So I said to Philip: 'Well – I suppose it could be done with suitable preparation and a bit of luck – but how would you get into a Hun airfield?'

'That's not your problem,' said Philip, a little sharply, I thought. 'The question is,' he said, 'if we got you into the cockpit of a FW 190, could you fly it without any training and could you get it back to England?' I had already flown a captured Me 109, there were plenty of German aeroplanes in the country, and their cockpit instrumentation and general conventions were thoroughly well known to us, and I was also well accustomed to flying a wide variety of different aircraft types including almost every available modern fighter. With reasonable preparation and fore-thought the FW 190 would, I concluded, be just another aero-plane. 'The answer to both questions is yes – in principle,' I said, 'provided there is reasonable preparation and planning. But you would have to get me into an aeroplane with the engine already running.' I explained that starting the engines of fighter aero-planes was not just a matter of pulling out the choke and pressing the self-starter button. The chances of getting an unfamiliar aero-engine started up from cold in a hurry were zero. We then discussed the idea at greater length and Philip's plan began to evolve and my requirements evolved also. Getting me into the cockpit of an aeroplane with the engine already running would mean doing it in the very early morning when airmen could be expected to be running the engines in the course of daily inspec-tions – probably just on first light – but before the station had come to full readiness.

Philip never asked me if I would do the operation – he just assumed that I would. We discussed the proposition more fully over the next few days and Philip began preparing a formal proposal for official approval by Combined Operations Head-quarters. This paper would have to be forwarded by Colonel Harrison, who was of course fully aware of the idea. I noticed that Philip's inner intensity and suppressed excitement increased markedly during this period and he became completely wrapped up in the scheme. I was taken round to be shown to Colonel Harrison by Philip, who adopted a somewhat proprietary atti-tude with a slight air of 'Look what I've got – a pilot for the FW 190 we're going to grab.'

As part of my initial preparation for the operation I said I required to spend about a week at the RAE Farnborough to become thoroughly familiar with German cockpit conventions and instrumentation and labelling from other captured German aircraft. There were experts on German aircraft at Farnborough and from them and perhaps from other intelligence sources, an informed guess about the main points of the FW 190 cockpit could be derived. An airfield should be selected which provided a chance for good preliminary observations and a reasonably favourable route home. I favoured Abbeville to Tangmere if other considerations permitted. Fighter Command would have to be informed in order to minimise the chance of my being shot down by some alert Spitfire pilot or, more probably, by the airfield defences during my approach to land. However none of these preliminaries could start until the plan had been approved in principle by HQ Combined Operations.

If I got airborne my intention was to proceed at wavetop height across the Channel. Apart from that the whole business of landing in France, getting to the selected airfield, penetrating the perimiter, shooting the German airman who was running the engine and dealing with any local difficulties which might arise was entirely a matter for the Army. I would be in Air Force uniform and simply do what I was told until the Army had got me into the cockpit.

From our original discussions I had pictured 'E' Troop, led by Philip, conducting this operation with me tagging along, as it were, as an honorary member, until I was ensconced in the cockpit.

Naturally the most rigid security was practised (for instance, the proposal put up to Combined Operations by Harrison and Philip was written in longhand to avoid any possibility of a leak) and I was told only what the Army thought it necessary for me to know. I could discuss the matter with nobody but Philip and all negotiations with RAE for my period of briefing would be done by Combined Operations and not by me.

I was decidedly startled, therefore, when I discovered that the plan was that Philip and I should go alone – mounting, as it seemed to me, a two-man invasion of France. However, this was not really my business but I did ask Philip how on earth he proposed to get back; at least I had some tangible means of homeward transport across the Channel, speculative though it might be on a number of counts. However, he refused to discuss that aspect of the matter in any detail.

We were to be taken to a point within a mile or two of a suitable beach in a Naval MGB (motor gun-boat) and then we would transfer to a 'Folbot' which we would paddle ashore and subsequently hide or bury. Accordingly, and while the proposal was still in preparation, Philip and I paddled about the Hamble River and in Southampton Water in a 'Folbot' so that I could become familiar with this abominably wet, cold, uncomfortable and, in my view, thoroughly unseaworthy little beast. I soon realised that flying the FW 190 back to England would probably turn out to be the least of my problems. All these 'Folbot' training sessions took place in the evening because I was flying all day and it was essential that there should be absolutely no visible change in my daily routine.

After a lot of thought and imagination I had concluded that, if I reached the cockpit of an aeroplane with the engine running, and provided the grass surfaces of the airfield were reasonable (they would be most carefully conned through powerful field glasses in advance), I had about a 50/50 chance of getting quickly airborne and back to an English airfield. As to the chances of ever reaching the cockpit I was not qualified to judge, but Philip was supremely confident. The fully detailed plan was delivered to Combined Operations Headquarters on 23 June 1942, marked 'Most Secret and Urgent'. There it was honoured with the code-name 'Operation Airthief' and steps were taken to decide on the most suitable 'target' airfield. The surviving documents indicate that they favoured a place called Maupertus, near Cherbourg.*

By a remarkable coincidence, on the very day, 23 June, that the paper was submitted to Combined Ops a Luftwaffe pilot, Oberleutnant Arnim Faber, landed an FW 190, undamaged, at Pembrey in south Wales. Precisely why he did this and why he made no attempt to destroy his aircraft is not clear. No public announcement of this was made at the time, however, and the information evidently took a little while to filter through to Combined Operations, for there was an exchange of internal minutes dated 25 June on the best choice of airfield. However, when the information did filter through 'Airthief' at once became a dead duck.

The first I knew of it was when Philip turned up at the aerodrome at Eastleigh on an Army motor bike. I walked out onto the tarmac to greet him because we always made a point of talking in the open air.

'The whole thing is off,' he said in a tone of the utmost dismay. 'Some bloody fool has landed an FW 190 in Wales and it's completely undamaged. We've been robbed.'

I took a few moments to absorb this sensational piece of news and it was only at that moment that I realised how much tension

---

* The detailed plan together with Colonel Harrison's and Philip Pinckney's covering letters and some Combined Ops internal minutes are filed in the Public Record Office at Kew.

had built up inside me during all this because its sudden release was quite unnerving. Had there been a chair handy I should certainly have sat down on it.

'Dear me,' I said to the outraged Philip, 'I *am* sorry.' I hoped that my face did not break into too broad a grin and that my craven sense of relief was not too apparent. There is no doubt that Philip was genuinely annoyed about the sabotage of his much prized plan.

Not long afterwards I had the chance to fly Arnim Faber's FW 190 at Farnborough. As I sat in the cockpit receiving my briefing from Willy Wilson (being 'shown the taps' as the expression was) I had some quiet amusement speculating whether I could have worked it all out for myself in the course of a rushed take-off had 'Airthief' come to pass. One unusual feature of the aeroplane was its electric press-button retraction system for the undercarriage. While this would have caused me some delay in getting the gear up, I felt I would have been able to puzzle it out quite quickly.

Thereafter, having been told that I must discuss 'Airthief' with no one as it was still classified 'Most Secret', I put the whole matter out of my mind until thirty years later when the Combined Ops files were opened in 1972, and an alert journalist, Alan Goddard, telephoned me out of the blue to ask about it. A flood of memories came back.

I saw quite a bit of Philip until No. 12 Commando left the Southampton area. He saw service in North Africa and Sicily and Italy and his exploits became a sort of local legend wherever he went. Finally – predictably – he was killed in Italy in 1943 when leading a group of SAS parachutists behind the enemies' lines ahead of the advancing allied armies. He is buried in the British Military cemetery in Florence.

Such men as Philip Pinckney appear from time to time in all ages, and seem set aside a little from their fellow men whether in peace or war. Robert Henriques, who knew him as well as anyone, dedicated *Through the Valley* to his memory, and his writings make it clear that, when I gained the impression that Philip could not survive the war, I was not alone in this belief. Philip also believed that he would not.

19

Griffon Spitfires:

Mks IV and XII

Not long before the war Rolls-Royce had begun to foresee the need for an engine of greater cylinder capacity than the Merlin. Amongst its applications would be as an engine of great power at low altitude for naval shipborne aircraft.

The old 'R' type engine, which had powered the Supermarine S.6 and S.6B Schneider seaplanes of 1929 and 1931, had, at 36.75 litres swept volume, been of some ten litres' greater capacity than the Merlin. It was a supercharged, 60° Vee 12, liquid-cooled engine and thus of similar basic layout to the Merlin – by then almost traditional for Rolls-Royce. Under sprint conditions the 'R' engines had, in 1931, produced a power output of 2,700 bhp on 'dope' fuel at sea-level and so its power potential had been amply demonstrated. It was entirely logical for Rolls-Royce to think of reviving this engine in modernised and production engineering form, to take over when the Merlin reached the end of its development life and by December 1939 the first Griffon was running on the test-bed.

When the 'R' type engine had been developed for the S.6 racing seaplane in 1929 the achievement of the lowest possible frontal area had been an obvious requirement. Now the Griffon, based on the 'R' type, came out with a frontal area of only 7.9 sq. ft compared with the Merlin's 7.5 sq. ft. This very small increase in frontal area for an engine of 10 litres' additional cylinder capacity at once suggested to Joe Smith that the new engine might fit into a Spitfire.

In October 1939 he submitted a design proposal (Supermarine Specification No. 466) for a Griffon-engined Spitfire. The idea at once received the support and encouragement of Sir Wilfrid Freeman, the Air Member for Development and Production (AMDP) on the Air Council, and N.E. Rowe, the Deputy

Director of Research and Development (Landplanes). This is significant because it suggests that Freeman's thoughts were turning actively towards the future development of the Spitfire whereas only six months previously he had been discussing the possibility of turning Supermarine over to Beaufighter production. On 9 November 1939, N.E. Rowe minuted the RAF Director of Operational Requirements with the details of the Supermarine scheme for a Griffon Spitfire, describing it as a long-term project requiring at least eighteen months to mature into production and saying that it would not interfere with current schemes to install improved versions of the Merlin. He also pointed out, however, that the larger Griffon would, if the standard fuel tankage was retained, reduce the aircraft's endurance and that the extra weight involved would have some impact upon such matters as tyre-pressures and landing speed.

At that stage, late 1939, opinion at Supermarine was that the future policy should be to exploit every power increase that might come from the Merlin but that sooner or later the bigger Griffon engine was sure to take over. Furthermore this view was apparently shared by Derby for Ernest Hives, the head of Rolls-Royce Aero engines, is on record as having referred to the Griffon as a 'second power string for the Spitfire'.

Joe Smith's attitude was – and I heard him say it so often – that, other things being equal, 'the good big 'un will eventually beat the good little 'un'. Therefore he was very determined to see a Griffon installed in a Spitfire and flight tested as soon as possible. In the event work was delayed by the impact of events in May 1940 but resumed again in the spring of 1941 and later that year the first Griffon engine, the RG 2SM, with two-speed single-stage blower was delivered to Supermarine and installed in what was basically a Mk III airframe. I made the first flight in this aeroplane, DP845, at Worthy Down on 27 November 1941. It was designated the Mk IV.

The main differences, insofar as they affected the pilot, were: because the Griffon engine rotated the opposite way to the Merlin, it caused the aeroplane to swing right-handed instead of left-handed on take-off; there was somewhat less ground clearance, resulting in a slight reduction in propeller diameter; the power available for take-off was much greater; and the engine RPM were lower than in the Merlin.

All this meant that the throttle needed to be handled judiciously on take-off but, once in the air, the aeroplane had a great feeling of power about it; it seemed the airborne equivalent of a very powerful sports car and was great fun to fly. Changes of trim with changes of power were much more in evidence, both directionally and longitudinally, and the aeroplane sheared about a bit during tight manoeuvres and simulated dog-fights. I realised at once that we should have to correct its directional characteristics and probably its longitudinal stability also, both of which, in due time we achieved. Indeed, DP845 eventually went through many phases of development, remaining in our flight development unit throughout and I, and others, flew in it a great deal; it became one of our favourite aeroplanes.

By the time I first flew DP845 in November 1941 the Mk III Spitfire with the Merlin XX engine had been cancelled as a production project. It was superseded by the Mk V with the Merlin 45 engine which was by then in full production at Supermarine and at Castle Bromwich.

Also by this time, the first Merlin 61 two-stage two-speed engine was flying experimentally in Spitfires N3297 and R6700 (see previous chapter). At that moment, therefore, the overall performance of the Merlin engine had, especially at high altitude, leap-frogged that of its younger but larger capacity brother. This was the result of the spectacular success of the two-stage supercharging with intercooler system which had been developed for the Merlin, but it did not take either Supermarine or the technical departments of the Ministry of Aircraft Production and the Air Ministry long to realise that whatever supercharger technologies had been developed to increase the performance of the Merlin could, in due time, be applied to the basically more powerful Griffon. Indeed, as early as June 1941 the Controller of Research and Development (Linnell) had, at a meeting of officials, stipulated that in the layout of the Spitfire Mk IV airframe the possibility of two-stage, two-speed supercharging (thus a longer and heavier engine) must be taken into account.

Thus, whilst the single-stage Griffon engine had produced a big jump in performance at lower altitudes, its engine characteristics were not yet fully what the critical situation in Fighter Command and in the air-war over the Channel and northern France in late 1941–2 demanded. All efforts were at that time being devoted therefore to getting the Merlin 61-engined Spitfire Mk IX into production and into service. The Mk IV thus had no immediate production future; but as a basis for longer-term development it remained very much alive. It had demonstrated the practicality of installing the Griffon engine in a Spitfire.

In 1941 the future fighter policy for the Royal Air Force was somewhat in disarray. The Hawker Tornado with the large 24-cylinder Rolls-Royce Vulture engine, intended as the replacement for the Spitfire in 1942–3, had run into trouble on two counts: first, compressibility trouble in dives necessitated moving the position of the radiator; and, second, the Vulture engine was so troublesome that it was eventually cancelled, bringing both the Tornado and the Manchester heavy bomber programmes to a standstill. A production order for 1,000 Hawker Tornados, which had been placed with Avro's, had to be cancelled, but the Manchester's two Vultures were replaced with four Merlin engines hung on a modified wing and this turned it into one of the most successful heavy bombers of the war – the Lancaster. In the case of the failed Tornado, Hawkers and Sydney Camm already had a back-up variant of this basic aeroplane using the newly developed 24-cylinder sleeve-valve Napier 'Sabre' engine (designed by Frank Halford). This aircraft, called the Typhoon, had made its first flight on 24 February 1940, but it also ran into trouble and delay over the Sabre engine so there was no chance of it coming into large-scale service in 1942. In any case it was by no means ideal for the type of 'air superiority' combat operations which had now developed. This remained the role of the Spitfire.

There was also confusion in fighter armament policy, which inhibited progress on the Mk IV aeroplane. This centred on whether future day-fighter armament should be six cannon, or four cannon, or two cannon and four .303 machine-guns, and overlaying this were possibilities of adopting 50 calibre or 13-mm machine-guns in place of the .303, a question much affected by problems of availability and supply. Little positive guidance was offered by Fighter Command; indeed, in the midst of it all, Air Marshal Sholto Douglas suddenly threw the idea of 12 × .303 machine-guns into the ring, thus adding to the confusion.

This created great problems for Joe Smith because, as the situation pointed more and more clearly towards the continued development of the Spitfire with the Griffon engine, the need for a settled armament policy was becoming vital from the design point of view. It was possible to fit almost anything into a Typhoon wing, but stowing greatly increased armament and ammunition into the thin and delicate wing of the Spitfire was another matter. To get things settled Joe Smith proposed a six-cannon installation for the Spitfire Mk IV and I flew this in mock-up form in DP845.

Then a most significant event happened. The Ministry of Aircraft Production decided in March 1941 to return to the procedure, abandoned in 1940, whereby a new design of aircraft should be based upon a specification issued to the contractor by the Ministry, deriving from an Operational Requirement clearly stated by the RAF. The Ministry had accordingly been instructed to prepare a specification for the design of the Griffon Spitfire to be called (officially now) the Mk IV. The official charged with this task said, reasonably enough, that he could not write a specification without a clear Operational Requirement from the RAF who, in turn, said they could not issue such a requirement until the armament question was settled and until there was more general agreement about essential aspects of performance. However, a file was opened in the design branch of the Ministry marked F.4/41 and a specification was prepared but without the appendix 'B' which normally stated the Air Staff's requirement in detail. At this point the Mk IV assumed the status of a new design which would form the mainstay of fighter force for 1942–3. Furthermore it was then clear that it would need to use the Griffon two-stage engine. Its performance potential estimated by Supermarine, based upon the assumption that two-stage supercharging would provide for the Griffon the same percentage power increase it had for the Merlin, would be very high indeed – something of the order of 470 mph at 28,000 ft. The opportunity would be taken to provide the weight of armament consistent with future requirements, additional fuel would clearly be needed to maintain the aircraft's range, let alone increase it, and much structural re-design would be needed to accommodate the increases in weight. The Spitfire Mk IV therefore grew in concept from being a relatively simple conversion of a Mk III airframe to take the single-stage Griffon into a substantially re-designed Spitfire able to accept the big two-stage Griffon. It would also have greatly strengthened wings able to accommodate extra fuel, as well as 6 × 20-mm cannon or 2 cannon and 4 × .303 machine-guns.

A contract was placed with Supermarine for two prototypes and it was the second one, DP851, which I flew on 8 August 1942, which became a more advanced prototype and in fact represented the first step towards what eventually became the Spitfire Mk XXI (21).

However little DP845, with the single-stage Griffon, by then almost my favourite aircraft with its spectacular rate of climb 'off the deck' and very good low-level performance, did not become entirely redundant. There had been much concern about the low- and medium-level performance of the FW 190, of course; and because of this I was told, one day in July 1942, to fly a Spitfire to Farnborough to take part in a demonstration for a small audience of very important people. Apart from that Jimmy Bird had very little information, so I immediately telephoned Willy Wilson at Farnborough to find out what it was all about. All I could gather was that it was to be a comparative demonstration of the low-level speed performance of the FW 190, the Typhoon and the Spitfire. 'How are you going to organise this, Willy?' I asked.

'God knows,' he said. 'I suppose we shall have to have some sort of a race.'

On reflection the general scheme became clear. The Spitfire was to be a sort of datum pacemaker – 'Mr Average Contemporary Fighter' – and its job would be to come in last, the real excitement of the proceedings being by how much it would be beaten by the FW 190 and the Typhoon, and which of these two bright stars would beat the other and by how much. Outside on the tarmac at Worthy Down stood the inoffensive-looking but highly potent DP845. Nobody had said what sort of Spitfire I should bring. Just a Spitfire. I rang up Joe Smith. 'Joe,' I said, 'about this thing at Farnborough. I reckon if I take DP845 I will beat the pair of them. Will that upset any applecarts?'

'You bet it will,' he said. 'Take it.'

At Farnborough I parked DP845 as inconspicuously as I could and walked into Willy Wilson's office. Kenneth Seth-Smith of Hawkers had arrived with his Typhoon, and we discussed the plan. We would all three take off together and fly to a point westward of the aerodrome at Odiham. We would then head back towards Farnborough in open line abreast at a moderate cruising speed at 1,000 ft, Willy Wilson in the centre with the FW 190 and Seth-Smith and myself on each side. At a signal from Willy we would all open up simultaneously to full power and head for the finishing line at Farnborough where the assembled VIPs would be waiting.

All went according to plan until, when we were about half-way between Odiham and Farnborough and going flat out, I was beginning to overhaul the FW 190 and the Typhoon. Suddenly I saw sparks and black smoke coming from the FW 190's exhaust and at that moment Willy also saw it and throttled back his BMW engine and I shot past him and never saw him again. I was also easily leaving the Typhoon behind and the eventual finishing order was, first the Spitfire, second the Typhoon, third the FW 190.

This was precisely the opposite result to that expected or indeed intended. It certainly put the cat among the pigeons, and among the VIPs. When I taxied in, everybody crowded round DP845, as the message sank in that it was the Griffon Spitfire which had handsomely beaten what were then supposed to be the two fastest fighters in service. The sensation was considerable.

It was 22 July, exactly one day after the Secretary of State for Air, Sir Archibald Sinclair, had addressed his letter to the Minister of Aircraft Production saying 'our mastery of the day-light air is threatened', and it was only a very few days also after the Chief of the Air Staff had issued his lengthy 'Most Secret' memorandum. I was, of course, quite unaware of this at the time and I must say I was somewhat startled by the general stir which our simple little exercise seemed to be causing.

Sholto Douglas came and examined the aircraft and in no time at all instructions arrived that some pilots from Fighter Command, including Jamie Rankin who was then leading the Biggin Hill wing, were to fly the aircraft and report to him. Bill Lappin of Rolls-Royce was quite annoyed, perhaps because I had not brought a Merlin Spitfire. There was unease in parts of Rolls-Royce at that time that the Griffon might pre-empt further development of the Merlin and Bill more or less accused me of pulling a fast one, which was to some extent true. 'Well, Bill,' I said, 'I had no spare aces up my sleeve – the aeroplane is faster than the other two and that's all there is to it.'

Eight days later, on 30 July, there was a meeting in the Secretary's of State's Office attended by the Chief of the Air Staff (Portal), the Vice-Chief (Freeman) and the Controller of Research and Development (Linnell) at which fighter development and production was discussed. This meeting was told that our performance figures showed the Griffon IIB Spitfire (i.e. DP845) was superior to the FW 190 in speed of climb up to 12,000 ft and it was agreed that, in addition to the various improvements to be made to the Mk IX, an immediate order should be placed for Spitfire Vs converted to the Griffon engine. The Ministry of Aircraft Production immediately went into action. The Mk Vc fitted with the Griffon IIB was designated the Mk XII and an order for 100 aircraft placed immediately. Because the Mk XII was intended only for operations at low and medium altitudes, it was decided that it should be produced without its wing tips, thereby improving its lateral manoeuvrability at speed. It was the first mark of Spitfire to be produced in this configuration but it was later adopted for many Mk IX aircraft with the Merlin 66. DP845 thus became the prototype Mk XII.

The Mk XII went into service with 41 Squadron at Tangmere in March 1943 and subsequently 91 Squadron was also re-equipped with Mk XIIs. The two squadrons were used primarily on low- or medium-level duties, in particular 91 Squadron operating from Hawkinge which performed fighter reconnaissance duties along the north coast of France. The Mk XII was essentially an interim type, produced quickly in small numbers to fill an immediate tactical gap, but by any standards it was a fine little aeroplane. The Air Fighter Development Unit, in its report No. 61, wrote:

17. The Spitfire XII handles in general better than the previous marks of Spitfire. Its longitudinal stability has been improved but its rudder control is not at present completely satisfactory as it needs constant retrimming and is rather heavy.
18. The aircraft fills the category of a low-level fighter extremely well, being capable of speeds 372 mph at 5,700 ft and 397 mph at 18,000 ft.

The A & AEE considered the type to be an excellent aircraft for fighter and intruder work below 18,000 ft, fast low down and very manoeuvrable. Generally, pilots who flew the type at Boscombe preferred it to the Mk IX.

The general characteristics of the Mk XII, from the viewpoint both of performance and handling, made it extremely attractive as a Naval carrier-borne fighter and in February 1943 two of these aircraft, EN226 and EN227, were fitted with hooks and delivered to the Fleet Air Arm Service Trials Unit at Arbroath for evaluation and aerodrome dummy deck landings (ADDLs).

Deck landing trials were flown by Lieutenant 'Winkle' Brown on 7 March, flying from Machrihanish to HMS *Indomitable*, when he made fifteen landings on the hooked XII EN226. These led to the development for the Fleet Air Arm of the Seafire XV and XVII aircraft, two of their most potent fighters. I also made landings on HMS *Indomitable* in a Seafire II that day, this being my first experience of carrier flying and very challenging I found it. I spent that night aboard *Indomitable* and had a long conversation with Admiral Lumley Lister, Flag Officer Carrier Training, and Commander 'Tubby' Lane, who was commanding the Carrier Trials Unit in which 'Winkle' Brown was a leading pilot. This began for me an insight into the problems of Naval aviation and the shortcomings of the Seafire as a Naval fighter, but I felt sure that a great deal could be done to the Seafire to make it a more practical Naval aircraft and I made up my mind I must find out more about the problems.

So the Mk XII had performed the important role of getting Griffon Spitfires into service, and now the introduction of the two-stage Griffon engines into Spitfires became the demonstrably logical next step.

20

Second Quantum Jump:

Spitfire Mk XIV

In war, time is at a premium. Consequently in between each planned and considered forward stride along the main path of Spitfire development, from Mk I to Mk V and Mk V to Mk VIII and from Mk IV to Mk 21, some intermediate or interim steps had to be taken on an opportunity basis in order to respond to urgent new operational demands or to make the earliest possible use of some n‿w engine development. Two outstandingly successful examples of this were the Mk IX (Chapter 17) and the Mk XIV. Both were developed extremely quickly, taking short cuts in various ways and both had a splendid performance. In fact, in the author's opinion, the Mk XIV turned out to be the best of all the fighter variants of the Spitfire. Furthermore, both marks became available in quantity precisely when they were most needed.

The method of issuing official specifications embodying carefully considered and detailed operational requirements, which the MAP had re-introduced in 1941, tended to be ponderous and to take time. Quite the reverse was the case in the much more 'ad hoc' method adopted in the case of the Spitfire Mk XIV. The history of that mark provided a model of how to procure and produce a new type of service aeroplane with a minimum of formality and delay. Credit for this must go both to the adaptability of the Supermarine design and production organisations and also to the MAP's technical departments under the leadership in 1943 of the Director of Technical Development, N.E. Rowe, and his Deputy in charge of Research and Development, Landplanes (DD/RDL), John Serby. Both were to play important and imaginative roles in getting the Mk XIV established as an operational type.

During the latter part of 1941 design changes to the Mk IV had proliferated under the influence of the F.4/41 specification, especially to the wing, undercarriage and armament. Nevertheless by the end of the year the type had become firmly committed for production at Castle Bromwich with the proviso, at CRD's insistence, that the production design should be such that the two-stage Griffon could be fitted at the earliest possible date without interrupting the flow of production. At this stage the description 'Mk IV with a two-stage Griffon' was dropped and it became the Mk XXI (or 21). The single-stage version became the Mk XX. Production forecasts being as usual optimistic it was thought at first that production of the airframe would start in September 1942 and that first deliveries of the two-stage Griffon would begin about six weeks after that. Two things were to happen to upset these plans.

First in March 1942, Hives informed the MAP that for technical reasons production of the two-stage Griffon could not start at Rolls-Royce until August/September 1943 and secondly the Air Ministry informed the MAP in June that there was no requirement for the Mk XX since the needs of Fighter Command would be met by the new Mk IX. This spelt the end of the Mk XX.

Hives then informed the MAP that six or a dozen 'pre-production' versions of the two-stage Griffon (now called the Griffon 61) could be delivered by the end of 1942. This ostensibly good news in fact created something of a problem for Rowe. In April 1942 the CRD (Linnell) had written to him to say that as soon as the Griffon 61 engines became available they should somehow be got into the air immediately for intensive flying in order to identify any early teething troubles. This clearly pointed to the need for some sort of flying test bed but there was by then no hope of any Spitfire 21 airframes from Castle Bromwich. Fortunately the Spitfire Mk VIII was about to enter production at Supermarine and this now became the obvious choice.

The decision was made to convert six of these aircraft to take the big Griffon engine. Design work was put in hand immediately at Supermarine and Spitfire Mk VIII numbers JF316 to JF321 were converted in the Supermarine Works. Changes to the aircraft were restricted to those essential to enable it to accept the new engine and I flew the first one, JF316 (generally known as a Spitfire Mk VIIIG) on 20 January 1943. I found that it had a spectacular performance doing 445 mph at 25,000 ft with a sea-level rate of climb of over 5,000 ft per minute. I remember being greatly delighted with it; it seemed to me that from this relatively simple conversion, carried out with a minimum of fuss and bother, had come something quite outstanding – another quantum jump almost on a par with the jump from the Mk V to the Mk IX.

The Mk VIIIG, with virtually the same tail surfaces both horizontal and vertical as the Merlin Mk VIII, was very much over-powered and the handling in the air was absolutely un-acceptable for an operational type. It was obvious that larger vertical tail surfaces would be required and probably larger horizontal surfaces too. I soon realised also that a new throttle unit would be needed giving a much greater angular travel for the hand lever. The existing throttle box was exactly the same as it had been on the prototype K5054 in 1936, controlling an engine up to $6\frac{1}{4}$-lb manifold pressure and around 1000 bhp. Now the same unit was unleashing 18-lb boost and over 2000 bhp so the slight-est movement of the throttle produced a rush of power. I asked Joe Smith to get the D.O. to design something with a much greater angular movement, better propeller control and a better friction device. This was duly done and a lovely new throttle box resulted which gave the pilot much better and sweeter control. The next essential before delivery of the VIIIG to Boscombe Down for official handling tests was an improvement in the directional stability and control and a new fin was drawn out with a substantial increase in area (7.42 sq. ft) and a much larger rudder and fitted to the second aircraft JF317. This, though not immediately ideal, produced a very marked improvement in directional characteristics and we were able to introduce minor changes thereafter and by various designs of trimmer tab and balance tab to reach an acceptable degree of directional stability and control. The enlarged fin of JF317 had a straight leading edge but for production a more elegant curved line was intro-duced.

Meanwhile intensive flying went on with the Griffon 61 engine both at the firm and at Boscombe Down and one of the Mk VIIIGs, JF321, was fitted with a Rotol six-bladed contra-rotating propeller. This consisted of two three-bladed propellers on con-centric shafts rotating in opposite directions but controlled by a single constant speed unit. It was a most remarkable device, rather complicated mechanically, but it completely eliminated propeller torque, both at take-off and during manoeuvres in the air. It also provided a much-needed increase in blade area within a given diameter which in itself tended to solve a fundamental problem for the Spitfire.

I had flown some of the early contra-propellers on a Mk IX aircraft and there had been trouble arising from failures of a thing called the translational bearing. The normal Rotol pitch change mechanism controlled the pitch on the front propeller and this then had to be transmitted to the rear propeller (which was rotating in the opposite direction) through the translational bearing mechanism. If this failed the pitch of the rear propeller was no longer under control and might do anything which was potentially dangerous. Indeed, one of the Rotol test pilots, Jack Hall, was killed in this way. He was the brother of my friend Noel Hall, who had taken over the Met Flight in 1936 and who was killed in the Battle of Britain in 1940.

I think I was the first to have a translational bearing failure and it happened one day when I had taken off from Worthy Down in a Spitfire IX JL349 and was climbing up for some performance checks. Suddenly there was a bang and a violent jerk and although I was running at quite a high power setting the airspeed began to unwind rapidly down to about 140 mph. A quick look over the engine instruments revealed that everything seemed to be quite normal. I put on more power and still the speed went on dropping. Eventually I had almost full RPM and Boost and still the speed was dropping. There seemed no doubt that the ASI was reading correctly. I was utterly puzzled. Here I was, in a very powerful aeroplane, going at full power with an airspeed steadily falling below 130 mph. It was a decidedly eerie feeling and I racked my brains for some explanation. I had flown close by a large and scattered formation of Dakotas towing Horsa troop-carrying gliders and the bizarre thought occurred that perhaps I had picked up a Horsa tow-rope on my tail wheel and was inadvertently towing one of these large and cumbersome gliders. I weaved sharply from left to right, looking behind – but no Horsa! If this goes on much longer, I thought, I shall subside gently but decisively into the ground with full power on, thus providing an interesting intellectual exercise for the Accidents

Investigation Branch. Middle Wallop was quite near so I decided
to put down there while the going was good. I put the flaps down
at the last moment and crossed the airfield boundary at 110 mph
at almost full power. It must have been a strange experience for
anyone watching to see a Spitfire approaching to land at a normal
speed but emitting the roar of an engine at nearly full power.

In fact the translational bearing had failed, causing the overall
propeller efficiency to drop to almost nothing and it had therefore
taken almost the full power of the engine to keep me in flight at
all.

We had a lot of other troubles with the early contra-props,
amongst which were high levels of vibration in some conditions
and a rather daunting amount of mechanical noise in flight
especially at low RPM. I kept in close touch with my friend
Bryan Greenstead, Chief Pilot of Rotol's, and of course had to
report officially all snags and difficulties which we encountered.
For some reason the idea got about that I was hostile to contra-
rotating propellers whereas it was only that it fell to me to report
many of the early troubles. In fact I was very much in favour of
them and thought they were absolutely the right answer for the
Spitfire. In particular I favoured them for Seafires and deck
operation. I wrote a letter to R.H. Coverley, CBE, the Managing
Director of Rotol's, assuring him of my full support for contra-
propellers and had a friendly reply.

The fourth Griffon 'flying test bed', JF319, was developed at
the firm to a standard at which it could be submitted to the A &
AEE for performance and handling tests, as a potential operational type. It was fitted with Griffon RG 5 SM engine No. 1282
driving a Rotol 10 ft 5 in. propeller through a .51 to 1 reduction
gear and the coolant radiators had been increased in area to be
compatible with the increased cooling requirements of this
engine which was running at +18 lb per sq. in. boost. It had a
neat tropical type air intake and the enlarged fin and rudder. The
all-up weight was 8,400 lb.

Our performance measurements (later confirmed by the A &
AEE) showed maximum speeds of 447 mph at 25,600 ft in FS
gear and 389 mph at 16,000 ft in MS gear. The recorded climb
figures were also outstandingly good: 20,000 ft in a shade over 5
minutes, 40,000 ft in 15 minutes with an absolute ceiling of no
less than 44,600 ft. The handling of the aircraft was also most

favourably reported upon by the A & AEE.

On the basis of these trials, enthusiasm for the new type blossomed at the Air Ministry. In October 1943 the Air Staff stated they would like to get the type (now officially called the Mk XIV) into production, to replace outstanding Mk VIII orders on a one-for-one basis as soon as possible so as to bridge the gap until the Mk 21 came into production. The AOC-in-C Fighter Command was advised that 120 Mk XIVs would be produced by 1 April 1944.

So the Mk XIV was in business and a very fine fighter it was. It fully justified the faith of those, who from the early days in 1939 had been convinced that the Griffon engine would eventually see the Spitfire into a new lease of life.

I flew the first production Mk XIV, RB140, in October 1943. It was a splendid and potent aeroplane. We still had some work to do to improve its longitudinal and directional characteristics, but it was powerful and it performed magnificently. The only respect in which the XIV fell short was in its range. As far as its flight characteristics were concerned, it could well tolerate more weight and it seemed that additional fuel in the rear fuselage would be the answer but we were up against the CG problem and longitudinal stability. After doing the early flights on RB140 the time was approaching for me to go into the Fleet Air Arm so I handed over the job of completing the contractors' trials to Frank Furlong, by now my number two at Worthy Down and almost as good as a test pilot as he was a steeplechase jockey.

The first squadron deliveries were on 1 January 1944 when RB 142, RB148 and RB150 were delivered to Exeter to start the re-equipment of 610 (City of Chester) Squadron. The next Squadrons to be equipped before D-Day were 91 and 322 (Dutch Sqn) and by September 1944 four more Squadrons, 41, 130, 350 and 402 (Canadian), were re-equipped with the F.XIV for service with 2nd Tactical Air Force on the Continent. The aeroplane came into service, as it happened, in good time to help counteract the threat from the German flying bombs, in which of course the Tempest played a prominent part.

In response to an urgent appeal to the MAP from the PRU at Benson for a new photographic reconnaissance Spitfire of even greater performance than the then current PR Mk XI a small batch of Mk XIVs was adapted on the production line for photographic reconnaissance work and delivered to the service, under the description PR Mk XIX, in time for D-Day. Unlike the later fully developed PR Mk XIXs these early aircraft were not equipped with pressure cabins.

Then on 1 November 1944 I flew a Mk XIV RM784 with a cut-down rear fuselage and a large 'teardrop' cockpit canopy designed to give the pilot a greatly improved rearwards view. This important and major modification had its origins in the strong recommendation which I made to Supermarine long before in the autumn of 1940 when I returned from attachment to 65 Squadron.

An improvement in the rearwards view for the pilot had impressed me as being of extreme importance and I had urged it upon Joe Smith since it was a commonplace in everyone's experience that most fighter pilots were shot down by an enemy they didn't see. Early in 1941 two experienced fighter pilots, Flight Lieutenants Jeff Wedgwood and Tony Bartley, had come to Supermarine on attachment to help with the test flying. We had had a long session one day with Joe Smith and the question of rearwards view came up again. Both Wedgwood and Bartley, on the basis of their own combat experience, strongly supported the need for major improvement in this respect, and Joe Smith was clearly convinced. It would mean a big change to the geometry of the rear fuselage and the pressures on production precluded such major changes at that time. Another factor was that the technology of producing large area one-piece canopies out of Perspex was not then developed, so this very desirable modification did not reach the production stage until it came in on the FR XIV, the Mk XVI and the Mk XVIIIs in 1944/5 but here it was at last.

Eventually a total of 957 Mk XIV aircraft was produced, not including its direct derivative, the Mk XVIII of which a further 300 were built.

The Air Fighting Development Unit (AFDU) carried out tactical trials of the Spitfire XIV against the Merlin-engined Mk IX. In their report No. 117 they wrote as follows:

The all-round performance of the Spitfire XIV is better than the Spitfire IX at all heights. In level flights it is 25 to 35 mph faster and has a correspondingly greater rate of climb. Its manoeuvrability is as good as a Spitfire IX. It is easy to fly but should be handled with care when taxiing and taking off.

Later, in another report, occurs the following:

GENERAL CONCLUSIONS

68. The Spitfire Mk XIV is superior to the Spitfire Mk IX in all respects.
69. It has the best all-round performance of any present day fighter, apart from range.

The Mk XIVs and Mk XVIIIs remained in Royal Air Force Service, mostly overseas, until the 1950s and on 1 January 1951 Spitfire XVIIIs of 60 Squadron, RAF, operating from Singapore, flew a ground-attack sortie against Communist forces in the Malayan jungle. This was the very last time that the Royal Air Force flew Spitfire fighters in anger against the King's enemies. On that occasion 60 Squadron was led by its Commander, none other than my good friend Squadron-Leader Duncan Smith, DSO DFC, who had commanded the first squadron of Spitfire IXs (64 Squadron) back in 1942.

To mark the occasion of the Spitfire's last fight in the hands of the Royal Air Force, Ronnie Harker of Rolls-Royce and I arranged for the two firms to join in presenting 60 Squadron with a silver model of a Spitfire, on the plinth of which we had had engraved the opening words of the *Nunc Dimittis*: 'Lord, now lettest thou thy servant depart in peace'.

21

Longitudinal Stability

and Increased Range

In the course of its development life the Spitfire greatly increased its overall weight, the disposition and configuration of the various loads it had to carry, its maximum speed and the range of heights at which it operated. As more powerful and heavier engines were installed the area of the propeller blades had to be increased to absorb the greater power. All this had a big influence upon the way the aeroplane handled in the air and particularly upon its longitudinal (or fore-and-aft) stability.

Stability in an aircraft can be simply defined as follows: the tendency of an aircraft when disturbed from a condition of steady flight to return to that condition when left to itself; conversely instability is the tendency of the aircraft to diverge further away from the condition of steady flight if once disturbed.

The vital importance to the pilot of having positive stability is obvious. For instance, if the pilot wishes to raise the nose of his aircraft a small amount, perhaps to aim his guns, but the aircraft itself decides to bring the nose up further than he wants before he has time to check it he will have great difficulty in aiming. He would probably come down and report: 'My elevators are too light and too effective – I can't fly the aeroplane accurately enough.' He would, however, almost certainly be wrong in blaming the elevators – what he should say is 'My aircraft is unstable longitudinally.' In a high-performance fighter, lack of longitudinal stability can also be exceedingly dangerous in the course of manoeuvring at high speeds for it can cause a pilot inadvertently to perform much more violent manoeuvres than he intended, thus perhaps dangerously overstressing his aircraft. This is by no means an academic case; a proper degree of positive longitudinal stability is a basic necessity in any aeroplane controlled by manually operated aerodynamic surfaces. Therefore in aeroplanes such as the Spitfire, which were entirely manually controlled, any inherent instability was unacceptable and potentially dangerous.

The provision of a sufficiency of inherent stability in an aircraft is therefore an essential task for the designer and it is normally provided by designing a fixed tailplane at a distance behind the main wing. The effectiveness of this tailplane depends upon its own aerodynamic qualities and its distance behind the aerodynamic centre of the mainplane, and its proper positioning in the 'wake' of the main wing.

Obviously, because a fixed tailplane produces both weight and drag, the designer normally wishes to keep its size as small as possible consistent with the right amount of stability. This would certainly be the case with an aircraft designed for the highest possible speed, as was the Spitfire. Another very important influence on stability is the position of the aircraft's centre of gravity, which usually lies at a point about one-third of the mean chord* of the wing. If the centre of gravity is moved backwards it tends to de-stabilise the aircraft and if forwards it makes it more stable. The limit to the amount that the centre of gravity can be moved forwards is determined by the position of the undercarriage (if the centre of gravity is positioned too far forward the aeroplane will tend to tip onto its nose when taxiing); and the limit to which it could be moved rearwards was fixed by considerations of longitudinal stability in the air. So the centre of gravity had to be kept within certain finite limits.

All aeroplanes must carry fuel and oil which is used up in flight, thus inevitably causing some shift in the centre of gravity. Fighter aeroplanes also carry quite big loads of ammunition which are used up in flight so, again, it is impossible to avoid some movement of the centre of gravity in the course of a sortie and, if it moves rearwards, the aircraft becomes less stable. So every aircraft should take off with a sufficient margin of longitudinal stability to accommodate significant rearwards shifts of centre of gravity whilst in flight. The greater the basic stability margins, the greater the amount of change which can be tolerated in flight and therefore the more flexibility there is for accommodating extra amounts of disposable load.

---

* The chord is the distance between the leading and trailing edges of the wing in the line of flight.

There were other factors which affected the aerodynamics of stability of the Spitfire. For example, the aerodynamic characteristics of the elevator itself (as opposed to the fixed tailplane) also had a major influence on stability and at Supermarine we exploited this and increased the stability margins as we moved from one mark of Spitfire to another. Furthermore, in the case of the Spitfire we found out early on that the stability margins decreased with altitude. As the aeroplane began to operate at greater heights and speeds this problem became progressively more acute.

Another de-stabilising influence in the Spitfire's development life was the necessity for continual increases in the area of the propeller blades. Aerodynamically the propeller blades, although rotating at quite high RPM, were, in fact, equivalent to a fixed horizontal surface equal to their projected area. This was equivalent to a fixed foreplane acting in the reverse sense to the fixed tailplane and therefore essentially destabilising. Adding more propeller blades simply made the matter worse. All these things combined to exacerbate the stability problem as time went on.

In 1936, before we delivered the prototype K5054 to the A & AEE at Martlesham,* I had flown it at a centre of gravity position at which it was very severely unstable longitudinally. This was unacceptable and so, before delivery, we arbitrarily fixed, by means of ballasting, a basic centre of gravity position at which we considered it acceptable. I remarked, however, that the stability margin was tight. The A & AEE pilots remarked also that the elevator was too light and too powerful and they recommended reducing the gear ratio between the elevator and the control column. I suspected at the time, and later with more experience and understanding of the problem I became quite convinced, that they were wrong in blaming the elevator for being 'too light'. It was much too simplistic a conclusion. The aeroplane was on the borderline of instability and making a heavier elevator, or even a smaller one, would have been no solution. Indeed it would have been counter-productive.

In general configuration the Mk I and Mk II production aeroplanes were almost identical to the prototype and so there

* See Chapter 6.

was no trouble with their stability. The adoption of the three-bladed De Havilland propeller (Mk I) and the three-bladed Rotol (Mk II) had a slightly destabilising effect but not one of any real significance. The next step thereafter was the first prototype Mk III, N3297, which I flew on 16 March 1940 and which had short span wings 'clipped' down to 30 ft 6 in. and the Merlin XX engine. This aeroplane was unstable as first flown and was tightening into turns quite severely. This tendency was accentuated with altitude.

It was Alan Clifton who came up with the idea of fitting a weight in the elevator control system. The object of this was that, when any g was applied to the aeroplane, the weight would react in the sense of pushing the stick forward thus counteracting the g. Any tendency on the part of the aeroplane to tighten into turns was therefore immediately corrected by the elevators. When I tested this device extensively on N3297 it worked extremely well. It was worth about two inches' rearward travel of the centre of gravity and provided in good measure the increased stability margins we were seeking. In fact, our very first tests of this idea were done by weighting the trailing edge of the elevator; later we fixed a lever arm in the control circuit with a weight which could be varied and we sent the aeroplane to the A & AEE at Boscombe Down with this device fitted. We started with a $3\frac{1}{2}$ lb bob weight and increased it to 7 lb. The only side-effect, so to speak, was that when taxiing over bumpy ground it showed a tendency to jerk the stick about a bit but this was a minor effect, and of no real consequence.

The Mk III Spitfire did not go into production, but the success of the bob weight experiment in curing its instability immediately opened up the possibility of its use for later marks of Spitfire. It could also easily be incorporated on a production line, which was just as well as we had to produce a large number of bob weights in a hurry to respond to a nasty situation which developed in 1942.

The Mk V aircraft was by this time in full service with Fighter Command and, since the Mks I and II had been phased out of front-line service, a fair amount of additional operational equipment had gradually crept into the aircraft, most of it stowed within the fuselage. The aftmost acceptable position for the aircraft's centre of gravity had been fixed in the normal course of flight testing by the firm and by the A & AEE, determined entirely on the basis of what provided a safe and acceptable degree of longitudinal stability. Any rearward movement of the centre of gravity in service, for whatever reason, would begin to destabilise the aircraft. Therefore for each sub-variant of the Mk V (and there were Va, Vb and Vc) detailed instructions for the correct loading of the aircraft were issued to squadrons to ensure that the centre of gravity remained within the limits laid down. It was not a simple business because the loading instructions had to take into account whether certain items of equipment were or were not fitted to a particular aircraft, such as, for instance, the new automatic signal cartridge firing device or additional oxygen bottles situated at the rear of the fuselage. However, the importance of these loading instructions was not generally appreciated in squadrons and in the daily round of operational activity they tended to be disregarded.

In February 1942 Tony Bartley, who had been test flying with us at Supermarine for many months, returned to operational duties with 65 Squadron at Debden, which was then commanded by Squadron Leader Humphrey Gilbert. As soon as Bartley started flying certain of the Squadron's aeroplanes he realised something was wrong. Tony had been test flying correctly loaded Mk Vs with us at Supermarine and he very well knew the difference between a stable and an unstable aeroplane. He rang me at Eastleigh to tell me that the Station Commander at Debden, Group Captain John Peel, in pulling out from a dive at high airspeed in one of the Squadron's aircraft, had inadvertently applied so much g that he had collapsed downwards in the cockpit and hit his head on top of the stick. This at once suggested to me that his aircraft might have been wrongly loaded and dangerously unstable. I at once flew to Debden. Tony took me to John Peel, who was an old friend from Duxford days when he was a Flying Officer in 19 Squadron. Having commiserated with John over his black eye – he had quite a shiner – I asked if I could fly his aeroplane. Sure enough, it was dangerously unstable. John Peel, who was an experienced pilot, had nearly lost control of it and might well have pulled the wings off if he had not recovered himself as quickly as he did. Clearly the centre of gravity of that aeroplane was well outside the limits and yet it was on the flight line of an operational squadron. I asked if I could test some other aeroplanes in the Squadron. I picked two or three at random and found they were all in much the same state.

How many more aeroplanes are there in the Command in this condition, I wondered. I persuaded Peel to let me take one of the Squadron's Spitfires back to Worthy Down for checking and weighing, whence I shot into Joe Smith's office at Hursley Park. Alan Clifton was there too and with all the emphasis that I could command I impressed on them both that something had gone seriously wrong either with the loading instructions or the Squadron's interpretation or implementation of them. There was thus a real chance that, as of that moment, in almost every squadron in the Command Spitfires were flying in a dangerous state of instability.

It was obvious that something very practical and quick must be done but sending signals through Command and Group Headquarters telling engineer officers to check all loadings on all aircraft was not the answer. For it was also obvious that, under daily wartime operational conditions, mistakes would be made and that a gradual aftwards creep of the centre of gravity was probably an inevitable fact of life, rather like middle-age spread.

No, the answer was bob-weights. I reminded them of the success of this device on the Mk III, and that we had also used it on the pressure cabin Mk VI high-altitude fighter. Furthermore, since our initial experiments with the Mk III, the bob-weight device had been fairly thoroughly tested on various aeroplanes at the A & AEE and at RAE, and its effectiveness had been established. Now was the time to introduce it as a matter of urgency.

Len Gooch, the Works Manager, was called in – how long would it take to make 1,000 or so mod. kits for installing bob-weights in every operational squadron Spitfire? Len said, 'I don't know but I'll soon find out.' Joe Smith and Clifton got down to this with a will and of course there was much discussion with HQ Fighter Command and MAP; signals did go round and plenty of wrongly loaded aircraft were identified throughout the Command. Bob-weights were introduced on a mandatory modification basis and Len Gooch and the Works excelled themselves by producing hundreds of sets of parts in an incredibly short time.

Up to that time there had been a distressing and increasing incidence of total structural failures of Spitfires in the air, which was causing great concern in the Ministry of Aircraft Production and especially at Supermarine. The Accidents Investigation Branch was largely baffled. The remains of Spitfires which had simply flown apart in the air were assembled on the floor of a hangar at Farnborough and experts from the firm, the RAE and Air Ministry tried to pinpoint some common factor in these accidents, in which the pilots were mostly (but not always) killed. I too had been much puzzled by it all and tended to think inexperienced pilots were somehow getting seriously out of control in cloud or some other circumstances and over-stressing the aircraft beyond their strength limits. In the course of test flying I used regularly to pull 7 or 8 g (measured by acceler-ometer) and I often dived Spitfires well beyond their limiting speed of 470 mph. I thus acquired the greatest possible faith in the aeroplane's structural integrity; yet a brand-new production Mark VB aircraft had come apart without warning on poor George Pickering, desperately injuring him and in the end in-directly resulting in his early death. So I, and many others more technically qualified than I, had reached the conclusion that there was no single identifiable cause for these accidents. Joe Smith's design team and the RAE studied every conceivable possibility and a number of precautionary structural modifications were introduced on a 'it might be that' basis, especially on the Mk VB which statistically was most prone to these structural failures.

Now I suddenly realised that, if there were a large number of longitudinally unstable aeroplanes flying around, the chances of pilots getting seriously out of control in various circumstances – especially in cloud flying – were greatly increased. I became convinced that this underlay the mounting numbers of structural failures of Spitfires in the air.

Therefore the introduction of bob-weights seemed a matter of pressing urgency and we had no trouble in getting the A & AEE and Fighter Command to agree to it. So bob-weights were in, at least until some more elegant solution to the problem could be devised (which later it was).

But this was not popular with pilots, especially in those squadrons where loading instructions had been properly adhered to anyway, because they did produce some side-effects. Also, most squadron pilots, at any rate in Fighter Command, spent most of their time as part of large wing or squadron formations proceeding at modest airspeeds, and a certain degree of longitudinal instability did not worry them much. But on the rarer occasions when they found themselves in a dive at very high speed serious trouble could arise – as was the case with John Peel.

Eventually we introduced various sizes of bob-weights according to different variants of the Spitfire. For instance, the Mk VI and Mk VII pressure cabin Spitfires had particularly bad stability characteristics. This was because the cables from the cockpit to the elevators had to pass through the pressure cabin bulkhead behind the pilot and the friction caused by the pressure seals meant that the elevators had somewhat impaired freedom of movement. This in itself was destabilising in effect and in these aeroplanes we had to use a heavy $6\frac{1}{2}$ lb weight. This was a practical demonstration of the fact that any interference with the free movement of the elevator was essentially destabilising, for it interfered with what was known as the 'stick-free stability'. From this it followed that the elevator itself had a positive stabilising function and so, if that stabilising influence of the elevator could be increased, the overall stability of the aeroplane would be improved. The bob-weight, of course, did just that – it increased the stabilising function of the elevator but by dynamic rather than aerodynamic means. If, however, the same effect could be achieved by changes to the aerodynamic design of the elevator itself, then we should be able to dispense with the bob-weights altogether.

It was W.E.W. Petter, Chief Designer of Westland Aircraft, who seems first to have appreciated that aerodynamic modification to the elevator itself could provide additional stability, although S.B. Gates, of the RAE, who had been doing advanced theoretical work on aircraft stability for several years, had already defined what he referred to as 'convergent' and 'divergent' elevators.

Westlands were building Spitfire Mk Vs under contract to the Ministry of Aircraft Production and I used to fly often to Yeovil to see Harald Penrose, the Chief Test Pilot there. Sometimes I would fly their Spitfires and he and I had one long talk with Teddy Petter specifically on the subject of the Spitfire's instability problem. Harald was recording some longitudinal stick-force data and trim curves on a Spitfire at various centre of gravity loadings, at Petter's behest. Eventually Petter produced an experimental plywood-covered elevator of modified (bulged) aerodynamic section. Harald flew it and found it produced a remarkable increase in stability, equivalent to a significant amount of centre of gravity travel. He telephoned me and I flew down to Yeovil and flew it myself and, sure enough, this seemed the answer. We at once brought one of those elevators to Worthy Down and tested it on one of our own Mk Vs, AB186, and the Westland aeroplane AR278 was sent to RAE at Farnborough. I was very enthusiastic about this but Joe Smith was not best pleased with me for what seemed to him to be my involvement in cooking up modifications to the Spitfire with the designer of another firm without proper consultation with him. However in due course I was forgiven. The 'Westland elevator', as it became known, demonstrated the way forward; but our aerodynamicists at Hursley Park thought that an even more effective answer could be obtained by enlarging the horn balance of the standard elevator and this we did by stages. The effect was astonishing.

At last a way had been found to improve the basic stability margins of the aeroplane, thus giving more flexibility in centre of gravity movement, without our having recourse to any enlargement of the fixed tail surfaces. Great credit for this breakthrough must go to Petter and Penrose who first demonstrated in practical form what could be achieved by relatively simple aerodynamic change to the elevator itself.

With aeroplanes, as in life, you seldom get something for nothing; there's no free lunch. The enlarged horn balance of the elevator produced a slightly unpleasant 'feel' of the aeroplane at low speeds and when coming in to land, especially if any yaw or sideslip was applied. This effect, however, was trivial by comparison with the gain in the stability margins.

During the period between the mandatory introduction of $6\frac{1}{2}$ lb bob-weights on the Mk V and their eventual removal, which became possible due to the introduction of the modified elevators, HQ Fighter Command bombarded the Ministry with arguments against having to fit them. This was inspired by a flood of complaints from operational squadrons who did not always understand the problem. Some pilots claimed that the bob-weights were causing them to miss enemy aircraft which they would otherwise have shot down. Other squadrons raised no objections at all and it was noticeable that reaction varied, not on a squadron basis but on a station basis, which suggested that discussions in the Mess were not unconnected with general attitudes.

In spite of the complaints, however, there was no doubt in my mind that the bob-weights were an essential safety measure and the A & AEE and the Ministry of Aircraft Production took the same view. In our minds were the large number of catastrophic structural failures in the air, the facts of which were not generally known in the squadrons. Even when the AOC-in-C himself, Sholto Douglas, entered the fray the Ministry (Rowe and Serby) stood firm and insisted on the retention of bob-weights until they were rendered redundant by the introduction of modified elevators. Also, it was statistically established that, as soon as the longitudinal stability of the Spitfire was thus brought under control, the problem of the unexplained breakings-up of aircraft in mid-air, like the baker in *The Hunting of the Snark*, 'softly and suddenly vanished away'.

By late 1943, the Spitfire's performance at all heights and its armament had been vastly improved. The great build-up of the daylight bomber offensive, mostly by the US Army Air Force, and especially the B17 ('Flying Fortress') raid on Schweinfurt in October 1943, had shown that daylight bomber casualties were too high unless the bombers were heavily escorted by fighters. By the end of 1943, therefore, the role of the long-range escort fighter, as opposed to the pure air defence role or that of achieving theatre air superiority, was becoming an important requirement.

Long-range escort was the role in which the Merlin Mustang was particularly excellent because of the large load of fuel it was able to carry. True, the Spitfire Mk VIII, in service in 1943, was carrying additional fuel in its wing roots and also in external jettisonable tanks under the fuselage, but it was serving overseas and the problem of accommodating larger loads of fuel in the Spitfire at home was acute. The only available space was in the fuselage behind the pilot, but a tank of significant size there would have a major effect upon the centre of gravity.

However, it seemed to both Joe Smith and myself that, for the purpose of escorting bomber formations in daylight, a degree of longitudinal instability in the *early* stages of a sortie would be acceptable. Therefore the fuel in a rear fuselage tank could be used for take-off and climb and during the early stages of the sortie, the main tanks and wing tanks remaining full. In this case the centre of gravity would be moving forward to an acceptable position by the time the aircraft reached hostile airspace. It was decided therefore to embody a rear fuselage tank in a derivative of the Mk XIV shortly due to come into production, the Mk XVIII.

In the meantime a 75-gallon tank was fitted in the fuselage of a Mk IX (ML186) behind the pilot and we also fitted a bob-weight in the elevator circuit, so what with this and the large horn-balance on the elevator we hoped for the best. However the best and most expeditious way to test this aeroplane was to fly it a good long way and see how everything worked out. So I took off from High Post on Salisbury Plain with all tanks full, carrying a 45-gallon drop tank in addition, and set off at economical cruising boost and RPM in the general direction of Scotland. The weather was unsettled, so I decided to fly at a low altitude which was not, of course, a favourable height for optimum air miles per gallon; but I thought that if I could fly a distance equivalent to John o'Groats and back non-stop at that rather unfavourable height, keeping to the east of the Pennines and the Grampians, it would be a useful demonstration.

The aeroplane was unstable to start with, but as soon as I had used up the rear fuselage fuel the handling was back to normal and I settled down to a long and enjoyable flight over a great variety of countryside from Salisbury Plain to the Moray Firth and back again, all below 1,000 ft. In distance, and not taking into account the various diversions for weather and terrain, it was roughly equivalent to flying from East Anglia to Berlin and back. It took five hours.

This flight demonstrated, if nothing else, that there was no fundamental reason why the Spitfire should not be turned into a long-range escort fighter provided that certain problems could be solved.

A demonstration of this basic fact was also given by the Americans. They had two Mk IX Spitfires at Wright Field and by local modification they added two Mustang overload fuel tanks under the wings and some additional fuel inside the wings. They flew them across the Atlantic by the Northern route – via

Greenland and Iceland – and eventually they were thoroughly examined by the Supermarine design department. Unfortunately some of the structural modifications carried out were detrimental to the strength of the aircraft and so could not be considered for production.

However the decision had already been made to fit rear fuselage tanks in production to a derivative of the Mk XIV Spitfire, the F.Mk XVIII which also had a strengthened centre-section and undercarriage as well as a cut-away rear fuselage for improved rear vision. The basic stability margins of this aircraft, with its more forward centre of gravity due to its heavier engine, and with the latest standard of modified elevator and the larger vertical tail surfaces, were thought likely to be adequate to enable the aircraft to be cleared for long-range escort duties accepting some instability in the early stages. However, we had more difficulty than we anticipated in reaching an acceptable standard of handling with the rear tank in use and the war was over before it was possible to clear the aircraft with the rear tank in full operation.

The next and final stage in the longitudinal stability story was the incorporation of what came to be known as the 'Spiteful' tail. This had greatly enlarged (27 per cent) horizontal and vertical tail surfaces and was fitted to some Spitfire Mk 22s, all Mk 24s, some Seafire 46s, and all Seafire 47s and all Spitefuls and Seafangs.

It was a major production change and, had the pressures of war permitted its earlier introduction, for instance on the Mk XIVs and Mk XVIII, the Spitfire would have become a very fine long-range escort fighter. As it was, although the Seafire 47 and the Spitfire 24 were both very long-range aeroplanes compared with the early marks of Spitfire, the fact is that throughout the period of Spitfire wartime operations problems of longitudinal stability imposed a severe limitation on its range.

Back in 1936 we had had no way of measuring stability other than by recording phugoids, so all we could do was make qualitative judgements in the air. As time went on much better instrumentation became available enabling us to get accurate recordings of elevator angles and elevator trimmer angles as well as stick forces. Also much work was done on the theoretical side of stability at the RAE, particularly by S.B. Gates, while the A & AEE contributed greatly towards developing techniques for the quantitative measurement of stability in the air. Towards the end of the Spitfire's life, therefore, although we did not completely solve the problem at least we knew where we stood.

22

Test Pilots

The test flying task at Supermarine, particularly the clearance of the output of production aeroplanes, began to reach such proportions that it was necessary to form a team of RAF and Fleet Air Arm pilots on attachment to the company. Altogether, and not including those pilots who went to Castle Bromwich to help Alex Henshaw, the list of pilots who were seconded to and served at Supermarine amounted to more than forty; and they included pilots from the Royal Air Force, the Fleet Air Arm, the Belgian Air Force, and Norwegian Air Force as well as those civilian pilots who already belonged to the company (Appendix 11). These service pilots were drawn in the main from Spitfire or Seafire operational squadrons and they were employed principally in the routine testing of production aircraft as they emerged from the factories. At Supermarine they came under my control operationally and under the resident Air Ministry overseer, who was a Group Captain, for service administration affairs.

Of Mutt Summers, George Pickering and Alex Henshaw I have already written. Flight Lieutenant George Snarey, AFC, with whom I had served in the Met Flight in 1933–4, had, at the end of his short-service commission, joined Westland Aircraft as a test pilot where he flew Lysanders and Whirlwinds. After Alex Henshaw moved up to Castle Bromwich in the summer of 1940 we took Snarey on at Supermarine and after George Pickering's accident in October 1941 he took over administrative charge of the production test flying.

The first of the RAF pilots to be appointed to Supermarine in late 1940 and early 1941 were Flight Lieutenants J.H. Wedgwood, DFC, and A.C. Bartley, DFC. Both had fought in the Battle of Britain, Jeff Wedgwood in a Hurricane squadron (253) and Tony Bartley in Spitfires in 92 Squadron at Biggin Hill. Both pilots quickly got the hang of testing the production aeroplanes for, as Air Force pilots, they thoroughly understood from their direct experience what the aircraft were required to do in service.

Tony Bartley served with us from July 1941 to February 1942 and Jeff Wedgwood from November 1940 to December 1941. Tony, when a member of 92 Squadron, had been one of the small number of RAF aircrew actually to go into action with the early 20-mm cannon installations, which had initially caused us so much trouble. In February 1941, operating from Manston, he attacked and shot down a Heinkel 111 flying Spitfire X4272 armed with $2 \times$ 20-mm cannon with drum feed. Tony was a very competent pilot with a gregarious and convivial disposition. On one occasion he was invited to a party at Heston. All the light ferry aircraft were busy and there was no Spitfire that I could allow away for the night. Having reluctantly said 'No' to Tony I took off in some DTD aeroplane and when I landed back at Worthy Down a very startled looking foreman met me. 'What's happened, Mr Woolridge?' I asked. 'You look as if you've seen a ghost.' 'It's Mr Bartley,' he said. 'Another officer arrived in a Spitfire – Mr Bartley got in with him and they both took off together.' At Heston, an operational conversion unit, there was at that time Group Captain 'Taffy' Jones, who had, during the First World War, made a reputation for himself as a fighter pilot serving in Mick Mannock's Squadron. Taffy, whom I had known at Duxford during 1935, was a very convivial character. He was doing an evening round of the station in his staff car when he observed a lone Spitfire come in to land and taxi to a distant dispersal pen. He instructed his driver to follow it so that he might see who the pilot was. It is said to have been one of the most notable double-takes in Air Force history when Taffy saw not one young officer but two emerge from the tiny cockpit of the Spitfire.

Neither Humphrey Gilbert (the other pilot) nor Tony Bartley were small men but they had managed to squeeze themselves into the tiny cockpit of a Spitfire and still control it. This had been done more than once in a Hurricane, which had a much larger and roomier cockpit, and it had been done once in a Spitfire when a pilot of 92 Squadron, Flying Officer Gordon Brettel, took a WAAF with him in his Spitfire but she was of fairly diminutive proportions. Brettel was subsequently court-martialled but got away with it on a technical point. Tony and Humphrey Gilbert managed to fly by removing the parachute from the bucket seat and disposing themselves so that they each had one foot on one rudder pedal and one had his left hand on the throttle and the other his right hand on the control column. As they were both experienced pilots this aeronautical pas de deux worked quite well. Fortunately, no disciplinary action was taken and Tony and Humphrey Gilbert got away with no more than a ticking off; but some months later Humphrey Gilbert tried to do it again at Debden with a controller, who was not a pilot, called Bill Ross. It ended in disaster and both were killed.

Jeff Wedgwood, who had been a year or two younger than me at Lancing, was promoted to Squadron Leader while he was serving with us and then posted to command 92 Squadron in the Western Desert. He was a successful and distinguished commander of this famous squadron and personally destroyed 13 enemy aircraft, winning a DFC and Bar. In December 1942 he was being flown home as a passenger in a Halifax. After a night take-off from Malta the aircraft crashed and all the occupants were killed. I felt the loss of this good friend very deeply.

The presence of both Wedgwood and Bartley in those early days was very valuable to Supermarine. They had an easy and informal relationship with the people in the Works and design department which contributed towards increased understanding of the outlook of squadron pilots.

In 1941 we took on Johnnie Wakefield. I had known Johnnie at Brooklands before the war when he was making his name as an international racing driver. I encountered him again when he was in the Fleet Air Arm fighter squadron after the outbreak of war. He showed great interest in test flying and his experience and demonstrable ability in handling high performance machinery, his knowledge and understanding of the mechanical side of things (he supervised the preparation of his own cars for racing), indicated that he had much of what was needed in a test pilot. To build up his experience we put him onto the testing of production aeroplanes. At that time we were producing Spitfire PR Mk IVs in the Reading area of the dispersal scheme and these we flight tested from a small grass aerodrome near Henley. This airfield was also used by the RAF for 'ab initio' training in Magisters and Tiger Moths. They had a hangar in one corner of the field and we had ours in another. There was no formal aerodrome control and it was, as at nearly all minor aerodromes at that time, a case of keeping a sharp look-out and every man for himself.

One day towards the end of April 1942, Johnnie taxied out in PR IV from the small apron in front of our hangar, turned into wind, or as near into wind as the tight dimensions of the airfield permitted, and opened up. At the same time a Magister started its take-off run from the direction of the RAF hangar. Their courses were slightly convergent. As Johnnie was becoming airborne he must have seen the Maggie on a collision course. He swerved to the right as he became airborne, lost control, crashed and burst into flames.

The death of Johnnie Wakefield was a sad blow for us and I had been looking forward to him taking some of the load of the development flying off my shoulders.

We had to cast around for another pilot. By this time the development of Seafires was under way and the Admiralty was keen that there should be at least one naval pilot at Supermarine. They recommended Lieutenant D.R. Robertson, RNVR, currently serving in 809 Squadron in HMS *Victorious*.

After leaving Rugby Don had served an engineering apprenticeship with the Armstrong-Siddeley Car Company and had learned to fly privately in the late 1920s. He had then found employment as a 'bush pilot' in Canada, in a small company carrying passengers or stores into the northern regions, the aircraft operating on skis during the winter. Don used to describe how, on occasions when camped for the night, the engine oil would be drained into a drum and spend the night in the tent with the crew to prevent it freezing. There was then a sporting chance of starting the engine in the morning.

Don came to Supermarine in July 1942. As he was a man with an analytical mind and a deep interest in technical matters, we used him primarily on the development flying unit at Worthy Down. Don was with us when I started flying the prototype Spitfire 21, DP851, and he did much useful work on that aeroplane as on the prototype Spitfire XIVs. Don was the ideal man for development flying, with an instinctive understanding of designers' and pilots' problems alike and the practical man's knowledge of what was feasible and what was not. He left us to return to the Navy in April 1943 having completed nearly 400 hours of test flying in nine months. He was sent to the Naval Test Squadron at the A & AEE, Boscombe Down.

At the outbreak of war George Errington was Chief Test Pilot of Airspeed Ltd and one of the small band of senior test pilots in the industry whose origins were entirely in civil aviation. Through flying a wide variety of light civil types he had graduated towards larger and heavier aircraft and had flown Mosquitos and Spitfires. He had been responsible for the flight development of the Airspeed Oxford which started life as a civil project and was developed to fulfil the role of a twin-engined trainer for the Royal Air Force. The Airspeed Company, based at Christchurch and Portsmouth, embarked upon the development of troop-carrying gliders, constructed principally out of wood and designed to be towed behind large transport or bomber aircraft. The largest was the Horsa, for the flight development of which George had been responsible. The Horsa played a prominent part in airborne operations including D-Day and Arnhem.

In early 1943 George told me that he was under-employed at Airspeeds so I said we could give him plenty of important work at Worthy Down but he would have to come and join us full-time and take up residence. To this he readily agreed and it was fixed up that George should come for a period on loan. Apart from being a safe, experienced and reliable hand with an aircraft he was an engineer and a man with all the insight that goes with a wide range of outside interests and a great love of nature and the countryside. I came to rely upon him very much.

To get another naval pilot to replace Don Robertson I made extensive inquiries amongst my contacts in the Fleet Air Arm and the Admiralty. One of the pilots strongly recommended was Lieutenant Frank Furlong, RNVR. Initially I had some misgivings, for Frank had no technical or engineering background; his father, Noel Furlong, trained horses privately near Banbury. Frank, after Sandhurst, had gone into the 9th Lancers, where with his friend in the same regiment, Fulke Walwyn, his activity as an amateur race rider grew and developed. Finally Frank left the Army, made a great name for himself riding 'over the sticks', won several important races and in 1935 rode his father's great horse, Reynoldstown, to win the Grand National.

Having learned to fly at a club he was amongst the band of young private aviators to whom the Admiralty offered RNVR Commissions on the outbreak of war and then trained as operational pilots. Frank graduated onto fighters and served in a

Fulmar Squadron aboard HMS *Illustrious* in the Mediterranean
and in the Indian Ocean. When the German battleship *Bismarck*
broke out into the Atlantic in May 1941, Frank's squadron was
hurriedly embarked in HMS *Victorious*. On 24 May 1941,
Victorious flew off three Fulmars to shadow *Bismarck*. Of these
three Fulmars, two did not return and one of them was Frank's.
In appalling conditions of wind, low cloud and rain, and unable
to find their way back to *Victorious* which was having to preserve
radio silence, Frank ditched his aircraft and he and his observer
managed to scramble into their inflatable dinghy. Cold, wet,
heaving about in mid-Atlantic seas to the south-east of Greenland
and as far north as approximately latitude 58° their chances of
survival seemed to them virtually zero. They existed miserably in
their dinghy for more than 48 hours and then, when all hope must
nearly have gone, they were miraculously sighted and picked up
at sunrise by a passing, unescorted, merchant ship. The officer of
the watch in that ship was taking the dawn sight with his sextant
when he saw their dinghy bobbing up and down in the direct line
between him and the sun.

At Supermarine Frank studied test flying carefully and became a very useful, conscientious and practical test pilot. With
him and George Errington at Worthy Down, I saw my chance of
getting away at last and when Rear-Admiral Sir Denis Boyd
invited me to serve a period in the Fleet Air Arm and study and
report on the problem of the Seafire I accepted with alacrity.

The unit at Worthy Down was working closely in liaison with
the design department at Hursley Park. We had a local branch of
the technical office in residence at the airfield, under Murry
White, helping to plan flight programmes and analyse results on
the spot; and we had a weekly meeting at the aerodrome with Joe
Smith, Clifton and Mansbridge and their staff in which the last
week's results would be carefully assessed and the next week's
activities planned. Frank Furlong and George Errington livened
up these meetings greatly as both were not only expert pilots but
also extremely coherent and effective in discussion.

One of our problems at this time was the unsuitability of the
aerodrome at Worthy Down. Situated on a small hill, much too
short for comfort in all directions, it was particularly dangerous
in its shorter direction. There was a tremendous amount of Naval
traffic on it and on one occasion I had a head-on collision with a

Naval Proctor. The Proctor had finished his landing run over the brow of the hill and instead of taxiing in round the perimeter he 'backtracked' and taxied up the slope towards the centre of the field. I was just approaching to land against the other slope and as I touched down over the brow of the hill I was appalled to see a pair of wing tips appear each side of my blind spot dead ahead. I hit him head on at about 70 mph and showers of plywood from his wooden structure flew in the air as my metal propeller sliced into the Proctor. I scrambled out of the cockpit expecting to find dead and mangled bodies. Instead I found a very dazed sailor lurching about and swearing volubly and the pilot, Lieutenant Howard, lying trapped in the wreckage of the demolished Proctor with his engine resting across his legs. I was able to lift the hot engine somewhat as the sailor dragged Howard clear just as the whole thing went up in flames, Spitfire and all. Fortunately Howard was not too badly injured but the whole incident added urgency to our plans to move the unit to an aerodrome we could have more or less to ourselves. We had, with the energetic help of an Air Ministry overseer, Group Captain Pat Thomson, requisitioned the airfield at High Post near Boscombe Down where a 2500-yd runway was being prepared and the erection of a hangar and of offices where we could accommodate all the Supermarine pilots, production and development alike, as well as a larger resident unit from the technical offices. We moved the whole Worthy Down unit to High Post in March 1944 but, sadly, it was when operating out of High Post that Frank Furlong was killed in one of the prototype Spitefuls and in rather unaccountable circumstances.

I felt the loss of Frank very acutely not only because he was a staunch and capable colleague as a test pilot but because we had become very close friends.

Lieutenant Pat Shea-Simonds, RNVR, came to us after attending the No. 1 course at the newly formed Empire Test Pilots School (ETPS) at Boscombe Down. The first Commandant of EPTS – who might be described as the founder/Commandant – was my old friend of Grantham and early Martlesham days, and now a Wing Commander, Sammy Wroath. The chief technical instructor on those early courses was H. McLaren Humphries. So Pat Shea-Simonds – 'Shea' to everyone – was the first formally trained test pilot to come to Supermarine and one of the first to industry generally. He arrived not long after Frank Furlong's death and was soon deep into the development flying at High Post as well as production testing around the many dispersal aerodromes. Shortly before coming to us, but after completing his ETPS course, he had been sent on an attachment to Fairey's where one day he was flying a production Albacore (a biplane torpedo bomber) when, somewhat to Shea's surprise, the engine fell out altogether and descended rapidly earthwards. Shea managed to land the aeroplane in a field and a working party came and fitted a new engine. Sometime later he flew it out of the field and back to Fairey's aerodrome. For saving his aircraft in these very unusual circumstances Shea was later awarded the MBE.

Although the requirements of industry and of the Government establishments, A & AEE and RAE, were becoming larger and increasingly difficult to fulfil with suitable pilots, and the need for some sort of training establishment was very apparent, I was nevertheless puzzled to know how ETPS was going to work. I sometimes discussed it with Sammy Wroath who had the very difficult job of starting it off and it was difficult to imagine a person better qualified to do it.

After Pat Shea-Simonds had been with us for a short while I realised that my doubts had been unfounded. It was a relief to me to have someone with a basic understanding of what the job was all about from the outset. We had enough difficulties with the Spiteful and Seafang and the Spitfire 21s and later marks of Seafires to provide plenty of scope and plenty of problems for anyone taking an intelligent interest in test flying.

I had ten or twelve pilots at Supermarine by then and at least four dispersal airfields producing Spitfires which had to be served every day as the aircraft rolled off the line. I based all the pilots at High Post and they flew out to the dispersals in light aircraft as required, so that in this way we were always in touch with each other and with the small technical office. We operated as a team; Squadron Leader Guy Morgan was in organisational charge of the production pilots and we did our best to maintain a consistent standard of production testing. I was extremely lucky with the service pilots who were from time to time attached to Supermarine. To mention only a few, there was Andy Andrews of 41 Squadron who after leaving us was shot down and killed in a Spitfire XII; Flight Lieutenant Philip Wigley, DFC, an ex-

Mustang pilot, and Flight Lieutenant Les Colquhoun, DFC, DFM, late of the PRU, who stayed with the firm after the war; Titch Havercroft who had been an instructor at ETPS; Lieutenant Johnnie Underwood, MBE, one of the most experienced deck landing and trials pilots in the Navy; the ebullient Michael Graham and Geoffrey Page, the latter terribly burned in a Hurricane in the Battle of Britain who was with us before going back on operational flying. There was 'India' Clive who had been in the AFDU, 'Gos' Gosling who served with us for more than two years before going back into operations, and many others.

One young Flight Lieutenant called Frank Banner stalled a Seafire when practising ADDLs on the runway at High Post with Johnnie Underwood on the bats and his aircraft burst into flames. Johnnie, with the aid of men who ran out from the hangar led by their foreman Tom Northeast, and the Fire Tender crew, managed to pull him out but he died in hospital.

Another young Flight Lieutenant in the early days at Eastleigh particularly sticks in my memory. His name was Jarred and he came to us from Douglas Bader's Tangmere Wing. Before he had been with us long he suffered an engine failure in a PR IV and in trying to land in difficult country near Petworth he crashed into trees and was killed. This came as a great shock to his parents, for it emerged that, from the time of his initial flying training and throughout the period that he had been fighting in Spitfires in the Tangmere Wing, he had hidden from them the fact that he was a pilot, and made them believe he was on ground duties in order to save them anxiety. To do this he always removed his wings from his tunic when he went home on leave. At a time when young men serving their country in the Royal Air Force were intensely proud of the wings on their tunics, it seemed a most impressive example of extreme consideration for the feelings of his parents and sacrificing his own natural feeling of pride to do so.

The next ETPS graduate to join us was Lieutenant Commander Mike Lithgow, RN. He was sent to us on a short attachment at the end of his course, as an integral part of it. Then he was posted to Patuxent River in the USA and by the time he came back the war was over and Shea had decided to return to his civilian occupation. So I offered Mike Lithgow the job and he took it. When, in 1947, I lost my medical category and had to stop test flying while I was in the middle of prototype trials on

Vickers' first jet aircraft, the Attacker, it was to Mike Lithgow that I handed over my job. Bitter and frustrated though I felt at being grounded, the blow was to some extent softened by handing over to a pilot whom I both respected and liked.

It has not been possible to write about all the pilots who served with me at Supermarine at some time between 1936 and 1946 but what I hope is a full list appears in Appendix 11. The contribution made by these men to the test flying task at Supermarine was highly valuable.

23

Seafires

and the Fleet Air Arm

Although the proposal for Sea-Spitfires had been dropped in 1940 (see Chapter 13) a variety of events in the early war years served to keep the Admiralty's interest very much alive.

The first was the remarkable achievement of 46 Squadron RAF, commanded by Squadron Leader K.B.B. Cross, in successfully landing their unhooked Hurricanes aboard HMS *Glorious* during the withdrawal from Norway in June 1940. Admittedly *Glorious* was steaming at 26 knots into a 15-knot wind but it was a practical demonstration that modern monoplane fighters could be successfully landed on aircraft carriers.

Then in January 1941 and again in May the need for high-performance fighter protection was demonstrated when first *Illustrious* and later *Formidable* were dive-bombed and seriously damaged in the Mediterranean despite their powerful anti-aircraft armament. These episodes served to re-emphasise the lesson learned in the North Sea in 1939 (see Chapter 13).

Diverting Spitfires from RAF production for conversion into Sea-Spitfires was obviously a matter of the utmost difficulty during 1940 and the early part of 1941 but eventually Seafires (as the Sea-Spitfire became known) were ordered into production in the second half of 1941 and were established in Naval Service in time to play a prominent part in Operation Torch, the Allied invasion of French North Africa in November 1942. Five Fleet Air Arm Seafire Squadrons were involved, operating from the carriers *Argus*, *Furious*, *Formidable* and *Victorious*. Torch was the first major Allied amphibious operation and the new Seafires acquitted themselves well but *Argus*, the oldest of the carriers with a very short flight deck, lost six Seafires in deck-landing accidents, twice as many as the combined losses of the other three ships from that cause. This was an advance indication of the problems of operating Seafires from the smaller ships, which was later to become acute.

In December 1942 the number of Seafire Squadrons grew and by May 1943 the Seafire had become the most numerous aircraft in Royal Navy Service. At this time delivery to the Royal Navy of the American-built Type G-3 escort carriers (CVEs) was getting into its stride. These were converted single-screw merchant ships with wooden-planked flight decks, arrester wires, crash-barriers between the landing area and the forward deck park, and adequate hangar space. They were, on the whole, very effective ships but their principal shortcoming was lack of speed; they could not raise more than about 17 knots and in some cases only 14. This was adequate provided there was at least 10 to 15 knots of natural surface wind to ensure a 25- to 28-knot wind over the deck which the Seafire liked to have for landing on. If the wind speed over the deck was below this, serious problems could arise especially for the less experienced pilots. Proof of this was to emerge in September 1943 during the Allied landings in the Bay of Salerno (Operation Avalanche). Salerno was some 230 miles distant from the nearest Allied airfields in Sicily so fighter cover for the landings would have to be provided in the main from ships at sea until airfields and landing grounds could be established ashore.

The ships of Force H, including the Fleet carriers *Illustrious* and *Formidable*, were to act as a heavy covering force to seaward of the main assault to provide air and anti-submarine support for an inshore force of carriers, Force V, under Rear-Admiral Vian in the cruiser *Euryalus*, comprising the carriers *Unicorn*, *Attacker*, *Battler*, *Hunter* and *Stalker*. Apart from *Unicorn* all these ships were escort carriers.

D-Day for the assault was 9 September and the first fighter patrols were airborne at 0615. By the end of the day Force V had flown a total of 265 Seafire sorties making an average of 2.5 sorties for every aircraft embarked. There was no surface wind throughout the day with the result that there was only 17 knots of wind speed over the deck for landing; also it was very hot. This led to a very high incidence of aircraft damaged in deck landing accidents; by dawn on D plus One the number of Seafires available in Force V had dropped from 105 to 65. As no shore base had been captured or established on the first day the carriers had to continue to provide the main fighter cover on the second day, D plus One, and they succeeded in turning back over 40 attacking enemy aircraft. By dawn on D plus Two the remaining force of serviceable Seafires was down to 39, but still 160 sorties were flown during that day. This was a high utilisation rate for carrier aircraft.

The inescapable conclusion to be drawn from Avalanche was that the accident rate in landing Seafires on the small escort carriers in conditions of no surface wind was unacceptably high. The bare statistics were frightening in their implication. A total of 713 sorties had resulted in 73 deck-landing accidents of which 32 were write-offs, 24 were damaged beyond immediate repair, and 17 sustained damage to their undercarriage. Throughout the operations four aircraft were lost due to engine failure and a further six from miscellaneous accidental causes not associated with deck landing. Altogether a total of 42 Seafires had been written off in accidents and a further 41 damaged out of a total embarked force, including those embarked with the covering force, of 121 Seafires.

Operating conditions were difficult primarily due to the slow speed of the escort carriers combined with zero wind at the surface and a glassy sea. The decks of the CVEs were 30 per cent shorter than those of the big Fleet carriers to which many of the Seafire pilots were accustomed, and their speed was a vital 10 knots slower. Most of the Seafire pilots were insufficiently experienced or practised to cope with these conditions which were often aggravated by lack of sea-room. The four escort carriers usually operated in a box formation and they flew off aircraft in fours and recovered them similarly. To quote David Brown*:

> The carriers' 'box', allocated by the naval planners, was far too small and too close to shore for comfortable operation in good wind conditions; in nil wind it left no margin for manoeuvre and in the event of a recovery commencing as the carriers approached the edge of the area the landings were often made in haste, the aircraft being too short of fuel to permit waiting until more sea room could be found.

The influence of the piloting factor was indicated by the

---

* *The Seafire*, Ian Allan, 1973, p. 53.

interesting fact that No. 834 Fighter Flight commanded by Lieutenant F.A.J. Pennington RNZNVR had been embarked in *Hunter* since 7 July and the pilots had been very thoroughly worked up and drilled in their deck-landing procedures. They operated throughout the three days of Avalanche and all six aircraft were serviceable at noon on 12 September. Thus, although there was obviously much to be done technically to improve the Seafire as a shipborne fighter, 834 Flight had also demonstrated that there was also much that should be done in improving piloting techniques and training methods.

The high wastage rate in deck-landing accidents during the Salerno landings at once called into question the suitability of the Seafire for flying off the small escort carriers. Inevitably I became involved in much discussion of this problem and was bound to say that as my experience of deck landing was limited to a few landings on one of the big Fleet carriers (*Indomitable*) I could have no properly informed view or opinion of the problem. At one such discussion which I attended the Fifth Sea Lord, Rear-Admiral Sir Denis Boyd, drew me aside afterwards and suggested that I should come into the Fleet Air Arm to gain some real experience of carrier flying. I accepted this chance with alacrity and very shortly afterwards received a formal letter from the Admiralty appointing me a Lieutenant-Commander (A) RNVR and instructing me to report to the Royal Naval Air Station at Easthaven in Angus to begin deck-landing training. I just had time to get measured for a uniform at Gieves and report to the Fifth Sea Lord's Office in London, and then, thus disguised as a Naval Officer, to take the night train to Easthaven. I thus found myself resplendent in the uniform of a Lieutenant-Commander but without benefit of any 'divisional' course or other arrangements to instruct me in the ways and customs of the Senior Service. It was some help that I had been brought up and trained in the Royal Air Force, but on arrival at Easthaven I certainly did have a feeling of having been thrown in at the deep end. Easthaven acted as a deck-landing training establishment and pilots came there for a course of ADDLs (aerodrome dummy deck landings) and other instruction before proceeding for their first real deck landings aboard HMS *Ravager*, an escort carrier allocated for training, or in the case of TSR pilots, to HMS *Argus*.

Lieutenant-Commander R.N. Everett, RN, was in charge of the school which also trained deck-landing control officers (DLCOs), the 'batsmen' who controlled a pilot's approach to the deck by signals from fluorescent objects resembling ping-pong bats.

Robert Everett, the son of an Admiral, was an energetic and very unconventional Naval officer strongly oriented towards aviation. Indeed, he coined the term 'Fishheads' to apply to Naval officers who were not aviators – which was most of them – and this caught on in quite a big way in the Fleet Air Arm. It did not endear Robert in some sections of the Service. Robert was very helpful to me, as was his second-in-command, Lieutenant Arthur Darley, RN, and we had a lot of fun during my deck-landing training. At Easthaven there was a dummy, and mobile, representation of the 'Island' of a carrier which could be wheeled out onto the starboard edge of the runway to accustom trainee pilots to landing with such a formidable obstacle very close to their starboard wing tips. It was dubbed 'HMS Spurious'. From Easthaven I was appointed to HMS *Ravager* for intensive deck-landing practice to build up my experience as quickly as possible.

In the five months I spent in the Fleet Air Arm, I accumulated many hours of carrier flying, did about 75 deck landings in a variety of types, which with subsequent trials work went up to well over 100. I flew Seafires most of the time, including some trials work of various sorts in the trials carrier HMS *Pretoria Castle*. I spent some while as a supernumerary Lieutenant-Commander flying Seafires in 886 Squadron and in 879 Squadron embarked in HMS *Attacker*, formerly one of the ships of Force V at Salerno and destined for the south of France landings (Operation Dragoon) in 1944. Apart from flying Seafires I also managed to get experience of operating from carriers in Wildcats, Hellcats and the F4U Corsair and I spent some while in a Corsair Squadron, 1837 (Lieutenant-Commander Pridham-Whipple). I was also asked to make an evaluation and write a report for the Admiralty on the suitability of the Corsair for operation from the small escort carriers.

The business of operating aircraft from ships was both interesting and challenging. Every landing of a fighter aboard a carrier was in itself an event fraught with far greater possibilities for error and disaster than any airfield landing. The results of an

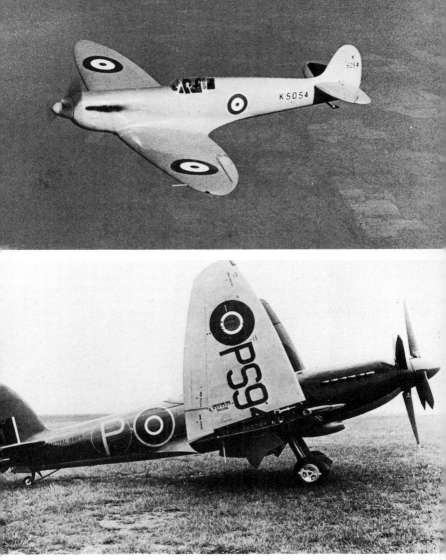

26/27 The first and the last: Spitfire prototype K5054 (1936) and Seafire 47 (1946)

28 A Seafire 45 aboard HMS *Pretoria Castle*. Deck landing: the perfect
    arrival—the aircraft has engaged No. 1 wire, is on the exact centre line of t
    deck and has landed gently. No prize for guessing the identity of the pilot

29 Deck landing: the imperfect arrival—the aircraft has failed to engage an
    arrester wire and hit the crash barrier aboard an escort carrier

Reginald Mitchell, the brilliant and inspired designer of the Spitfire

Alan Clifton, head of Supermarine technical office and most able lieutenant to both Mitchell and Smith

31 Joseph Smith, who took over when Mitchell died and led the extensive development of the Spitfire

33 Ernest Hives, the dynamic and shrewd leader of Rolls-Royce Aero engines

34 The old drawing office at Woolston, *c.* 1934, where the original Spitfire was designed

35 Woolston Works after enemy bombing, September 1940

36 Part of the fitting shop of a typical dispersal site. Note the number of female workers

37 One of six F.Mk VIIIs converted to take the Griffon RG 5SM; they were, effectively, prototypes of the Mk XIV

38 The first production F.Mk XIV, RB140

39 A PR Mk XIX, photographic reconnaissance derivative of the F.Mk XIV. A pressurised aircraft of exceptional range and performance

40 Cyril Lovesey, Rolls-Royce Merlin development engineer

41 Stanley Hooker, Rolls-Royce supercharger expert who worked closely with Lovesey

42 A Merlin III engine, with single-stage single-speed supercharger

43 A Merlin 61 engine, with two-speed two-stage supercharger and intercooler

44 (*top left*) F/Lt (later S/Ldr) Jeff Wedgwood. Killed in Malta after winning a DFC and Bar in the Western Desert

45 (*top right*) F/Lt (later W/Cdr) Tony Bartley, DFC and Bar

46 (*bottom left*) F/Lt Alan J. Andrews, DFC. Shot down and killed in a Spitfire XII of 91 Squadron after leaving Supermarine

47 (*bottom right*) F/Lt R.C.Gosling. Flew in a Meteor Squadron after leaving Supermarine

48 Lt Pat Shea-Simonds, MBE RNVR

50 Frank Furlong and Reynoldstown;
this combination won the 1935
Grand National

49 Lt Johnnie Wakefield, RNVR.
Killed in a PR Mk IV

51 Rear-Admiral Sir Denis Boyd,
Fifth Sea Lord (*left*) and
Commander Don Robertson, AFC
RNVR

Alex Henshaw, pilot extraordinary, who took over and ran
the test flying at Castle Bromwich
S/Ldr Guy Morgan, DFC (*left*) and
F/Lt Philip Wigley, DFC

53 George Errington, test pilot,
engineer and raconteur

55 Lt/Cdr Mike Lithgow, OBE (*left*)
and F/Lt Les Colquhoun, DFC GM
DFM

56 Spitfire MkV Floatplane. J.K.Q. taking off from Hamble on an early
   flight test. Several of these aircraft went to the Mediterranean

57 A Spiteful in a steep turn to starboard

58 'Dumbo': Supermarine type 322 designed to Spec. S.24/37. The world's first aircraft with a wing of incidence variable in flight. First flown by J.K.Q. on 6 February 1943

59 A recently restored Spitfire F.Mk XIV. The starkly simple paint scheme emphasises the aeroplane's beautiful lines

60   Spitfire F.Mk XIV RB140. Perhaps one of the best action photographs ever of a Spitfire. It was taken through the side-door of an Oxford by Supermarine photographer Frank H. Burr. The Oxford was flown by Frank Furlong and the Spitfire by J.K.Q. The main problem was to avoid a collision

error could be immediate and dramatic. Failure to engage an arrester wire with the aircraft's hook meant an immediate crash into the cable barrier which separated the landing area from the forward deck park. Misjudging the approach speed, or getting a few feet off line could result in a broken undercarriage and a damaged hook and a fair chance of going over the ship's side into the sea. The deck was 70 ft above the sea and it was extremely difficult to get out of a Seafire cockpit before it sank even if the pilot remained conscious after the impact. Not many pilots survived an 'over the side' in a Seafire.

On the other hand, a correct approach and landing, at the right speed, bang on the centre line of the deck, and engaging numbers one or two wire produced a great feeling of satisfaction and of security. A sharp deceleration as you engaged the wire and the ship had firmly got you – and as soon as the flight deck party had unhooked you from the arrester wire you taxied forward to the deck park and up went the barrier behind you as the next man approached to land. A well-worked-up Squadron could land four aircraft on in succession in the space of two minutes, but it had to be very well judged by the pilots, spacing themselves out at precisely the right distance one behind the other for the approach, and the batsman had to be quick and alert, ensuring that the previous aircraft was ahead of the barrier, and the barrier up, before accepting the next one who by this time would be in the very last stages of his approach. Wave-offs (the batsman signalling the aircraft to go round again if he was dissatisfied with its approach) were time-wasting and disrupting. A crash on deck was worse, for it meant that no other aircraft could land on until it was cleared. In cases of extreme urgency it was normal to get the pilot out and then heave the crashed aircraft over the side in order to clear the deck and continue operating. Thus the success and smoothness of operations depended very largely upon the precision and accuracy with which the pilots flew. Nevertheless it was great fun working all this up. Returning with 16 aircraft to the carrier group, breaking into one's own four to land on one's own ship with three other ships simultaneously doing the same thing, was exciting and competitive and could be a source of great satisfaction when it all worked smoothly and slickly. The Seafire was not an easy aeroplane to land on the deck, partly because of its restricted view and partly because it had to be flown very carefully if the approach speed was to be kept steady and accurate. Neither was it a very robust aircraft, never having been designed for deck operation in the first place, but if it was properly flown it was quite up to the job. However, if pilots were not adequately trained or practised, or if, as was obviously often the case, they returned from an operational sortie tired or otherwise a bit rattled the Seafire was undoubtedly accident prone.

Every deck landing was a challenging affair even for experienced and well-worked-up pilots. I had reached the stage where I felt I could land a Spitfire in my sleep on an aerodrome if need be, but I soon found that during a sortie from an aircraft carrier, there was always in the back of one's mind, however many other things there were to engage attention and concentration whilst in the air, the consciousness that at the end of the sortie one had to get this damn thing back on the ship again. It gave each flight from a carrier a certain special character of its own, not experienced when operating from a shore base. There was never any question of giving less than one's full concentration and effort to a deck landing. There is no doubt that it added a significant new dimension to the task of training young pilots as well as to the requirements affecting the aeroplane which did not exist in normal shorebased operations. It also added to the mental and psychological strain on young Naval fighter pilots which was additional to that normally associated with operational flying. It is a factor all too easily forgotten. In this area, therefore, the human element and its fallibility was of vital significance to the success or otherwise of Fleet Air Arm operations.

It became very evident to me that there were two distinct approaches to the Seafire deck-landing problem. One was to develop some of the technical shortcomings out of the aircraft and the other was to establish the best flying techniques and train pilots intensively in it and give them plenty of practice. Both would take time and neither could be expected to produce 100 per cent results, but a very significant improvement over the situation as it was at Salerno could surely be achieved.

When I felt I had done sufficient deck landings and gained enough variety of carrier flying I wrote my report to the Admiralty along these lines. The report was addressed directly to the Fifth Sea Lord at the Admiralty and was dated 29 February 1944. It has survived in the files and I am indebted to Alfred Price and Peter Arnold for the loan of a copy.

In the introduction to the report I wrote:

> there are four main factors which contribute to the success and practicability of deck landing in ships under conditions as they exist today.
>
> (1) the method of approach
> (2) the view from the aeroplane
> (3) the speed controllability of the aeroplane
> (4) the robustness of the aeroplane to withstand the degree of rough usage which may be expected on the deck under sea-going conditions.

I went on to point out that No. 1, the correct method of approach, needed clear definition and then training of pilots and DLCOs, whereas the remainder depended largely upon the design features of the aeroplane. The report went on to discuss correct and incorrect methods of approach. It pointed out that if the Seafire made a straight approach from dead astern it soon got into an area astern of the ship in which the pilot's view of the ship was obscured by the aircraft's nose. At that point the pilot tended to wander off towards the ship's starboard quarter in order to restore his view of the deck. He was then off the correct line, would have to do a last-minute jink to try to realign himself with the deck, and arriving thus untidily from the starboard quarter he would touch down with a lot of drift, probably damage his undercarriage, quite likely miss a wire or pull his hook out and finish up by going over the ship's port side. It happened all too often. A straight approach from astern was therefore absolutely ruled out. Another method, which had been used by Commander Peter Bramwell, the first man ever to land a Seafire on deck and subsequently by Lieutenant 'Winkle' Brown of the FAA Service Trials Unit at Crail, was to make an approach from dead astern of the ship and solve the view problem by crabbing the aircraft sideways, thereby pushing the nose away sideways to starboard and so keeping the deck just in view. Both Peter Bramwell and 'Winkle' Brown were very skilful and very experienced pilots and this was fine for them, but I disapproved of the method for young and relatively inexperienced pilots. A deck landing approach had to be made at a speed very close to the stall – a speed which in the Royal Air Force would be considered dangerously slow for airfield approaches – and to ask a young pilot when flying with such a narrow speed margin over the stall deliberately to apply yaw was in my view asking for trouble. I pointed out that 'the accepted way of putting an aeroplane into a spin is to stall it and then apply yaw'. I had tried it often enough myself and didn't care for it. 'Winkle' Brown went on doing it with clockwork precision over and over again but he was an exceptional pilot and even he did not recommend it for general use.

The proper method was to approach the ship in a gently curving left-hand turn with a thoroughly well-controlled rate of sink, sneaking in, as it were, just in front of the Seafire's blind area astern of the ship. This could be done quite safely due to the Seafire's excellent lateral stability characteristics right down to the stall. If the circuit was correctly flown and the moment of turning in correctly judged it really wasn't difficult but very accurate flying was still the name of the game.

I quote from my report:

The following are considered to be reasonable rough rules for Seafire deck landing:

(1) Circuit height – 300 to 400 feet.
(2) Fly ahead of ship for 10 to 15 seconds according to windspeed before commencing circuit.
(3) Keep circuit small.
(4) Lower hook, undercarriage and flaps during circuit before getting abeam the ship on the downwind leg.
(5) While still ahead of the beam slow down to 80 knots and watch for the moment to turn in which can only be a matter of judgement but it will be easier to judge when you have nothing else to concentrate on.
(6) When on the port quarter during your turn settle down to your correct approach speed (70 to 75 knots with a IIC); keep steady rate of descent; watch the DLCO and your speed; make up your mind that you are going to arrive from the port quarter and *not* the starboard quarter.
(7) If you have difficulty seeing the batsman lean your head over the port side of the cockpit.
(8) Wear Mk VII or Mk VIII goggles.

As to the aeroplane itself my report pointed to the importance of speed controllability on the landing approach. I defined this as:

the quality in an aeroplane (which is dependent upon the features of its design) which renders it either easy or difficult to fly at a steady or accurate speed under conditions of a deck landing approach. Factors in the design which go towards providing either good or bad speed controllability are firstly a good degree of fore and aft stability at slow speeds and secondly the provision of plenty of drag when in the flaps and undercarriage down position, or, more simply, a low lift/drag ratio.

I went on to say that the Seafire was decidedly lacking in both these respects and that these, added to the poor view from the pilot's cockpit, were the principal causes of pilots' difficulties in landing Seafires on the deck. I also drew attention to the immediate need for an improved undercarriage design having higher energy absorption and reduced rebound ratio, the incorporation of a 'sting' hook with its thrust line passing more nearly through the aircraft's centre of gravity, the incorporation of a hydraulic damper to eliminate hook bounce (which we had already tried experimentally) as well as sundry other refinements.

Much of this I had already discussed at length with the Supermarine design department and modifications were in preparation to deal with the points in later marks of Seafire, which naturally took time. The Seafires XV and XVII had improved undercarriage legs, more stability and more drag in the approach configuration and sting hooks. Personally I found them easier to land on the deck.

The Seafire 47 (of 1946 vintage) was better still but by the time it entered service the Navy had changed over, for reasons of inter-Service standardisation, to the very different American methods of deck landing and 'batting' which involved a lower and flatter approach path and a high cut. This usually involved a faster and heavier touchdown and a more violent arrival into the arrester wires and a spate of buckled fuselages on the Seafire 47 resulted. It was my opinion at that time that this would not have occurred had the Navy not abandoned its previous landing technique.

The period I spent flying with 886 and 879 Squadrons embarked in HMS *Attacker* (Captain Shirley-Rollason) was in many ways the most interesting and enjoyable. Val Bailey, with Dick Law as his senior pilot, commanded 886 and David Carlisle 879 Squadron. HMS *Attacker* was a unit in the Escort Carrier Group being worked up (although we did not know this specifically at the time) for Operation Dragoon – the Allied landings in the south of France. The other ships in the Group were *Hunter*, *Pursuer* and *Stalker* and the Force was under the command of Rear-Admiral A.W. La T. Bisset flying his flag in the cruiser HMS *Royalist*. From these working-up exercises I began to get an insight into Naval fighter operations and the methods of mounting such operations from aircraft carriers. Hitherto I had been much involved in various 'trials' – operating a lot from the carrier *Pretoria Castle* (Captain Caspar John) – but now, in *Attacker*, I was getting an insight into an operational Squadron and getting to know and understand young front-line pilots and their attitudes. I found it of the greatest value and I longed to stay in that ship – but it was not to be. By the time Operation Dragoon actually came off on 15 August 1944, Rear-Admiral Bisset, who had been responsible for planning the carrier operations, had been taken ill and replaced at short notice by Rear-Admiral Sir Thomas Troubridge who commanded Task Group 88.1 comprising *Emperor*, *Pursuer*, *Searcher*, *Attacker* and *Khedive* (the last two with Seafires) and the Flagship *Royalist*, while Task Force 88.2 commanded by the American Rear-Admiral Durgin comprised two US carriers *Tulagi* and *Kasaan Bay* and the British ships *Hunter* and *Stalker*, both with Seafires.

Operations for the first five days of Dragoon were at a somewhat lower intensity than at Salerno; nevertheless there was continuous dawn-to-dusk flying. The Seafire Squadrons maintained a good deck landing record and low accident rate in spite of low windspeeds. In fact, *Hunter* and *Stalker*, which had both maintained a high sortie rate during those first five days, did not suffer one deck landing write-off although the accident rate somewhat increased later due to pilot fatigue and the onset of an increasing swell.

When, on 28 August 1944 (D Plus 13) the Royal Navy's escort carrier Squadron was released from Dragoon it had flown 1,073 Seafire sorties, 252 Hellcat sorties, and 347 Wildcat sorties. Seafire deck-landing losses amounted to only 14 (1.4 per cent all returning sorties) and the overall wastage rate from all causes was 2.8 per cent of all sorties flown.

So Dragoon did much to restore the Seafire's reputation which had suffered so badly at Salerno. Undoubtedly the higher standard of pilot training and experience and the somewhat more favourable operating conditions had their effect.

In the middle of March I was sent back to Supermarine, much against my will. I had flown every type of operational aircraft in the Fleet Air Arm (British and American) except the Firefly and the Albacore and I had deck-landed most of them. I had an all-too-short experience of the inside of a Naval Fighter Squadron and I had certainly crammed in plenty of deck landing experience. At least I had got some sort of grasp of the problems of Naval aviation and of life and conditions aboard an aircraft carrier.

I had badly wanted to stay in HMS *Attacker* with the Seafire Squadrons, but I suppose, inevitably, I had to go back to Supermarine. There were many things crying out to be done back at the firm and I got an undertaking that I could participate henceforward in the carrier trials of all new marks of Seafire and indeed I did this in the case of the Seafires XV, XVII, 45, 46 and 47.

Most valuable of all I had established many excellent and lasting friendships, and I acquired, during my brief period of service in the Fleet Air Arm, a deep and lasting respect for the Royal Navy.

24

Variations

on a Central Theme

The main trail of Spitfire development was blazed by the fighters, and determined by the changing requirements of war. In tracing its main path, I have concentrated on the fighters and inevitably devoted less than adequate attention to the Spitfires of the Photographic Reconnaissance Unit (PRU) which operated them and the value of the contribution they made to Allied Intelligence from the very early days of hostilities until the war came to its final successful conclusion.

These Spitfires which were modified to carry cameras in order to photograph targets deep in enemy territory, relying upon their speed and height for survival, were derivatives of the highest-performance fighter versions of the aeroplane currently in production. Thus the PR Mk IV was developed from the F. Mk. V, the PR X and XI from the F. Mk VII and the F. Mk IX respectively and the PR XIX from the Griffon-engined F. Mk XIV. Because the PR aeroplanes carried neither guns nor ammunition it was possible to cram much extra fuel into their wings. Unusually, the main structural strength of the Spitfire wing was concentrated in a box-like spar structure forming the whole leading edge section of the wing; this part of the structure was converted into a fuel tank, thus more than doubling the internal fuel capacity. This represented one of the very earliest examples of the use of integral fuel tanks in aircraft.

Notwithstanding a great deal of pioneer work in the use of aerial photography for artillery and tactical purposes during the First World War, practically nothing was done to develop or improve this technique during the days of peace. The result was that by 1939 the Royal Air Force found itself with no resources or equipment for long-range strategic aerial photography and no suitable camera equipment to cope with high-altitude or low-temperature operation. Aerial photography had become simply a residual tactical activity for the Army Co-operation squadrons equipped with low-performance aeroplanes (with low-perform-ance cameras) such as the Audax and Lysander. Furthermore, camera equipment was out of date.

However, activity in aerial survey for commercial purposes had taken place in the civilian field using some modern civil aircraft and when some clandestine aerial photography of Italian positions in Libya was urgently needed by the Special Intel-ligence Service (SIS) it was to civilian sources they turned. This led to a liaison between an energetic and forceful aviation entrepreneur called Sidney Cotton and Squadron Leader Fred Winterbotham of the SIS, and some sub rosa photographic operations by Cotton using a modern, civil registered Lockheed 12 transport aircraft, operating from Malta and financed secretly by SIS.

Later, in the immediate pre-war period, Cotton extended his clandestine photographic activities, still in liaison with the SIS through Winterbotham, to cover Germany, still using his Lock-heed 12 transport aeroplane. Indeed when the Germans overran France in 1940 they discovered in the files of the Deuxième Bureau a comprehensive pre-war coverage of the Siegfried line fortifications, taken by Cotton, and supplied by the SIS to the French.

During Cotton's Libyan operations from Malta he had met a young RAF Flying Officer, M.V. Longbottom, a member of a flying boat Squadron, who, in his off-duty hours, sometimes flew Cotton's Lockheed on photographic missions and who showed great interest in the techniques and possibilities of aerial photo-graphy. Longbottom conceived the idea of using the highest performance available fighter, equipped with suitable downward-facing cameras, and relying upon its speed and height to avoid detection or interception. In effect this meant the Spitfire. There is little doubt that a close and friendly relationship had developed between Longbottom and Cotton and so it is almost certain that this somewhat revolutionary concept developed from discussion between them. Longbottom as a serving officer was in a position to put proposals forward officially to the Royal Air Force; Cotton, although enjoying a close and fruitful relationship with the SIS, would certainly, as a somewhat flamboyant civilian entrepreneur, be heartily distrusted by the pre-war senior officer hierarchy in Whitehall. Moreover they would not take kindly to being told that their own photographic reconnaissance capabilities were out of date, moribund and ineffective, a point which Cotton would certainly have made in no uncertain terms.

In August 1939 Longbottom, then on leave in the UK, submitted a lengthy memorandum to the Air Council in which he spelt out in detail the proposal that Spitfires suitably modified should be used to obtain photographic reconnaissance coverage of enemy territory and shipping movements. The memorandum has survived and it is very comprehensive and certainly it made all the relevant points especially about the use of altitude, camouflage and speed to achieve invulnerability from enemy defences. It is evident from the memorandum that he had no knowledge of the existence of radar (very few people had) but that did not really affect the validity of the points he was making. He was certainly very well informed about the performance of the Spitfire. Whatever part Cotton may or may not have played in the preparation of this memorandum, it was a most remarkably prescient document, for although many of the points made may now seem obvious with the benefit of hindsight, they had certainly not occurred to anyone else then. The story of how Sidney Cotton got the early PRU formed with tacit and semi-official RAF support, almost on a private army basis, and how he got the early experimental versions of the Spitfire modified, and of the early operations in which 'Shorty' Longbottom participated and earned a DFC has been well told by Constance Babington Smith*. In due course, when this somewhat irregular Unit had become a going concern and proved its worth it was skilfully absorbed into the administrative and command structure of the Royal Air Force by Wing Commander Geoffrey Tuttle, DFC, its first regular commander.

The PRU pilots flew alone and unarmed deep into enemy airspace. It was seldom known what happened to those who did not return, a fact clearly somewhat daunting for their comrades. Mostly they flew at extreme altitudes and until the advent of heating systems and pressure cabins in their aircraft they suffered considerable hardships. Their contribution to the pool of Allied

---

* *Evidence in Camera*, Chatto & Windus, 1958.

Intelligence, upon which the success of our military operations depended, was enormous and can hardly be overstated. Many of them were happy that their contribution could be made without drawing blood but still at great personal risk to themselves.

Until the arrival of jet-propelled fighters with swept-back wings, such as the North American F-86 Sabre the highest recorded subsonic Mach number to be achieved by any fighter aircraft was the M 0.9 achieved in a dive by a specially modified and instrumented PR Mk XI Spitfire at the RAE Farnborough. This was achieved in 1944 by the late Squadron Leader Martindale, AFC (and Bar) in the course of some dives carried out with the object of obtaining full-scale data of the drag co-efficient of the Spitfire wing in flight at high Mach numbers. The aeroplane had been fitted with a fully feathering Rotol propeller in order to prevent overspeeding of the engine at the high altitudes at which these dives would necessarily have to be made. Martindale had two forced landings in the course of these tests due to engine failure, in the second of which he injured his back.

An earlier series of tests, carried out by the late Squadron Leader Tobin, AFC under the technical supervision of John Charnley* and Ron Smelt, was designed to compare the high Mach number characteristics of the Spitfire, the Mustang Mk I and the P-47 Thunderbolt. These tests resulted in the Spitfire achieving a corrected Mach number of a shade under M 0.9 against the Mustang Mk I which achieved just over M 0.8 with the Thunderbolt in the 'also ran' category.

Technical opinions vary as to the reason for the Spitfire's extraordinary high Mach number capabilities but certainly Mitchell's decision to go for a wing of very low thickness/chord ratio (13 per cent at the root and 6 per cent at the tip) had much to do with it. Ron Smelt (who went on to a distinguished post-war career as Technical Vice-President of Lockheed in California) has recently expressed the view to me that Mitchell's choice of wing section also had much to do with it.

Even more remarkable than the achievements of a modified aeroplane under special test conditions at Farnborough was the fact that in the pilot's notes of the standard Spitfire F. Mk IX

* Now Sir John Charnley of MOD

in 1942 'never exceed' figures were quoted at heights which represented a Mach number of M 0.85 (there were no Mach-meters available for production aircraft then). That any operational aircraft off the production line, cannons sprouting from its wings and warts and all, could readily be controlled at this speed when the early jet aircraft such as Meteors, Vampires, P-80s, etc could not, was certainly extraordinary.

Wartime operations and training brought in their wake an incidence of damage to Spitfires ranging from being peppered with bullet holes to more serious damage from belly landings, broken undercarriages and other crashes. Simple economics and logistics demanded that damaged aircraft be repaired and returned to service with minimum delay. It was neither economic nor practical to return them to the manufacturers' works so a specialised repair organisation under civilian management (CRO, Civilian Repair Organisation) was set up with works at Cowley near Oxford and at Air Service Training Ltd, Hamble.

A feature of aircraft accidents is that no two are the same, so each repair scheme was an individual case needing technical or design approval in order to safeguard the integrity and strength of the aircraft structure. This was an additional task devolving upon the Supermarine design organisation and a senior design engineer, Jack Rasmussen, was appointed to liaise with the repair organisations and approve repair schemes, and later to serve with the RAF.

Some Royal Air Force Maintenance Units (MUs) also undertook repair and rebuilding work under the auspices of the MAP and they always had a senior RAF technical officer in charge. An enormous number of damaged Spitfires passed through the CRO or the Maintenance Units and were returned to active service.

As production rates built up the problem of getting new and flight-tested aircraft delivered from the manufacturers' works to the Squadrons or MUs became acute. At a time when the RAF had a severe shortage of trained air crew the job of ferrying aircraft was a chore which could not sensibly be put upon the Service, nor upon Industry.

Accordingly a uniformed civilian organisation, the Air Transport Auxiliary (ATA), was formed and staffed with pilots who were either too old or otherwise unfit for RAF service.

Many of these were pilots who had served in the First World War and somehow kept their flying up privately – others had private pilot's licences and varying backgrounds of experience.

The organisation had its headquarters at White Waltham and established 'ferry pools' at various points in the country from which pilots would go and collect aircraft from the various manufacturers' works and deliver them to their destination. They therefore had to be trained to fly a wide variety of types and an excellent training organisation was set up which reduced the training task to the minimum needed to enable them to make these ferry flights. Then women began to come into the ATA; first in small numbers and then more and more. First they flew light and slow aircraft but soon they graduated onto Hurricanes and Spitfires and Mosquitos. Before long practically every Spitfire which left our works was collected by a woman. In their dark blue uniforms they always looked neat and smart and they did the job quietly and efficiently with a minimum of fuss. Many of them graduated into 'heavies' – that is, Lancasters, Halifaxes and Stirlings. They had an excellent accident record and by and large they did their job superlatively well. I greatly admired them.

During the crisis following the German invasion of Norway in 1940 the idea of putting a Spitfire on floats was conceived. There was no time to design and build special floats so it was decided to use the nearest existing alternative designed by Blackburn for their Roc two-seat turret fighter. The Roc was a much heavier aircraft than the Spitfire so its floats were bigger than necessary, nevertheless the urgency was such that a trial installation was started at Woolston. In the meantime the design of a pair of floats suited specifically for the Spitfire was put in hand and a contract to build them placed with Folland Aircraft. Before the Roc float installation was ready for test flight the Norwegian campaign was lost and the project cancelled.

The idea was revived some two years later and the special Spitfire floats, designed by Arthur Shirvall, who had been responsible for the floats of the S.5 and S.6 Schneider aircraft, were built by Folland Aircraft and fitted to a Mk V aircraft W3760 which I first flew on 12 October 1942, launching from the Hamble slipway.

It was a most beautiful floatplane and all we had to do, predictably, was to increase the fin area to compensate for the float area ahead of the centre of gravity. The loss of speed performance was surprisingly low and it handled easily on the water and in the air. I was also able to clear it for spinning. We converted and flew two more Vc aircraft to floatplanes and they were sent together with W3760 to the Mediterranean where a flight was formed under the command of Squadron Leader D.S. Wilson McDonald. However, for various reasons the requirement 'died' and the flight was soon disbanded. Later we converted a Mk IX to a floatplane. With its floats fitted it was still faster than a Hurricane I.

The Spitfire owed much to its racing seaplane ancestry, for it was the experience gained with those Schneider racers which had enabled Mitchell's team of designers and engineers to respond so splendidly to the challenge of fighter design in 1934/6 and subsequently. It was fitting, perhaps, that at least some Spitfires should have taken to the water on floats.

25

Spitfire 21, 22 and 24

The Spitfire 21 was the fastest and also the most controversial of the fighter variants. It was never a very satisfactory aeroplane but it sired two more fighter variants in the form of the Mk 22 and the Mk 24 which were superb aircraft. These, the last of the Spitfire line of fighters, were produced only in small quantities for they were overtaken by, first, the end of the war with Germany; second, the end of the war with Japan; and, third, the advent of jet propulsion which rendered further development of piston-engined fighters less important and attractive. But for those circumstances the Mks 22 and 24 would certainly have had very significant operational careers.

Initially the design of the Mk 21 represented one of the large forward design strides in development planned a good time in advance. It took longer to come to fruition than it should have, because of the pressures on both the design and production organisation of Supermarine over the interim types, such as the Mks IX, XVI, XII and XIV, during the period of intense hostilities.

Conceptually the Mk 21 grew from the Mk IV prototype, the first Spitfire to be fitted with the Griffon engine back in 1941. Its design was strongly influenced by the developing fighter armament requirements of the war and also by the desire of Supermarine to achieve major improvement in the lateral manoeuvrability of the Spitfire. This had been the ambition of Joe Smith and his team, as well as my own ambition, ever since the Battle of Britain. The metal-covered ailerons of 1940–1, whilst a vast improvement over the previous situation, were never completely satisfactory, and this became increasingly evident as time went on. However, had we, in 1941, been able to produce a design of aileron capable of allowing much greater control displacements at very high speed we should very soon have been in serious trouble with what was known as 'aileron reversal', arising from lack of torsional stiffness of the wing. In other words, the load applied to the wings by more powerful ailerons would have caused the wings to twist, thereby nullifying or reversing the effect of the ailerons and, incidentally, causing danger to the wing structure as a whole. So any major increase in aileron effectiveness would have to be accompanied by a major increase in the torsional stiffness of the wing itself which would mean extensive structural redesign.

Nobody appreciated this situation better than the head of our technical office, Alan Clifton. Therefore the design of a much stiffer wing was put in hand in 1942 and at the same time it was proposed to carry more fuel and much heavier armament – at least 4 × 20-mm cannon and armour plate for the increased load of cannon ammunition. It also became clear that nothing less than the two-stage two-speed Rolls-Royce Griffon 61 or 65 engine would suffice, and a better and longer undercarriage was designed in order to allow an 11-ft diameter propeller to be carried for improved performance. Thus a considerably re-designed aeroplane began to emerge. The new wing of much increased stiffness (47 per cent) had a theoretical aileron reversal speed of 825 mph as opposed to the 580 mph of earlier marks. The new Supermarine Type No. 356 with this redesigned wing was designated Mk 21. The first experimental aeroplane which could be called a prototype of the Mk 21 was DP851, fitted with a Griffon 61 engine and a modified wing with extended tips, and also with a new design of aileron which had plain piano hinges rather than inset hinges and Frise balances, and with geared balance tabs at the trailing edges. I first flew this aeroplane from Worthy Down on 1 December 1942. This wing was by no means representative of the final redesign of the Spitfire 21 wing. The extended wing tips, then very much the same as on the early Mk VIII aeroplanes, were meant to enhance the high-altitude performance which at that time was considered all-important.

The performance of DP851 was very good but the handling directionally and longitudinally was appalling. While we were trying to cope with this problem I crashed the aeroplane at Worthy Down in May 1943. We were operating from Hartford Bridge Flats (Blackbushe) at the time because of the unsuitability of Worthy Down aerodrome, but I flew the aeroplane back there on this day to have some work done in the 'shops'. In one area of Worthy Down, by the northern end of the hangar, there was quite a severe ridge. I happened to touch down just short of this ridge and as I crossed it there was a loud crack as the starboard undercarriage leg failed at the pintle fitting at the top. The wing went down and the propeller dug into the ground and the aeroplane swizzled right round and skidded along the ground backwards. I had on previous occasions found myself sliding along the ground in Spitfires but hitherto I had always been able to see where I was going. This time I considered putting in a claim for the world speed record in reverse!

The next prototype Mk 21 aircraft, and more truly representative of the Type 356 design, was PP139 which I first flew on 24 July 1943. This aeroplane, with its piano-hinged ailerons, had an enormously improved standard of lateral control with a greatly enhanced rate of roll. Like DP851 it had a redesigned, lengthened and slightly wider track undercarriage and it carried an additional 35 gallons of internal fuel in bag tanks in the inner wing leading edges. The performance of this machine, enhanced by some 10 mph of top speed over the Mk XIV with the same engine, was extremely good and represented the highest so far achieved on any fighter variant of the Spitfire, in spite of its increased all-up weight. But the handling remained a problem both directionally and longitudinally. It needed substantially larger tail surfaces, vertical and horizontal, but production was already falling behind schedule and there was no hope of getting such modifications in time. So we had to do the best we could with the aeroplane in its existing configuration, confining ourselves to relatively simple modifications to control surfaces and careful control of loading. In hindsight, it might have been better to have grasped the nettle at once and gone straight for much bigger tail surfaces at the expense of some delay in production, but in that critical phase of the war, hold-ups in production were anathema to everyone.

The first production aeroplane came out in January 1944 and the handling was still not good. Nevertheless my view was that, whilst it undoubtedly had difficult handling qualities, requiring plenty of concentration and attention by the pilot, these would nevertheless be acceptable because of the remarkable performance of the aeroplane. My underlying philosophy was that we were not trying to produce the most elegant possible flying machines but the most *effective* possible fighting machines and there was no doubt that the Spitfire 21, with its remarkable performance, its 4 × 20-mm cannon armament and its greatly enhanced rate of roll and diving speed of 525 mph was a very effective fighting machine indeed.

The pilots of the A & AEE and Air Fighting Development Unit thought otherwise, however, and reported very unfavourably on the aircraft. It was perhaps a case where my judgement, at any rate in the short term, was at fault. Perhaps by that time I had done so much flying on Spitfires that I could cope automatically and instinctively with almost any problem that arose. Also, my experience had taught me to have the greatest confidence in the abilities of young aircrew. It was a great mistake to underestimate them, and I felt that establishments such as A & AEE and AFDU often tended to do this. I also believed in the paramount importance of performance and agility in an air combat fighter and the Spitfire 21 seemed the ultimate in those respects.

However by that stage in the war the operational scene had shifted. The Allies now enjoyed an air supremacy in Europe due to sheer weight of numbers. Great emphasis upon attacking ground (and sea) targets had naturally arisen due to the development of tactical air forces in support of land operations; the need for very long-range escort fighters to accompany massive daylight bombing raids deep into enemy territory had resulted in the development of a somewhat different category of long-range fighter, the best example of which was the Merlin-engined Mustang.

The AFDU, in one of their early reports on the Spitfire 21, went so far as to recommend that all further development of the Spitfire should cease, suggesting that it had reached the end of its development life. This was an ill-judged and premature recommendation, as the excellent performance and handling of Spitfires Mk 22 and Mk 24, with the enlarged tail units, were later to demonstrate. Furthermore we soon managed to improve the characteristics of the Mk 21 by modification to the control surfaces and in their report No. 17 (AFDU Report 163) of 18 March 1945 the newly formed Central Fighter Establishment (CFE) wrote as follows:

> para 22. The elevator control is light and positive in action and the aircraft is stable in pitch.

para 23. The aircraft is unstable in the yawing plane especially at high speeds. The rudder control is however sufficiently heavy to make positive control possible but is sensitive to very small movement.

para 25. The general handling characteristics of this aircraft are good at all heights if careful trimming is carried out.

para 30. The general handling of this aircraft allows the pilot to fly on his instruments smoothly and the aircraft is considered acceptable for cloud flying by formations of aircraft. The pilot can maintain a steady rate of climb with hands off the control. It is recommended that sudden movements of the throttle be avoided.

para 33. The good control of the Spitfire 21 enables the pilot to anticipate the manoeuvres of other fighters and the average pilot should be able to hold his sight on the target throughout all combat manoeuvres.

para 45. *Conclusions*
The Spitfire 21 possesses the following advantages over the Spitfire XIV:

(I) It has the greater fire power.
(II) It is faster at all heights by some 10 to 12 mph.
(III) It has slightly better acceleration in the initial stages of a dive.
(IV) It has better aileron control at speeds above 300 mph.
(V) It has slightly greater range.

para 46. Despite its unsuitability in the yawing plane at altitude and high speeds the Spitfire 21 is considered a satisfactory combat aircraft for the average pilot.

So in spite of earlier difficulties and in spite of its unfavourable early reception we got the Spitfire 21 right in the end. But I still hankered for much larger tail surfaces, and those eventually came into production with Mks 22 and 24.

On these aircraft we introduced a completely new tail unit with much greater vertical and horizontal surfaces (see page 191). To quote a well-informed historian, Harry Robinson: '. . . a completely revised and superbly handsome rudder and fin that increased overall length by 3 in. to 31 ft 11 in. Once the first Mark 22 had been fitted with this revised tail the stability problem ceased to exist . . .'*

The final version of the Supermarine Type 356 was the Mk 24

* See *Aeroplane Monthly*, February 1980.

which was really a Mk 22 improved and modified in certain operational details, with cut-away rear fuselage. As Harry Robinson wrote: 'This was indeed the ultimate Spitfire, it had speed climb and ceiling far in excess of earlier Marks. Manoeuvrability and handling were as delightful as ever, while ailerons were far superior to those of earlier versions. When fitted with the (enlarged) tail the Mks 22 and 24 belied the oft-repeated claim against Griffon-engined Marks "It ain't a Spitfire no more". To Jeffrey Quill whose experience in this context is unsurpassed it was "a little overpowered, perhaps – but a magnificent aeroplane".'

Personally I, and most others at Supermarine, felt extremely proud of the Spitfires 22 and 24 and I was only sorry that so few people, particularly amongst my fighter pilot friends in the Royal Air Force of a slightly earlier wartime vintage, ever had the opportunity to fly them.

The totals of aircraft produced in this series were as follows: Spitfire 21: 120; Spitfire 22: 260; and Spitfire 24: 81.

There were no PR derivatives, but the Seafire 47 was the Naval equivalent of the Spitfire 24 although substantially different in detail.

Spitfire 22s and 24s served with the Royal Air Force overseas in Malta, Cyprus, and Hong Kong and in Auxiliary Squadrons at home. Mark 22s were purchased after the war by the Air Forces of Southern Rhodesia, Syria and Egypt.

During 1954 I flew several of the Egyptian Air Force Mk 22s from England to Cairo. I had only recently recovered my flying licence after being medically grounded for some three or four years. Therefore I came back to flying these reconditioned Mk 22s after a long pause and so with a very fresh mind. I had also flown quite a few jet aircraft by then and I well remember thinking at once what a magnificent aeroplane the Mk 22 was.

On one of those delivery flights Archie Boyd and I flew two Spitfire 22s in formation at night on the leg from Rome to Malta, passing over the red glow of Stromboli illuminating the cloud cover below, and when we arrived at Luqa it was very dark indeed with heavy cloud cover. I remember setting the trimmers carefully, with a small amount of power on, for a gently curving and steady landing approach, and as I chopped the throttle at the threshold of the runway the aircraft virtually landed itself. I had the same thought that I had had so many years before after my first flight in the prototype – that this aeroplane was a real lady; albeit by then a much more powerful, noisy, tough and aggressive lady, but a lady just the same.

26

Spiteful, Seafang

and E.10/44 Jet Spiteful

In late 1942 information about the drag characteristics of the Spitfire's wing at the higher subsonic Mach numbers was available only from calculations and wind-tunnel tests. Although at that time we were diving Spitfire Mk IXs to speeds slightly in excess of Mach 0.86 (in the official pilot's notes of the Mk IX aircraft there was a table of 'never exceed' speeds at various heights one of which worked out at about M 0.85). We had not at that time developed methods of measuring drag coefficients in full scale or real life flight conditions. So the wind tunnel still ruled the roost and it tended to be pessimistic.

When an aircraft reaches a speed in level flight where the total drag equals the total thrust available from the engine and propeller it can no longer accelerate. It has therefore reached the maximum level speed of which it is capable. In general the drag of an aircraft's wing increased progressively with speed, but when a certain percentage of the speed of sound (Mach number) was reached compressibility effects were encountered which would cause the drag to increase very sharply and suddenly. This would then limit the level speed performance of the aeroplane more or less regardless of how much more power was applied. This compressibility or Mach number effect was a function of speed and height and the Spitfire was already achieving high Mach numbers in level flight at 28,000 ft. It was therefore feared at Supermarine that, as Rolls-Royce produced engines of even greater power at greater heights, we could find ourselves in a situation whereby the power of the Rolls-Royce engines would have outstripped the aerodynamic capabilities of the aeroplane. We certainly could not allow that to happen.

So a new design of wing with better drag characteristics at the high subsonic Mach numbers would be needed in the forseeable future, and the design of such a wing was put in hand towards the end of 1942. It was further decided to design this wing in collaboration with the National Physical Laboratory at Teddington. Our chief aerodynamicist S.R. (Sammy) Hughes was in charge of the design at Supermarine and his chief collaborator at the NPL was Dr S. Goldstein, who was doing research into the aerodynamics of high Mach number flight under Professor Relph.

The prime objective of the new wing was, graphically speaking, to move the point where the drag curve cocked sharply upwards over towards the right hand side of the page. That point represented a drag barrier as well as a controllability barrier which was somewhile later to be somewhat dramatically dubbed 'the sound barrier'. In 1942 'laminar flow' was very much at the forefront of aerodynamic fashion. It was known that the airflow over the surface of a wing flowed smoothly and adhered closely to the surface initially (this was called laminar flow) but that eventually it broke away from the surface and became turbulent and it was this turbulent flow which caused a sharp increase in drag. The point on the surface of the wing where the laminar flow broke down and became turbulent was known as the transition point and the further back on the surface of the wing that this occurred the lower the overall drag. In other words the more laminar flow there was and the less turbulent flow (or the further aft the transition point) the better were the aerodynamicists pleased.

Experimental work had shown that there were two principal factors which influenced the matter. The first was the shape of the wing section and the second was the accuracy of the profile and the smoothness of the surface finish. One was a problem for the wing section designer and the other for engineers and the production shops.

The new wing was designed to have a section thought to be favourable to laminar flow and it was given a simple straight tapered plan form for ease of accurate manufacture and it was given a heavy gauge skin to help preserve the integrity of its profile and it had very sharp leading edge sections. As it came out it was, in fact, a beautiful piece of production engineering built to very high standards of precision.

The elegant beauty of the Spitfire wing's elliptical planform had disappeared – sacrificed in the interests of high-precision production engineering – but the new wing destined for the Spiteful was nevertheless well proportioned and by no means inelegant and it had a purposeful and businesslike appearance. The first pair of these new wings was fitted to a standard Spitfire Mk XIV fuselage with Griffon 61 engine with five-bladed propeller in order to provide a direct performance comparison. The wing was designed for an aileron reversal speed of 850 mph IAS, as was the Spitfire 21 wing. This aeroplane, NN660, was therefore a standard Spitfire XIV with a completely new design of wing.

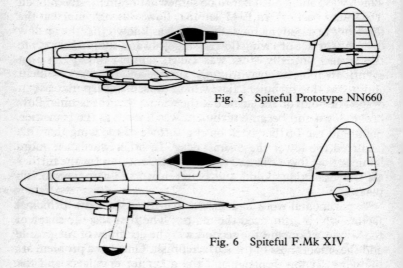

Fig. 5   Spiteful Prototype NN660

Fig. 6   Spiteful F.Mk XIV

I made the first flight on NN660 at High Post on 30 June 1944, just about 18 months after the initiation of the design of the wing. Two things were very soon apparent. The first was that the speed, although comfortably in excess of the Mk XIV which formed the direct Spitfire comparison was disappointing. The second was that the flight characteristics of the wing at and near the stall tended to be unpleasant. The ailerons showed a tendency to snatch as the stall was approached and occasionally a wing would drop but not to any serious or potentially dangerous extent.

However, after the Spitfire's impeccable behaviour at the stall, to which so many pilots had become accustomed, this characteristic was clearly undesirable. When the ailerons began to twitch and the wing showed signs of incipient lateral instability, it created the impression that at the moment of touchdown for landing it was about to do something nasty (which in point of fact it never actually did). After I had flown the aeroplane a few times, and well and truly stalled it in every conceivable attitude, I realised that it was very much a case of the aeroplane's bark being much worse than its bite. Although whilst it seemed to make a great fuss when it was getting near the stall it never actually did anything. By analogy it was rather like a fidgety but otherwise perfectly well-mannered horse which you had to get to know in order to trust. I realised that we should have to do something about this characteristic because apart from anything else it would create a bad impression on pilots flying the aeroplane for the first time and this would never do for Boscombe Down. Indeed although we achieved a marked improvement in the characteristic before sending it there, one very senior officer damned it out of hand on the basis of a single flight.

However, for the early flights on NN660 performance testing and general functioning testing took priority and we decided to deal with the handling problems as we went along. I personally had done 32 flights in the aeroplane up until 11 September and Frank Furlong had begun to fly it at intervals from its fifth flight onward. On 13 September he was returning to the circuit after a test flight and encountered Philip Wigley in a Spitfire XIV. The two began to 'mix it' in a sham dog fight and when they were at a fairly low height and both pulling g Frank, in NN660, flicked over onto his back and before he could recover had hit the ground close to the airfield. He was killed instantly. This tragedy brought an abrupt end to our tests on NN660.

The next prototype was virtually a new aircraft for which Specification F.1/43 had been issued. It had a redesigned fuselage as well as the redesigned wing. It could not with any justification whatever be called a Spitfire and so it was renamed Spiteful. The new fuselage had been given a humped-back appearance rather like the Hurricane, in order to raise the level of the pilot's sight line for deflection shooting thereby eliminating one of the operational shortcomings of the Spitfire. Certain aspects of the cockpit had been finalised while I was away in the Fleet Air Arm. During this finalisation process some big changes had been introduced in the pilot's seating position in the course of visits to the mock-up* by the branch of MAP responsible for representing the customers' views in these matters. By this time (the latter part of 1943) these departments had expanded considerably in personnel and it is no criticism of the undoubtedly useful work which many of them did to observe that individuals in the department were sometimes able to ride some pet hobby horses as hard as they pleased. A certain Wing Commander concerned with cockpits had persuaded himself that the most important thing about a fighter cockpit was that the pilot should be seated in a posture which provided the maximum resistance to black out† under high g. The ideal position for this was, of course, lying on one's back but as this was scarcely practical when flying an aeroplane the Wing Commander persuaded Supermarine to seat the pilot with his feet on rudder pedals set very high and with the seat sloping backwards to an uncomfortable degree.

He had clearly been much influenced by the FW 190's seating position, which I had thought was bad if only because with the body leaning backwards it is difficult to turn your head to look behind you. In the Spitfire we had a 'top storey' for the rudder pedals and if you put the feet on these the g threshold was very adequate.

I took the view that a fighter cockpit should be such that pilots felt comfortable, happy and confident in it and particularly that they should have the best possible view rearwards. God knows they had enough to worry about without being seated in an idiotic attitude. I was extremely angry when I returned from the Fleet Air Arm and found what had been done to the Spiteful's cockpit but it was then too late to do anything about it. In other respects,

---

* A wooden full-scale model used for deciding upon equipment and cockpit layout, etc.
† Black-out, in pilot's language, is loss of vision due to blood draining from the head under conditions of high g. Vision is restored virtually immediately the g loading is relieved. It is nothing whatever to do with fainting or passing out, meanings it has unfortunately acquired in recent lay usage.

however, such as instrument layout, the Spiteful cockpit was very good indeed.

NN664, the first real Spiteful as opposed to Spitfire/Spiteful hybrid, was ready in the new year and I made the first flight on 8 January 1945. NN664 still had the tailplane, fin and rudder of a Spitfire XIV but in other respects it certainly looked a completely new aeroplane. We concentrated in the ensuing months on improving the performance and in smoothing out its behaviour at the stall. In the latter we succeeded to an acceptable degree as the later deck-landing trials on the Naval variant, Seafang, were to demonstrate.

During all this time I had been extremely puzzled about Frank Furlong's crash. Philip Wigley saw it and gave a coherent account. The easy answer was to assume that Frank simply stalled the aeroplane under high g and spun into the ground, but Frank was an experienced and skilful pilot and there was nothing foolhardy about his flying. I could not accept the easy theory of 'pilot error'. And then one day something happened to me in NN664 which gave me the clue. The Spiteful's ailerons were operated by solid push/pull rods and not by cables running over pulleys as the Spitfire's were. I was in a high g turn to the left when my ailerons jammed. I at once eased off the g, gave the stick a mighty wallop with the palm of my hand and they were free. It was momentary but it was enough; had I been near the ground I would have been in trouble. I became convinced that this is what happened to Frank. Thereafter a most thorough check was made of all Spiteful ailerons and the runs of the rods. It never happened again.

On 2 May 1945 the production order for 150 Spitefuls was cancelled by the Ministry of Aircraft Production and replaced on 5 May with an order for 150 of the Naval variant, Seafang, to Naval Specification N.5/45. The reasons behind this cancellation were various. Firstly the new wing had not shown the expected performance improvement over the Spitfire wing. This was partly due to laminar flow having become in the meantime somewhat discredited in practical terms. Also in the meantime full-scale measurement of the drag coefficient of the Spitfire's wing in flight had shown it to have far better drag characteristics at high subsonic Mach numbers than anyone had dreamed in

1942, when the Spiteful wing was conceived. The Spiteful wing had turned out not so good as hoped and the Spitfire wing a lot better than expected. It had been found that for a laminar flow wing to pay the dividends which aerodynamic theory had originally indicated it was necessary to have an absolutely smooth surface finish. The slightest degree of surface roughness, defined as a grain size as small as .0022 in., could reduce the speed of a 380 mph aircraft dependent upon laminar flow by as much as 43 mph. In short, for practical purposes laminar flow was a busted flush.

Next, in the interval between late 1942 and early 1945 jet propulsion had developed from a very experimental state (Whittle's engine had first flown only on 15 May 1941) to the point where it was becoming very much a practical proposition. Early versions of Meteors and Vampires were already flying in 1944/5 and the German Me 262 was operating in Europe. It was already clear that the future of high performance fighter aircraft lay with jet propulsion. The war had changed dramatically and the cancellation of the Spiteful preceded the German surrender in Europe by six days. Nevertheless it was logical that Naval interest should continue because of the uncertainty about how jet aircraft would behave on aircraft carriers.

The preoccupation of Supermarine's design effort with Spitfire development in all its forms and with the enormous manufacturing effort had precluded early experimental work with the new concept of jet propulsion. However, towards the end of 1943 it was proposed to take the Spiteful wing, already being tooled up for mass production, and apply it very quickly to a simply and rapidly produced circular cross-section fuselage which would take a projected Rolls-Royce jet engine (eventually to become the Nene). This proposal was put by Joe Smith to MAP (N.E. Rowe) on 6 July 1944 and was referred to as the Jet Spiteful.

I well remember attending a meeting at Rolls-Royce Barnoldswick, chaired by Ernest Hives and attended by Joe Smith, Clifton and Arthur Shirvall of our project office, at which Stanley Hooker outlined the basic design features of the new engine of which the main parameters, and final dimensions and thrust levels, were not then finally decided. From this meeting the main parameters of the Nene engine (including a static thrust level of

5000 lb) were tailored to the proposed fuselage to be applied to the new Spiteful wing in order to get a jet-propelled aircraft into the air in the shortest possible time. The fuselage was to be as simple as possible, the engine to be installed in a plenum chamber behind the pilot and because it was desired to make no change whatever to the already tooled up wing. The normal under-carriage was to be retained so the aircraft would have a tailwheel. A MAP specification, E.10/44, was issued to cover the design and an experimental prototype was ordered. VE Day came before the aircraft was finished, and the immediate rush to get a new jet-propelled fighter into the air in Europe had vanished overnight but it was decided to go ahead with it on an experi-mental basis at much reduced tempo.

As a result I flew the E.10/44 prototype TS409 in July 1946, using the new runway at Boscombe Down. In the meantime flying continued on various Spitefuls all of which was basically devoted towards improvements in performance and handling and gathering the maximum amount of data which would be relevant to the development of the Naval variant, the Seafang N.5/45. The E.10/44 was also destined for production for the Royal Navy. At that stage the circumstance that it had a tail wheel undercarriage commended it to the Navy because of un-certainty about the suitability of the nose wheel layout for deck landing and catapulting.

I did a total of 69 sorties on the first E.10/44 TS409. The immediate problems with it were that the pressure cabin was inoperative causing me to spend a lot of time at very high altitude in an unpressurised cockpit and secondly the elevators were too heavy. It certainly did not take after the Spitfire in the matter of its longitudinal stability margins. It was a natural for a spring tab elevator and we fitted one. One day when I was going at around 600 mph ASI at a very low height the tab fluttered; the stick and the entire aircraft shook and vibrated violently and I thought it was breaking up. I pulled the nose up and took off the power hoping to get some height before anything catastrophic hap-pened. Eventually when the ASI had dropped off the vibration damped out. I came in to land feeling somewhat relieved; and that was the end of the spring tab elevator idea. It was a pity because the production Attacker also had much too heavy an elevator. Indeed it was the aircraft's only real defect from the handling point of view in the air. Its top speed was just under 600 mph.

Fairly early on in the trials I had a total engine failure due to trouble in the fuel system. Although there was a lot of cloud cover I managed to get within reach of Farnborough and put it down safely on the main runway.

The Nene engine itself always ran remarkably well and I became very confident in it. In its plenum chamber installation it made some pretty odd noises from time to time, especially when throttled back but on the whole it was very sweet. It was giving around 5000-lb static thrust in those early days of the trials and was still giving 5000-lb thrust several years later in production Attackers and Sea Hawks. I never understood why it was not developed to give more power. After Sir Stafford Cripps sold the manufacturing rights to the Soviets they developed it to over 7000 lb for their MiG 15, which operated against us in Korea. The E.10/44 had a critical Mach number of about .82; exactly the same as the Spiteful but quite a bit less than the Spitfire!

In my view it really needed a tricycle undercarriage for the second prototype because tricycles were bound to come in for Naval aircraft and I pressed this upon Joe Smith but unsuccessfully.

One day, in June 1947, when climbing the E.10/44 between 35,000 and 40,000 ft I passed out. As I felt it coming on I took the power off and trimmed the aircraft into a gentle dive. I came to at about 10,000 ft and immediately assumed the oxygen supply had failed. I landed back at Chilbolton and investigation showed the oxygen system to be in full working order. CO_2 contamination of the cockpit became the next explanation and I made another flight with instrumentation to check it. I passed out again but the CO_2 reading was negative. A series of medical checks ensued and tests in the decompression chamber at Farnborough. I, who had always had absolute confidence in my own physical fitness in the air, and never even thought about it, at once became suspect in the eyes of the doctors. It was true that I was extremely tired – I had been flying continuously and hard for sixteen years without a break – and perhaps too much recent very high flying in unpressurised cabins had taken its toll. Certainly I was very run down and unwell. I was sent on three months' leave, most of which I spent sailing, and then various tests – mostly irrelevant in my opinion – continued and I had some strange turns even when flying the Auster or the Dominie and when driving my car.

Aviation medicine, although it had made great strides at Farnborough during the war years, was still a relatively new study and did not seem to be able to do anything for me other than tell me to stay on the ground. To cut a long story short it was the end of my career as a test pilot for high-performance fighters, for as soon as my physical fitness was under grave suspicion other people's confidence in me, so essential to my proper functioning as a Chief Test Pilot, evaporated overnight.

After a few months of inconclusive medical checks I decided I had no alternative but to give up. I went one evening to Joe Smith and told him and recommended the job should be taken over by Mike Lithgow.

There was talk of my becoming Flight Test Manager – a sort of non-playing captain. I thought about it but realised it was not for me – I had to lead from the sharp end or not at all.

I went home full of sad and bitter thoughts. I could never again be a test pilot; I would have to learn to fly a desk.

Epilogue

It was in 1966 when I made my last flight in a Spitfire. It was in an old Mk V aeroplane AB910, which we had restored at Supermarine in the early 1950s and which I had flown at various charity air shows each summer since; and which we had then just presented to the Royal Air Force Historic Flight at Coltishall*.

That last flight was at the behest of a French television company which was making a documentary film. As I taxied in afterwards and shut down the engine I remained for a few moments in the cockpit, listening to the gentle ticking noises as the engine cooled off, and savoured the indefinable yet so familiar smells of the Spitfire cockpit. It had been thirty years since my first flight in a Spitfire and eighteen since I had been an active test pilot, although I had flown AB910 from time to time when I could escape from the not inconsiderable preoccupations of my post-war job.

My mind went back to the day in 1936 when I stood with R.J. Mitchell and Mutt Summers around the unfinished prototype in the old works at Woolston and to the day, some two months later, when, as a very young test pilot, I had made my own first flight in it. I remembered all the activity and bustle of those pre-war days and my friends in the firm and in the Royal Air Force; the young fighter pilots of the first Spitfire squadrons who came to Eastleigh to be checked out in the Spitfire and then fly them away to their stations. Many of those young men were destined to become distinguished wartime fighter pilots and many, sadly, were to die.

Looking back on it I began to realise the extent to which the Spitfire had dominated my life and energies during those ten years from 1936. I had come to know the aeroplane intimately and thoroughly, not only as a test pilot but by flying it in the RAF and the Fleet Air Arm. It had been my business to criticise it and

---

* It is now at the Battle of Britain Memorial Flight at Coningsby.

identify its faults; I had had no illusions about it and knew its problems only too well. Indeed, they had caused me sleepless nights all too often.

Yet it was impossible to look back on the Spitfire without recognising it as something unique in aviation history. By the efforts of the many thousands of people who were in some way involved the Spitfire threaded its way through the historical tapestry not only of Britain but of the continent of Europe and of a great overseas Empire. I am referring to those who helped to design it, build it, maintain it, administer it and fly it – never ever forgetting those, all too many, who died in it. For the Spitfire was flown in combat not only by Britons but by Australians, Canadians, New Zealanders, South Africans, Rhodesians, Indians and by pilots from many of the smaller then British Colonies; by Free Frenchmen, Belgians, Dutchmen, Czechoslovaks, Poles, Danes, Norwegians, and by Americans who flew in the Eagle Squadrons in 1940/2 and in the US Army Corps in North Africa in 1942/3.

The Battle of Britain was a very public affair, fought mainly over southern England in full view of the people, who at once felt a sense of personal involvement. That the Spitfire and the Hurricane became absorbed into the folklore of Britain is therefore neither surprising nor inappropriate. Certainly it was in 1940 that the little Spitfires, so easily recognisable in the air, suddenly captured the imagination of the British people and became a symbol of hope and of victory. Later, in 1941, 1942 and 1943, the sound of the Spitfires sweeping daily over northern France, Belgium and The Netherlands, challenging the enemy to come up and fight, brought the hope of victory and liberation to the people of those occupied countries.

The Spitfire was very much a pilot's aeroplane. It had an indefinable quality of excitement about it – an unmistakable charisma – which greatly appealed to young and eager pilots, added to which it was the fastest and highest performance fighter of its day and most pilots wanted to fly the best.

It is to the eternal credit of a generation that to be a Spitfire pilot became the dream and pride of so many of its young men.

As I climbed out the cockpit of AB910, I felt the sadness of bidding farewell to an old and trusted friend.

APPENDIX 1

Company Organisation 1940–5

VICKERS Ltd
|
Vickers-Armstrongs (Aircraft) Ltd
|
MANAGING DIRECTORS
Sir Alex Dunbar
Sir Hew Kilner

Supermarine Works　　　　　　Weybridge Works
|
GENERAL MANAGER
S/Cdr James Bird

COMMERCIAL MANAGER	WORKS SUPERINTENDENT	CHIEF DESIGNER
A. E. Marsh-Hunn	W. T. Elliott	J. Smith
(See Appendix 1A)	(See Appendix 1B)	(See Appendix 1C)

APPENDIX 1A

Commercial Department

|
COMMERCIAL MANAGER
A. E. Marsh-Hunn

- Chief Storekeeper
- Contracts Manager　　CHIEF ACCOUNTANT
- Chief Buyer　　　　　　N. Sims
- Chief Estimator
- Subcontract Officer　　　　- Cashier
- Canteen Manager　　　　　- Wages
- Embodiment Loan Officer　　- Bought Ledger
　　　　　　　　　　　　　　- Inward Invoices
　　　　　　　　　　　　　　- Post Office
　　　　　　　　　　　　　　- Plant Records & Insurance

APPENDIX 1B

Works Department

SUPERINTENDENT
W. T. Elliott

- CHIEF INSPECTOR
C. Johns
  - Detail Inspection
  - Sub-Assembly Inspection
  - Process Inspection
  - Outside Inspection
  - Final Erection Inspection

- PERSONNEL MANAGER
  - Trainees
  - Security
  - Medical
  - Female Supervisor
  - Employment Office
  - Apprentice Supervisor
  - Air Raid Precautions

- WORKS MANAGER
L. G. Gooch
  - Area Managers
    - Hursley Park (including Winchester and Eastleigh)
    - Southampton Area
    - Salisbury Area
    - Trowbridge Area
    - Newbury Area
    - Reading Area
    - Miscellaneous Units

  - Works Engineer
    - Buildings and Services
    - Plant Layout
    - Plant Purchase
    - Buildings and Plant Maintenance
    - Airfield Maintenance

- PRODUCTION MANAGER
J. Butler
  - Transport Manager
  - Chief Planning Engineer
  - Pre-Production Manager
  - Production Controller
  - Jig and Tool Design
  - Job Planning
  - Finished Part Stores
  - Progress Department
  - Works Orders

APPENDIX 1c

Design Department

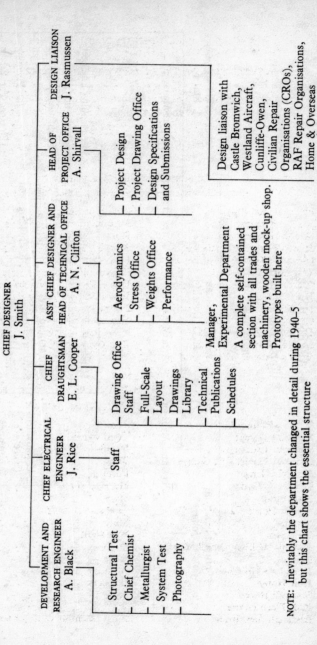

CHIEF DESIGNER J. Smith

DEVELOPMENT AND RESEARCH ENGINEER A. Black
- Structural Test
- Chief Chemist
- Metallurgist
- System Test
- Photography

CHIEF ELECTRICAL ENGINEER J. Rice
- Staff

CHIEF DRAUGHTSMAN E. L. Cooper
- Drawing Office Staff
- Full-Scale Layout
- Drawings Library
- Technical Publications
- Schedules

Manager, Experimental Department

A complete self-contained section with all trades and machinery, wooden mock-up shop. Prototypes built here

ASST CHIEF DESIGNER AND HEAD OF TECHNICAL OFFICE A. N. Clifton
- Aerodynamics
- Stress Office
- Weights Office
- Performance

HEAD OF PROJECT OFFICE A. Shirvall
- Project Design
- Project Drawing Office
- Design Specifications and Submissions

HEAD OF DESIGN LIAISON J. Rasmussen

Design liaison with Castle Bromwich, Westland Aircraft, Cunliffe-Owen, Civilian Repair Organisations (CROs), RAF Repair Organisations, Home & Overseas

NOTE: Inevitably the department changed in detail during 1940-5 but this chart shows the essential structure

APPENDIX 2

Supermarine Southern Region Dispersal Scheme

Premises occupied for Spitfire production, July 1940–December 1945
(Total floor area of all units: 1,385,337 sq. ft)

HURSLEY PARK HOUSE
(375,512 sq. ft)

Administration and Management
Design Department and Drawing Office (see 1c)

Experimental Shops	Prototype build
Southend House	Accounts
Sleepy Hollow Barn	Store
Short's Garage, Winchester	Machine shop
Chisnell's Garage, Winchester	Press shop
Wonston Stores	Embodiment loan
Worthy Down RN Air Station	Experimental flight test
Hursley Road	Raw materials store
Hendy's Garage	Pre-production build
Leigh Road Cable Works	Raw materials store
Garrett's Garage	Transport & transport repair
Moore's Garage, Bagshot	Transport centre
Ekin's Garage, Kenilworth	Transport centre

SOUTHAMPTON AREA
(330,987 sq. ft; Area Manger: A. Nelson)

Weston Rolling Mills	Tanks, pipes
Seward's Garage	Toolmakers
Sunlight Laundry	Details
Hants & Dorset Bus Garage	Wings
Hendy's Garage	Fuselages
Lowther's Garage	Machine shop
Hollybrook	Store
Austin House Garage	Tanks
Sholing	Store
Newtown	Woodmill
Bishops Waltham Brick Works	Store
Botley	Store
Deepdene House	Accounts
Holt House	Inspection
Marwell House	Store
Park Place House	WVS
Eastleigh Aerodrome	Final assembly & flight test

SALISBURY AREA
(195,262 sq. ft; Area Manager: W. Heaver)

Castle Road	Fuselages
Castle Road West	Leading edges
Assembly Rooms	Canteen
Anna Valley Garage	Sub-assemblies
Wessex Garage	Fuselages
Wilts & Dorset Bus Garage	Wings
Castle Garage	Transport
Chattis Hill Training Gallops	Final assembly & flight test
High Post Aerodrome	Production & experimental flight test

TROWBRIDGE AREA
(185,846 sq. ft; Area Manager: V. Hall)

Bradley Road	Wings & details
Hilperton	Sub-assemblies
Red Triangle	Canteen
Forest Street Garage	Details
Rutland Garage	Pipes
Southwick Steamroller Works	Leading edges
Westbury Glove Factory	Cowlings
Westbury Cloth Mill	Store
Red Hat Lane	Canteen
Keevil Aerodrome	Final erection & flight test

NEWBURY AREA
(167,202 sq. ft; Area Manager: T. Barby)

Shaw Works	Press & machine shop
Stradling's Garage	Details
NIAS No. 1 Garage	Toolmakers
NIAS No. 2 Garage	Store
Pass Garage	Process
Mill Lane Works	Sub-assemblies
Hungerford Garage	Machine shop
Baughurst Garage	Store

READING AREA
(126,888 sq. ft; Area Manager: K. Scales)

Vincent's Garage	Fuselage sub-assembly
Great Western Garage	Wings
Caversham Works	Fuselages
Central Garage	Canteen
Henley Aerodrome	Final assembly & flight test
Aldermaston Aerodrome	Final assembly & flight test

APPENDIX 3

Supermarine Southern Region Dispersal Scheme, 1940–5

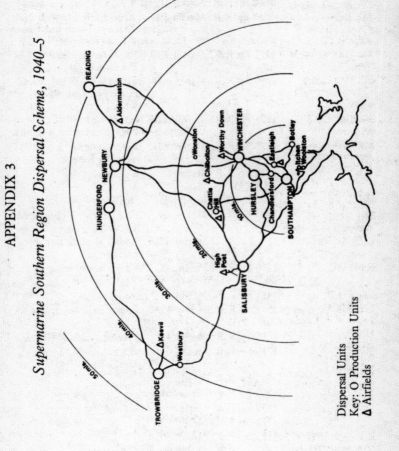

Dispersal Units
Key: O Production Units
△ Airfields

APPENDIX 4

Spitfire and Seafire Operational Marks

SPITFIRES: FIGHTERS

Mk Iᴀ	1030 hp R.R. Merlin II, III	8 × .303 machine guns
Mk Iʙ	1030 hp R.R. Merlin III	Armed initially with 2 × 20 mm cannon only; later 2 × 20 mm plus 4 rcmg
Mk IIᴀ	1175 hp R.R. Merlin XII	Produced at Castle Bromwich
Mk IIᴀ (L.R.)	1175 hp R.R. Merlin XII	Fitted with 30 gal. long range fuel tank under port wing
Mk IIʙ	1175 hp R.R. Merlin XII	Mk II with 'B' Wing – 2 × 20 mm plus 4 remg
Mk IIᴄ	1175 hp R.R. Merlin XII	Later designated ASR II (Air Sea Rescue)
Mk Vᴀ	1470 hp R.R. Merlin XLV (45)	8 rcmg
F.Mk Vʙ	1470 hp R.R. Merlin 45	'B' Wing
	1415 hp R.R. Merlin 46	Engine with higher rated altitude
L.F.Mk Vʙ	1585 hp R.R. Merlin 45M	Lower altitude rating engine
F.Mk Vᴄ	1470 hp R.R. Merlin 45, 50, 50A, 55, 56	'C' Universal wing
	1415 hp R.R. Merlin 46	
L.F.Mk Vᴄ	1585 hp R.R. Merlin 45M, 50M, 55M	Lower altitude rating
Mk VI	1415 hp R.R. Merlin 47	Pressure cabin (PC)
Mk VII	1710 hp R.R. Merlin 64	PC & 2-speed, 2-stage Merlin
	1565 hp R.R. Merlin 61	
F.Mk VIII	1565 hp R.R. Merlin 61	
	1650 hp R.R. Merlin 63	
	1710 hp R.R. Merlin 63A	
L.F. Mk VIII	1580 hp R.R. Merlin 66	
H.F.Mk VIII	1475 hp R.R. Merlin 70	
F.Mk IXᴄ	1565 hp R.R. Merlin 61	
	1650 hp R.R. Merlin 63	
	1710 hp R.R. Merlin 63A	

L.F.Mk IXc	1580 hp R.R. Merlin 66	
H.F.Mk IX	1475 hp R.R. Merlin 70	
F.Mk IXe	R.R. Merlin 61, 63, 63A	'B' Wing 2 × 20 mm mgs + 2 × 0.5 in. mgs
L.F.Mk IXe	1580 hp R.R. Merlin 66	
H.F.Mk IXe	1475 hp R.R. Merlin 70	
Mk XII	1735 hp R.R. Griffon III, IV	
Mk XIVc	2035 hp R.R. Griffon 65	'C' Wing
F.Mk XIVe	2035 hp R.R. Griffon 65	'E' Wing
F.R.Mk XIVe	2035 hp R.R. Griffon 65	Rear-view fuselage. Oblique camera in rear fuselage
L.F.Mk XVI	1580 hp Packard R.R. Merlin 266	'C' Wing
L.F.Mk XVIe	1580 hp Packard R.R. Merlin 266	'E' Wing
Mk 21	2035 hp R.R. Griffon 61	

Spitfires: Photo Reconnaissance

Type 'A'	1030 hp R.R. Merlin III	No extra fuel
Type 'B'	1030 hp R.R. Merlin III	Extra 30 gal. tank in fuselage behind pilot
Type 'C'	1030 hp R.R. Merlin III	As 'B' with additional 30 gal fuel tank under port wing
Type 'D'	1030 hp R.R. Merlin III	Special long range. Leading edge wing tank, + 30 gal. fuselage tank
{ Type 'F' (PR Mk VI)	1030 hp R.R. Merlin III 1470 hp R.R. Merlin 45	{ As 'B' with additional 30 gal. tank under each wing
{ Type 'G' (PR Mk VII)	1030 hp R.R. Merlin III 1470 hp R.R. Merlin 45	{ Armed low level PR Aircraft
P.R. Mk IV	1470 hp R.R. Merlin 45 1415 hp R.R. Merlin 46	Production version of Type D, fitted with Merlin 45/46
P.R. Mk X	1475 hp R.R. Merlin 77	P.C. 2-stage, 2-speed s/c
P.R. Mk XI	R.R. Merlin 61, 63, 63A, 70	
P.R. Mk XIII	1645 hp R.R. Merlin 32	Armed low level P.R. produced by conversion
P.R. Mk XIX	2035 hp R.R. Griffon 65, 66	All except first 22 with PC
F.Mk VI (P.R.)	1415 hp R.R. Merlin 47	6 Mk VI fighters sent to ME in 1942 for P.R. work

SEAFIRES

Mk I в	1470 hp R.R. Merlin 45	Produced by conversion
	1415 hp R.R. Merlin 46	from Spitfire Vв
Mk IIc	1470 hp R.R. Merlin 45, 50A	'C' Wing
	1415 hp R.R. Merlin 46	
Mk L.IIc	1645 hp R.R. Merlin 32	
Mk L.R. IIc	1645 hp R.R. Merlin 32	F.R. version of L.IIc
Mk L.IIc (Hybrid)	1585 hp R.R. Merlin 55M	26 basic Mk IIIs produced by Westlands with fixed 'C' Wing
Mk F.III	1470 hp R.R. Merlin 55	Folding 'C' Wings
Mk L.III	1585 hp R.R. Merlin 55M	
Mk F.R. III	1585 hp R.R. Merlin 55M	
Mk XV	1815 hp R.R. Griffon VI	
Mks F & FRXVII	1815 hp R.R. Griffon VI	
Mks F & FR 47	2145 hp R.R. Griffon 87	
	2350 hp R.R. Griffon 88	

NOTES

1 Spitfire Mk IIA (L.R.) is an unofficial designation, but is a convenient way of distinguishing the IIA with the extra under wing fuel tank from the standard IIA. Approximately 100 were produced.

2 Spitfires F & F.R. Mk XVIII and Mk 22 did not become operational in the Royal Air Force until after the cessation of hostilities.

3 Spitfire 'P.R. Type E': There was only one known example and I have omitted it from the list.

4 Spitfire F.Mk VI (P.R.). This again is an unofficial designation. These aircraft were soon relegated to communications duties, but two operational sorties took place with 680 (P.R.) Squadron in 1943: one in April to Crete, the other in May to Crete and Piraeus.

5 Seafire XV. This aircraft received its Service Release in April 1945.

6 The Seafires Mk XVII and 47 entered Squadron Service after the cessation of hostilities. The Mk 47 was operational in the Korean War.

APPENDIX 5

Spitfire Level Speed Performance

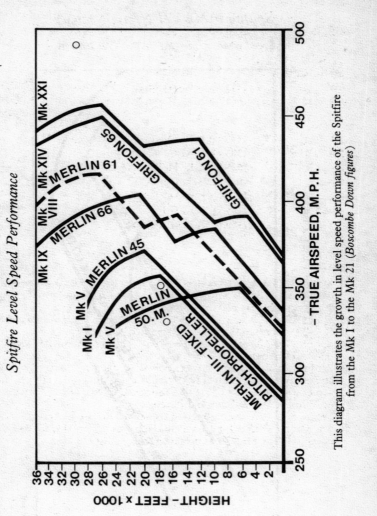

This diagram illustrates the growth in level speed performance of the Spitfire from the Mk I to the Mk 21 (*Boscombe Down figures*)

APPENDIX 6

Spitfire F.Mk VII (pressure cabin)

Speed performance (MD 176, TOW 7990 lb)

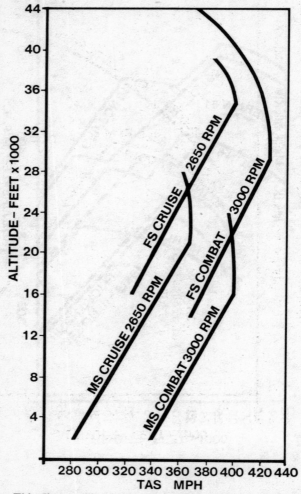

This diagram illustrates the excellent performance of the Spitfire F.Mk VII pressure cabin interceptor fighter of 1942/3, up to 44,000 ft (*Boscombe Down figures*)

APPENDIX 7

Spitfire PR Mk XI Speed Performance

(MB 789, TOW 8040 lb, Merlin 63)

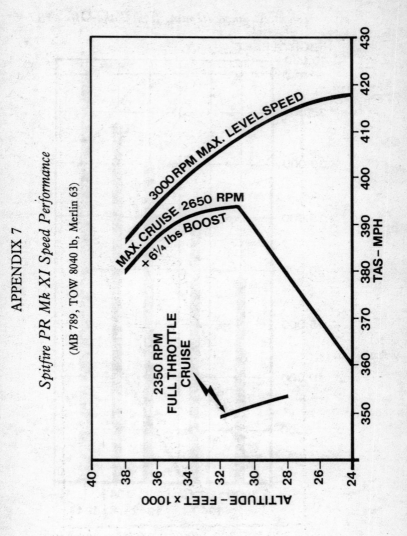

APPENDIX 8

Height Attained 10 min. from Take-Off

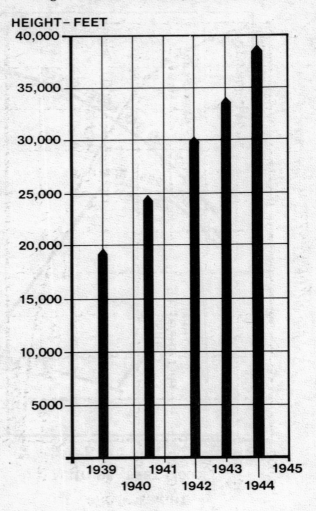

APPENDIX 9

Weight Growth

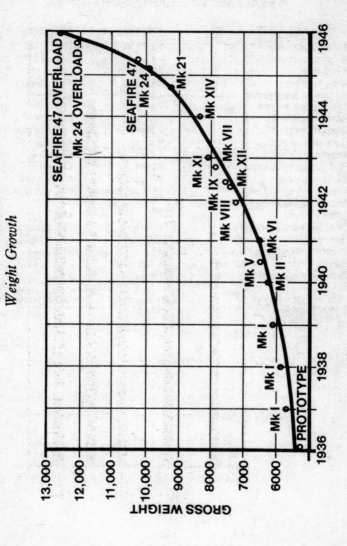

APPENDIX 10

Spitfire Mk I/Seafire 47 Comparison

	SPITFIRE Mk I	SEAFIRE 47
Weight, normal	5,820 lb	10,300 lb
Weight, overload	—	12,500 lb*
Wing area	242 sq. ft	244 sq. ft
Wing loading	24 lb/sq. ft	42.2 lb/sq. ft
Maximum horsepower	1,050	2,350
Power plant weight	2,020 lb	3,650 lb
Maximum speed	362 mph	452 mph
Maximum rate of climb	2,500 ft/min	4,800 ft/min
Time to 20,000 ft	9.4 min	4.8 min
Weight of fire/sec	4.0 lb	12.0 lb
Fuel capacity, internal	85 gal	154 gal
Maximum range	575 miles	1,475 miles
Rate of roll at 400 mph	14.0 degrees/sec	68 degrees/sec
Permissible CG range, percentage mean chord	2.7	11.5
Factored wing loading	240 lb/sq. ft	464 lb/sq. ft
Maximum diving speed	450 mph	500 mph
Structure weight, per cent	33.0	31.0
Energy absorption of undercarriage	8,300 ft/lb	26,600 ft/lb
Undercarriage stroke	4.9 in	9.0 in

* This weight is the equivalent of a Spitfire Mk I carrying 32 airline passengers each with 40 lb of baggage

APPENDIX 11

Test pilots serving at Supermarine at some time between 1936 and 1946
(Rank as at time of joining)

Almack	F/Lt J.P.B., RAF
Andrews	F/Lt A.J., DFC RAF (killed)
Arend	F/Lt P., RBAF
Banner	F/Lt F.S., DFC RAF (killed)
Bartley	F/Lt A.C., DFC RAF
Beaumont	F/Lt W.R.L., RAF
Burke	F/Lt T., RAF
Clive	F/Lt P.J., RAF
Colquhoun	F/Lt L.R., DFC DFM RAF
Comerford	F/Lt H.A.G., RAF
Cooke	F/Lt, RAF (administration only)
Craxton	F/Lt T., DFC RAF
Deytrikh	F/Lt A., RAF
Errington	G.B.S. (Airspeed Ltd)
Farquharson	F/Lt G., RAF
Furlong	Lt F.C., RNVR (killed)
Gosling	F/Lt R.C., RAF
Graham	F/Lt M., DFC RAF
Harris	Lt S., RNVR
Havercroft	S/Ldr R.E., RAF
Henshaw	A.H., MBE (Vickers-Armstrongs Ltd)
Hill	Lt P., RNVR
Hillwood	F/Lt P., DFC RAF
Jarred	F/Lt C.R., RAF (killed)
Jennings	F/Lt, RAF
Lithgow	Lt/Cdr M.J., OBE RN
Louis	F/O R., RAFO
Lowdell	G. (Vickers-Armstrongs Ltd)
Lundsten	F/Lt L., RNAF
McNicol	F/Lt I., RAFO
Manlove	S/Ldr R., RAF
Morgan	S/Ldr G., DFC RAF
Page	F/Lt G., DSO DFC RAF
Parry	F/Lt H., RAF
Payn	S/Ldr H.J., AFC RAFO
Pickering	A.G., AFC (Vickers-Armstrongs Ltd) (killed)
Quill	J.K., OBE AFC (Vickers-Armstrongs Ltd)
Robertson	Lt D.R., DFC RNVR
Rudland	F/Lt C., RAF
Shea-Simonds	Lt P., MBE RNVR
Snarey	G.N., AFC (Vickers-Armstrongs Ltd)
Summers	J., OBE (Vickers-Armstrongs Ltd)
Taylor	F/Lt H.A., RAF

Thomas	F/Lt, RAF
Ullstad	F/Lt O., RNAF
Underwood	Lt J., MBE RNVR
Wakefield	Lt J., RNVR (killed)
Wedgwood	F/Lt J.H., DFC RAF
Wigley	F/Lt P., DFC RAF

Index

BESTSELLING NON-FICTION FROM ARROW

All these books are available from your bookshop or news-agent or you can order them direct. Just tick the titles you want and complete the form below.

☐	THE GREAT ESCAPE	Paul Brickhill	£1.75
☐	A RUMOR OF WAR	Philip Caputo	£2.50
☐	A LITTLE ZIT ON THE SIDE	Jasper Carrott	£1.50
☐	THE ART OF COARSE ACTING	Michael Green	£1.50
☐	THE UNLUCKIEST MAN IN THE WORLD	Mike Harding	£1.75
☐	DIARY OF A SOMEBODY	Christopher Matthew	£1.25
☐	TALES FROM A LONG ROOM	Peter Tinniswood	£1.75
☐	LOVE WITHOUT FEAR	Eustace Chesser	£1.95
☐	NO CHANGE	Wendy Cooper	£1.95
☐	MEN IN LOVE	Nancy Friday	£2.75

Postage ———
Total ———

ARROW BOOKS, BOOKSERVICE BY POST, PO BOX 29, DOUGLAS, ISLE OF MAN, BRITISH ISLES

Please enclose a cheque or postal order made out to Arrow Books Ltd for the amount due including 15p per book for postage and packing both for orders within the UK and for overseas orders.

Please print clearly

NAME ....

ADDRESS ....

....

Whilst every effort is made to keep prices down and to keep popular books in print, Arrow Books cannot guarantee that prices will be the same as those advertised here or that the books will be available.